States and collective action: the European experience

States and collective action: the European experience

PIERRE BIRNBAUM

Professor at the University of Paris I

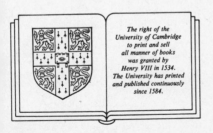

The right of the
University of Cambridge
to print and sell
all manner of books
was granted by
Henry VIII in 1534.
The University has printed
and published continuously
since 1584.

Cambridge University Press
Cambridge
New York   New Rochelle   Melbourne   Sydney

Published by the Press Syndicate of the University of Cambridge
The Pitt Building, Trumpington Street, Cambridge CB2 1RP
32 East 57th Street, New York, NY 10022, USA
10 Stamford Road, Oakleigh, Melbourne 3166, Australia

First published 1988

Printed in Great Britain at the University Press, Cambridge

British Library cataloguing in publication data

Birnbaum, Pierre
States and collective action: the European experience.
1. State, The. 2. Europe – Politics and government – 1945–
I. Title
320.1′094   JN94.A2

Library of Congress cataloguing in publication data

Birnbaum, Pierre.
[Selections. English]
States and collective action: the European experience / Pierre Birnbaum.
p.   cm.
Collection of extracts from previously published works by the
author, newly translated.
Bibliography. p.
Includes index.
ISBN 0 521 32548 X
1. Collectivism. 2. Corporate state – Europe. 3. Europe – Politics
and government. 4. State, The.   I. Title.
HX36.B537213 1988.
306′.2 – dc19   87-23284 CIP

ISBN 0 521 32548 X

CE

Contents

Acknowledgements

The author and publisher are grateful to the following for permission to utilise material first published elsewhere:

Presses Universitaires de France, for material extracted from *Dimensions du pouvoir* (Paris, 1984)

Librairie Arthème Fayard, for material extracted from *La Logique de l'Etat* (Paris, 1982)

The journal *Politics and Society*, 11:4 (1982), in which the bulk of chapter 6 first appeared

Unesco, for material in chapter 4 extracted from the *International Social Science Journal*, 32:4 © Unesco 1980

Introduction

In recent times the question of the state has been central to political sociology and it has become, in a quite unexpected manner, an academic industry. Indeed, one might well suppose from the astonishing number of books published on the state that one was dealing with the most important of all such industries. The fact that the Congress of the International Political Science Association held in Paris in July 1985 was wholly devoted to this question is just one more proof enabling us to measure the distance travelled since the Congresses of the 1960s, and even of the 1970s, which were dominated by developmentalist, modernising and behaviourist perspectives. It is not so long ago that the most industrialised societies in the West, Great Britain and the United States in particular, were still living in a period which they believed to be characterised by the end of ideologies, the disappearance of conflicts, and by consensus; in short, during this period the societies in question reckoned that the end of politics had come[1] and, at the same time, the end of history. Political scientists turned their attention wholly towards the study of the political system, to which a number of specific functions, inasmuch as they were subsystems of the global social system, were devolved. There was a convergence between structural–functionalist perspectives derived from Talcott Parsons' model and the systemic paradigms associated with general systems theory and with cybernetics, and this despite the real differences separating them. As a result, politics came to be regarded as a technique of demand management, demands which were 'incorporated' and 'converted' by various instruments, such as political parties, prior to being transmitted to the political authorities, who would then take it upon themselves to respond with decisions that were compatible with the available resources. This approach seemed to confirm that Western societies could be governed in a manner which was at once technical, apolitical, and compatible with a degree of depoliticisation of their citizens.[2] Systemic models and analyses in terms of decision-making thus lie at the basis of the pluralist vision of the social order, according to which power, and, *a fortiori*, the state, have disappeared: groups argue over resources in a permanent bargaining process, in which decisions are arrived at as a result of the opposition between various rival and specialist élites.[3] During this period international political science was dominated by a handful of writers, namely David Easton, Karl Deutsch and Robert Dahl. These political scientists regarded Western societies – with the exception of France and Italy, which had failed to carry through their modernisation process successfully and were still faced with a dualistic opposition between traditional and modern roles (such as African societies experienced during the same period)[4] – as being basically homogeneous, sheltered from history and pacified by the affluent society. For pluralist political science, which was the dominant school at the time and which took its inspiration from the division of labour perspective of thinkers like Durkheim or indeed, in many respects, Weber, politics was thereby restricted to a specific locus, and one whose functioning was guaranteed by legitimate authority and not by power. All Western societies were thus presumed, as the division of labour advanced, to undergo a modernisation which would eliminate the archaisms upon which power depended.

This evolutionist and developmentalist interpretation of history[5] helps to account for the particular preoccupations of the dominant currents within the political science of the time, a science which focused upon parties, elections and the activities of pressure groups in an attempt to analyse the translation into politics of social pluralism. Furthermore, the most radical critiques, such as those of Wright Mills,[6] Bachrach and Baratz,[7] or even Steven Lukes,[8] although they do admittedly reintroduce the roles of power élites, of the unequal capacities of groups, of non-decisions or indeed of structures, remain silent regarding the role of the state. Indeed, the concept of the state is employed neither by the advocates of an, often positivist, pluralist political science nor by its critics. It would seem never to have crossed their minds that the history of each of these Western societies has, in all probability, given rise to a particular type of state, some of which – especially in Great Britain and the United States, whose societies seem to function pluralistically – may well be less structured than others.

Which is as much as to say that the pluralist model of politics, together with the criticisms which have been advanced of it, may be situated squarely within a linear and evolutionist interpretation of political modernisation which cannot produce historical reasons as to why in the United States, or in countries such as Germany, Great Britain and so on, which seem to be the last word in rationalisation, the state remains so little structured. Such accounts testify to the absence of the state but, instead of enquiring more deeply into this feature, which is the key property of a certain type of society, they stave off historical explanation and hold to a purely developmentalist perspective.

There emerged, during this same period, in opposition to the pluralist paradigm and to an evolutionism conceived in terms of a division of labour serving to negate historical diversity, a Marxist structuralism which was just as blind to history. In the writings of Althusser,[9] in the works of the *Kapitalstaat* school and in a number of similarly oriented researches, a new kind of evolutionism became apparent. Its practitioners are concerned to recognise the autonomy of the state while at the same time insisting upon its functional character, a character that means it is all the better equipped to serve as an expression of the power of the hegemonic class. They see the state as endowed with its 'own selectivity', which enables it to tackle fiscal crises more effectively and to resolve the problem of its lack of legitimacy both by guaranteeing, by its action, the governability of the system and by resolving the various crises likely to occur in a political space in which depoliticisation might otherwise undermine support for the authorities, and therefore their legitimacy.[10] Whereas the earlier pluralist and evolutionist sociology rested upon the concept of the division of labour, these new theoretical tendencies depended more on that of relations of production, yet in both cases politics was considered to have one and the same function, regardless of the type of society involved or of its history. In the case of the former, politics was reduced to the operation of a subsystem, one serving in all modernised societies to guarantee the functioning of a specific pattern variable. In the case of the latter, whether directly or through processes of mediation guaranteeing it a degree of independence, politics was regarded as an instrument whose functioning principle lay outside itself, in the ruling class.

In spite of the differences between them, these two kinds of evolutionism are both profoundly ahistorical, whereas the founding fathers to whom they owed obeisance, be it Marx, Weber or Durkheim, displayed a much more serious regard for the diversity of historical processes.

If political sociologists have often, in recent years, rediscovered history, this has been achieved by turning back to the works of the founding fathers and by advancing a more serious reading of the latent models which may be discovered in them. One of their discoveries has, not surprisingly, been the crucial *œuvre* of Alexis de Tocqueville, who may be regarded as the real founder of a comparative approach of this kind. In distancing itself from any and every variety of evolutionism, in rejecting reductive schemata based upon the concept of modernisation or upon relations of production, political sociology encountered, towards the end of the 1970s, a properly historical approach and, from that time on, a debate has been joined which is very far from being closed even today. When political sociology seeks to retrace the distant origin of each type of state by pursuing a thread far back into the past, is it simply turning itself into a historical discipline? When historical sociology takes account of the theoretical gains made by historians, and in particular by the *Annales* school which, from the time of Marc Bloch and Lucien Febvre on, has worked on a very long time scale, is it simply applying research methods appropriate to historians or to facts which the historians themselves have often somewhat neglected in recent years because of their preoccupation with economic data? The truth is that many historians can see very little justification for sociology.[11] Does 'the meeting between sociology and history' represent, on the other hand, a progressive fusion and unification of theories and methods?[12] Are sociologists, who have never applied themselves either to archive work or, plainly, to fieldwork, settling for a superimposition of their abstract and general models upon realities whose extreme diversity they are ignorant of? When they are working on historically quite distant periods, are sociologists of politics in any position to apply their own methods? More specifically, are they able to use verification techniques, such as factorial analyses or the multivariant method, with which their colleagues try these days to assess the weight of each variable in the explanation of a particular vote, suicide or deviancy? Where political sociology endeavours to be both historical and comparative – in, for example, its enquiry into the origin of each type of state – is it forced to apply an approach which is Weberian and involves ideal types, and which is based upon the necessarily subjective and partial choice of a limited number of variables serving to construct a provisional picture of reality?[13] For, as Bendix observes, 'comparative studies . . . can only deal with a few cases and cannot easily isolate the variables (as causal analysis must)'[14]. On the other hand, can political sociology employ a causal analysis as rigorous as the kind which sociologists apply in other domains of contemporary reality?[15] The recent spread of a comparative historical sociology admittedly enables one to reject evolutionist perspectives regarding the state, while at the same time disqualifying the political philosophy which historical sociology had from the start laid claim to as its own. But, in setting out to be resolutely comparative, this historical sociology is faced with the problem of proof. What are the variables which may be held to account for one or other type of state? Which states should be compared with one another? Should one choose countries which are linked both by their geography and their history, keeping these variables constant, or should one instead select quite contrasting countries so as to bring out the differences more strongly, with each country representing a prototype of its own, and thereby risk exaggerating the homogeneity of each ensemble and not taking into account the differences within these opposed ensembles? What precisely is the value of a binary comparison between different or similar ensembles? In spite of the endorsement which the procedure suggested by John Stuart Mill, involving the use of both the 'method of agreement' and the 'method of difference', has often earned, it has its limitations, for the context of the situations being compared cannot be considered so homogeneous for environmental differences to be disregarded entirely, that is to say for the context to be considered a variable to be arbitrarily excluded from the analysis by being kept constant.[16] Generally speaking, comparative historical sociology therefore sets out to establish correlations rather than to discover relations of causality, for these latter seem still to be beyond the scope of this kind of research.

When applied to the problem of the state, this kind of sociology has proved very fruitful. Indeed, in the hands of Perry Anderson, Charles Tilly, Stein Rokkan, Schmul Eisenstadt and Theda Skocpol, it has, to varying degrees, broken with all evolutionist approaches and has placed the emphasis instead upon the specific weight of a number of variables which give rise to specific types of state. By elaborating on a number of Peter Nettl's brilliant intuitions,[17] and by combining different variables, this form of sociology has managed to construct what is virtually a typology of the state. Admittedly, this typology has grave faults,[18] but it is increasingly giving encouragement to others to embark upon researches whose end result will be to refine it ever further.

There is not space for me here to present yet another summary of the present state of the debate. I would simply observe that it is my intention not so much to distinguish between three possible approaches to the state (the pluralist, the managerial and the Marxist approach),[19] with it being demonstrated how each of them sheds light in its own way on the analysis of the state, nor indeed to investigate in an unspecific way the autonomy of the state,[20] but rather to proceed, in an interpretative and ideal-typical manner, to an examination of the multiple 'lineages' of the various states. I have adopted this approach because I hold that use of the concept of state implies the historical completion of a process of differentiation with respect to a set of social, religious, ethnic and other peripheries. This differentiation implies the institutionalisation of the state, the formation of a tightly knit bureaucratic apparatus which is both meritocratic and closed-off to various external intrusions, an administrative law and a secular approach – all of which are barriers marking off the boundaries of the space of the state. In this sense, a state cannot be a capitalist or a worker state, a democratic or a totalitarian state, a Catholic or a Jewish state, and so on. If the state is, for example, capitalist or totalitarian, or indeed Catholic, it is because, in each case, the bourgeoisie, an organisation with totalitarian claims, or indeed the Church, have attributed state power to themselves. Considered as an ideal type, the state – as locus and as process – cannot function in a particularist manner so as to become the more or less tame instrument of a class, party, religion, or indeed of a specific ethnic group. I would argue that, in purely heuristic terms, the state would then lose the very qualities that enable one to define it as such. Seen in ideal-typical terms, very few states are really states: they are states from the point of view of international relations, juridical sovereignty and so on, without being such in terms of the Weberian interpretative approach advanced here, an approach which could result in a comparative historical sociology of the state as fruitful as it is provisional.

Given a perspective of this sort, we are in a position to analyse actually existing state systems in order to assess how closely they approximate to a model built up on the basis of an examination of historical processes. So as to present things more clearly and, in addition, to avoid the needlessly provocative gesture of describing the majority of states as non-states, I have decided to call states that approximate most closely to the model 'strong' states, while those that diverge most sharply from it will be regarded as 'weak' states. In order to ensure that this typology is effectively employed, we can choose, in accordance with the requirements of the comparative approach, to consider examples located within one geographical space (Europe), all with an economic system based upon the private ownership of the means of production, all with an identical cultural code (Christianity),[21] and all with a basic democratic system. I have therefore deliberately chosen, on a provisional basis, a geographical space and definition of the state which will serve as a framework for the application of a comparative approach likely to bring out differences which can therefore no longer be the outcome of, for example, dissimilar economic structures (like collective ownership of the means of production), opposed religious codes (for example, the Islamic Umma, which cannot tolerate the idea of differentiation) or a different political system (like primitive or feudal society). In arguing thus, to take up the terms of the debate rehearsed above, we are certainly depriving ourselves of examples which would accentuate the oppositions. It may, moreover, be the case that the differences internal to the populations of the states selected may be less significant than those which would involve their being broadly contrasted with examples illustrating these latter categories, such as the USSR, Iran, and Indonesian and African societies, or indeed that of the Guyaki Indians. However, in order to restrict the parameters of my research, I wish merely to account for the profound differences which differentiate the states within the set being studied. Consequently, we can advance the hypothesis that, even if the USSR and Iran are, for reasons other than those under consideration here, non-states by comparison with France, the same may be said, again in relation to France, of Great Britain or Switzerland. These are the sorts of difference which concern me here and we can, with the help of historical sociology, identify the origin of these dissimilarities in the history particular to each of the societies within the chosen set. I would not claim, however, even within this limited framework, to advance an explanation which is causal in nature; I would merely wish, on the basis of correlations between these provisionally selected variables, to ıed some light on the origin of political differences. Hence, within the palette, as it were, of the examples under consideration, there is a typology opposing 'strong' states such as France, or to a lesser extent Prussia, and to still less of an extent Spain, to 'weak' states ('non-states') such as Great Britain, the United States (though it is outside Europe) or Switzerland.[22]

Once constructed, each of these states seems to preserve its own logic, so that each type of state would seem to be an independent variable. It is therefore in relation to its particularities that social groups are organised; henceforth, instead of explaining the type of state in terms of a particular arrangement of variables, I shall treat it as a variable which will serve to account for the behaviour of groups, parties, classes and nationalist movements which, in every case, are organised as a function of the type of state in relation to which they operate. Thus the logic of each state[23] influences the mode of action of actors in 'civil society'; the usual correlation is, as a consequence, reversed. In analysing the mobilisation process of the actors, I propose, in the present book, to assess the logic of each state by always considering the type of state involved. That is to say, within the limited context of a relatively homogeneous area such as Europe may be taken to be, I shall not refer again to the particular origin of each type of state, to its particular history as it unfolds in different (geographical and cultural) contexts. Within a set of in many respects similar states, it is therefore possible to undertake more effectively 'huge comparisons' between 'big structures' and 'large processes',[24] by employing as far as possible an interpretative and provisional ideal-typical approach, a strategy which returns us quite conclusively to 'bringing the state back in',[25] and therefore to taking seriously the role peculiar to each type of state. I would wish here to emphasise the state as a variable, but, in contrast to, for example, Theda Skocpol,[26] I would not claim to have arrived at a genuinely causal analysis of the consequences of the action of the state as variable. I also prefer now to work on 'what happened' rather than on 'why' questions,[27] even if, in earlier research, I have raised, in interpretative terms, the question 'why'; finally, I have imposed a fairly stringent limit upon the variations on display by retaining no type of state which seems (as is the case with Russia, China or with African or, indeed, Islamic countries) to be in many respects too dissimilar, and to have emerged from very distant histories produced in the context of quite other cultural codes. I have been mainly concerned, in the present work, to account solely for the effects particular to each type of state. I would thus hope to advance my thinking as far as possible in this direction, to reverse, for heuristic reasons, the correlation between 'state' and 'society', and to see to what extent such a partial and provisional approach sheds new light upon a set of social phenomena whose organisational or ideological diversity can only be understood in terms of the specific type of state with which they can be correlated. I would thus propose to treat the type of state as an independent variable in order to assess its particular effects upon the mode of organisation of the working class, upon the strategy adopted by strikers and upon nationalist movements.

I seek to emphasise the influence of each type of state upon the formation and development of collective action, analysis of which, along with that of the state, has without doubt allowed some particularly original models of political sociology to be formulated in recent years. It is the aim of this book to combine an examination of the logic of various states with that of collective movements, to enquire to what extent there is a close connection between them, to wonder if there exists a notable correlation between a strong state and a collective action structured around particular networks and ideologies, and to entertain the possibility that the opposite correlation – between a weak state and a collective action less holistic in nature – holds good too. The book is concerned as much with the logic peculiar to each type of state as with that which does or does not foster the emergence of a collective action on the basis, for example, of the aggregation of individual choices realised in multiple social contexts. As I propose to show, a wholly crucial debate has been entered into, one concerning the conditions for the production of collective action: the advocates of a holistic approach and those of methodological individualism are ranged in opposite camps. The former reify social movement; the latter interpret it in terms of the actors' intentionality and of their interest in mobilising, and therefore undertake a careful analysis of the 'free rider' strategy. I will give an account of this wholly crucial debate – involving Charles Tilly, Anthony Oberschall, Mancur Olson, Albert Hirschman, Raymond Boudon, Jon Elster, Adam Przeworski, Samuel Popkin and Alessandro Pizzorno[28] – below. I would merely note for the time being that this debate has generally been expounded without much attention being paid to the state, and that the crucial argument of the present book, underpinning its various chapters, hangs precisely on establishing a connection between type of mobilisation (whatever the internal difficulties accompanying its formation) and type of state. As I have already indicated above, I propose to interpret the many forms of collective action – strikes, demonstrations, nationalist claims, the social impact of ideologies, the formation of both left- and right-wing extremism, together with actual revolutions – in terms of the type of state involved, which will be treated as an independent, explanatory variable whose actual impact I have deliberately chosen to assess. While adopting a comparative approach which holds constant a large number of variables within a limited and relatively homogeneous social space, that of Europe from the end of the nineteenth century to the present day (though the USA and the USSR are introduced once or twice, for the sake of comparison), I therefore propose, with the aid of historical sociology, to arrive at an understanding of the influence of the structure of the state and of the actors who put it into operation (the nature of the élite involved being linked to that of the state) upon the constitution and strategy of movements of collective action. My ambition and my purpose in the present work consists, in the last instance, in treating the type of state as a variable which will account for the extraordinary diversity of forms of collective action still evident nowadays in the various countries of Europe.

1 ✥ Mobilisation theory and the state: the missing element

From the end of the nineteenth century, the economic system has been disrupted by the emergence of new social categories. The first sociologists, in response to this, emphasised the need for a permanent and quasi-organic social organisation which would limit mobilisation and the risks of fracture to which it gave rise. For the sociologists, society as it actually is has nothing in common with the metaphysical perspectives adopted by revolutionaries in their conceptual reconstruction of a new world. In the wake of Louis de Bonald and Joseph de Maistre, Auguste Comte and Saint-Simon thus sought to stand firm against the rise both of social confrontation and of an abstract individualism which threatened the collective and organic aspects of order. For these theoreticians, the whole (society) had necessarily to prevail over the parts (the individuals). Society therefore seemed to them to be a complex mechanism in which each part depended on all the others. They feared, much as Edmund Burke had done, that the destruction of social structures and the abolition of the estates or of the intermediate groups would in the end only result in the disintegration of the whole and therefore in the triumph of an uncontrollable individualism. They likewise foresaw a time when millions of men would no longer sustain any social relation with each other and would be, as it were, atomised, and would live out their lives under the lofty protection of an all-powerful state. For them, mass society represented just such an agglomeration of isolated individuals, incapable of ruling themselves and liable to adopt the most extreme ideologies. This society would therefore also be deprived of any of the kinds of value or tradition that are to be found in concrete, collective and quasi-organic societies. Alexis de Tocqueville also helped to formulate the notion of a mass society. In his *Democracy in America*, he emphasised the effect of the establishment of equality of conditions for all, which to his mind was crucial, upon the advent of a society composed of atomised individuals, deprived of any hierarchical system and little concerned with the preservation of liberty. It was in order to stave off the emergence of a new Leviathan, to which each man would be only too willing to abandon his fate, that de Tocqueville advocated having recourse to various means which would serve to restrict any disintegration, so destructive of all capacity for self-determination, of the social body. 'I see', wrote de Tocqueville, 'an innumerable multitude of men, alike and equal, constantly circling around in pursuit of the petty and banal pleasures with which they glut their souls. Each one of them, withdrawn into himself, is almost unaware of the fate of the rest.'[1] Likewise, for John Stuart Mill, 'the individuals are lost in the crowd . . . the only existing power is that of the masses'.[2]

One could give any number of quotations testifying to the disillusionment felt during this period by the theoreticians of liberalism, when confronted with the sudden changes occasioned by industrialisation and urbanisation.[3] Progress seemed to them to be leading to social disorder, and the Enlightenment to be leading to what Taine, in *Les Origines de la France contemporaine*, called 'popular fanaticism'. What I wish to emphasise here, however, is the crucial part played by this notion of 'popular fanaticism' in the formulation, which became current at the end of the nineteenth century, of the theory of crowds. Taine reckoned that the spirit of Jacobinism was behind this domination of the 'plebs', an 'urban mob' consisting of *déclassé* elements, who sought to simplify overmuch and who propagated a 'revolutionary sickness'.[4] He was the first to advance a genuine theory of crowd psychology, in terms of instincts, passions, irrationalism and illness. It is worth noting that both Le Bon and Tarde were influenced by Taine's writings. According to Taine, 'from the moment that they are in a crowd, the ignorant and the wise become equally incapable of observation'.[5] In a crowd, the conscious personality disappears, and the feelings and ideas of all the units involved become oriented in one and the same direction.

Through a process of mental contagion and hypnotism, 'the individual belonging to a crowd . . . is no longer conscious of his acts'.[6] Le Bon considered his theory of crowds to be validated by Charcot's studies, at La Salpêtrière, of hypnotism and suggestion.[7] For him, 'it is not from the rational but from the irrational that great events are born; the rational creates science but the irrational is the driving force of history'.[8] I would merely note here that, in Le Bon's terms, political mobilisation assumes a pathological character, depending in no respect whatsoever upon the choice of the actor. It is produced quite independently of the kinds of resource which he has at his command, requires no prior organisation and unfolds, in an ahistorical manner, quite independently of the political context or of the type of political power. *The Psychology of Crowds* is therefore presented as an anti-sociological work, in the sense that mobilisation derives neither from the deliberate choice of specific social actors nor from the nature of the social group. Society, when it is atomised, no longer exists; conversely, when a crowd gathers, it is the individual who disappears. Action does not result here from intention. Similarly, in the work of Gabriel Tarde, the individual is in no sense the master of his own action. It matters little if his position evolved originally from an absolute individualism towards a form of interactionism;[9] what is of significance here is that, for Tarde, a social group is 'a collection of beings who are apt to imitate each other',[10] imitation being 'an interpsychical photograph, so to speak, regardless of whether it is willed or not, or whether it is passive or active'.[11] Once again making a comparison between social movement and contagion, Tarde observes that 'when there is a new announcement over the telegraph, the insurrection spreads still more freely from capital to capital, from factory to factory'.[12] Movements of imitation and of counterimitation are therefore always elaborated without reference to any specific social structure, nor do they depend upon an intentional choice of the actors involved. Thus, 'society is imitation and imitation is a kind of sleep-walking'.[13] Mobilisation, therefore, belongs to the domain of the irrational.

This purely psychological interpretation has given rise to a great deal of research in the modern period. Most of the studies in question have reckoned that a high human density in a given place tends to provoke an irrational reaction on the part of individuals. Georg Simmel also adopts this perspective, regarding towns as the ideal framework for the formation of collective movements; for him, 'the *absolute* numbers of the total group and of the prominent elements . . . remarkably determine the relations within the groups',[14] and the nature of the great metropolises, on account of the high densities of population which are the rule there, influences the mental life of the inhabitants. The Chicago School has tried to establish similar correlations.[15]

The high population densities of towns are thus held to render the 'personal space' of each actor more precarious, so that he believes himself to be subject to intrusion.[16] In this sense, one can define a crowd as 'a large group of people so closely assembled that they feel oppressed'.[17] However, as Daniel Stokols observes, density would seem to be a necessary but not a sufficient condition for the formation of a crowd for, considered not from a purely physical point of view but rather from a psycho-sociological one, density does not always have the same meaning, nor the same consequences, for the actors confronting each other in such a situation.[18] While it is true that some writers maintain that the type of income or the ethnic origin, say, of individuals has no significant effect upon the behaviour of actors and upon their propensity to adopt or to reject attitudes which are peculiar to crowds,[19] one should nevertheless bear in mind, in order to account for noteworthy differences in behaviour, the traditional opposition between primary and secondary groups. In the context of the first kind of group, the potential oppression constituted by a crowd would be very strongly felt (for example, in relation to places of residence) for the actual personality of the actor, as determined by his face to face relations with other actors to which he is attached, would be undermined; conversely, in an environment of the second kind, such reactions would be less likely.[20] This opposition seems close to that already formulated by Cooley. It appears, however, to be open to criticism, inasmuch as social spaces of the second kind can also offer high levels of integration and protection. It nevertheless implies that individuals react to physical constraints in a way that is related to their social environment and not in a purely emotive manner. In this sense, group psychology such as it is now conceived has moved away from the atomistic models proposed by its founding fathers and has come to place more emphasis upon the social aspect of density, in its moulding of actors' perceptions. Finally, collective action, together with the spreading of rumours, or even the manner in which political propaganda is propagated, should simply be examined as social facts:[21] setting aside the question of density, it really is the nature of the social relation which can be held to explain the emergence of such phenomena, so that, even from the merely socio-psychological point of view, a network of interactions must necessarily serve as their basis.[22]

Drawing his inspiration explicitly from the Durkheimian tradition, Ralph Turner rejects any interpretation of crowds in terms of suggestion and contagion; for him a crowd, from the moment it is formed, is invariably constructed on the basis of social norms.[23] Durkheim and his school were in fact quite consciously opposed to all unsociological conceptions of social facts and, in particular, to those which derive from the notion of imitation. 'Doubtless', Durkheim writes, 'every social fact is imitated and has, as we have just shown, a tendency to become generalised, but this is because it is social, i.e. obligatory.'[24] Borne by a social structure, movement then assumes a collective dimension. For Durkheim, 'the states of the collective consciousness are of a different nature from the states of individual consciousness; they are representations of another kind. The mentality of groups is not that of individuals; it has its own laws.'[25] Consequently, a collective movement expresses 'a group state which repeats itself in individuals because it is forced upon them'. Durkheim thus rejects both the psychological explanation of crowds and the individualist and utilitarian perspective which he is out to challenge in, for example, *The Division of Labour in Society*. He holds that normal evolution, as the division of labour advances and therefore redistributes social roles in terms of functions, leads from one state of integration to another. Only where there is a constrained or anomic division of labour does solidarity turn out to be impossible. With the passage to a new form of community depending upon a functional division of tasks becoming impossible, social conflicts or anomie emerge. On the basis of the second hypothesis, Erik Allardt has sought to reduce the Durkheimian model to systematic form: his interpretation involves locating the moment of mass society in a period at which the beginnings of industrialisation had destroyed collective beliefs but the new principles of integration, based upon a genuine division of labour, had not yet been able to blossom.[26] In this sense, Durkheim can be compared with all those who predict the advent of a mass society in which the majority of primary groups and other forms of social organisation disappear.[27] Mobilisation would therefore take place in a society whose communal framework had been destroyed.

Allardt thus advances a stimulating interpretation of the rise of mobilisation in a non-integrated society. It would be as well, however, to emphasise that the theoreticians of mass society predict its advent in a society which is already highly industrialised and urbanised; it is therefore inaccurate to describe as mass society the state of non-integration which might arise when the emergence of a division of labour is accompanied by a disappearance of collective norms. This is all the more the case given that Durkheim himself never examined this latter hypothesis. Furthermore, when Charles Tilly considers the Durkheimian theory of mobilisation, he reckons that anomie would provoke confusion in individuals and would engender a collective conflict whose basis was essentially a psychological one.[28] However, Durkheim never considered mobilisation to be a consequence of anomie; he regarded the latter as occasioning individual attitudes, such as anomic suicide, but not collective forms of behaviour.[29] In the chapter of *The Division of Labour in Society* which is devoted to the anomic division of labour, Durkheim does admittedly describe the antagonism between labour and capital, which is especially evident in heavy industry, where an excessive division of labour prevails. Yet the truth is that it is only in the chapter where he examined the forced division of labour that Durkheim really turns his attention to the consequences of the still too great inequality of 'the external conditions of struggle', with the hereditary transmission of wealth impeding the emergence of a meritocracy in which each would exercise a function in accord with his competence. In such a society, for Durkheim, 'subversive tendencies . . . emerge more readily'.[30] Mobilisation would therefore not result from anomie but from an unequal distribution of resources which is structural in character; it appears in a class not a mass society.

For Durkheim, the social question that gives rise to conflict and favours the growth of socialism has, as a consequence, a collective basis.[31] Unfortunately, Durkheim never gave a more precise account of his theory of mobilisation; he never studied the manner in which it unfolded or its organisation. In this sense, he never presented a systematic theory of the birth and development of collective movements in industrial societies, nor did he pay much attention to the other forms of mobilisation which occur there, and which do not always depend upon class conflict.

Analysis of the dysfunctional character of inheritance can nevertheless allow one to construct a theory regarding the frustration felt by actors who have to limit their ambition to performing a function in the world that does not measure up to their actual competence, with these individual reactions having a structural character.[32] This perspective therefore differs fundamentally from that of a writer such as Ted Gurr, who holds that frustration is, above all, a psychological reaction arising, unexpectedly, in an institutional and sociological context.[33]

If we reject Durkheim's position, while at the same time not favouring a psychological explanation of frustration, we then have to consider rational choice theories, which are a modern version of the utilitarian perspective challenged by Durkheim himself. In a society in which individualism prevails and which also displays all the characteristics of a market society, the actors do in fact seek to maximise their own self-interest on the basis of a calculation in terms of costs and benefits. If the benefits gained end up by being less than the expenditure invested, revolt may take place, revolt based not only on a psychological attitude of frustration but expressing also a genuinely intentional choice on the part of an actor whose original calculations have been baulked. Conversely, in *The Wealth of Nations*, Adam Smith advanced for the first time an economic justification of the absolute defence of individual self-interest, with the invisible hand tending in general to guarantee both economic growth and the social order. Passion and self-interest would thereby again become synonymous, with the absolute passion entertained by each in the name of the maximisation of his individual self-interest thus guaranteeing the social order.[34] If we consider Helvétius, who maintained that personal self-interest is the source of all the passions upon which the social order rests, or Bentham's utilitarianism, or the generalised market society advocated by Adam Smith, who believed that 'Every individual is continually exerting himself to find out the most advantageous employment for whatever capital he can command. It is his own advantage, indeed, and not that of society, which he has in view. But the study of his own advantage naturally, or rather necessarily leads him to prefer that employment which is most advantageous to the society',[35] we must acknowledge that economic ideology became dominant in late eighteenth-century Europe[36] and that the space given over to politics thereby became circumscribed.[37] The theory of economic individualism, which from then on assumed an ever greater influence in Western thought, culminating, in the wake of the studies of Ludwig von Mises and F. A. Hayek, in the present-day 'public choice' school,[38] is therefore presented as an expression of an assuagement of collective relations which rests upon a defence by each actor of his own interests. This theory claims to eliminate the sources of collective conflict and renders all forms of political mobilisation anachronistic. The economic theory of individualism gains by rejecting the psychologising theory of relative frustration and, in addition, it renders every theory of mobilisation by atomisation alone null and void.

Mancur Olson was the first, on the basis of this reversal of perspective, to formulate a new logic of collective action which, in fact, is more like a logic of the absence of mobilisation. Olson's analysis begins with an examination of very large groups, which he calls 'latent' and which arise in situations where there is atomisation. He observed that 'an individual in a "latent" group, by definition, cannot make a noticeable contribution to any group effort, and since no one in the group will react if he makes no contribution, he has no incentive to contribute. Accordingly, large or "latent" groups have no incentive to act to obtain a collective good'.[39] From then on,

Marxian class action . . . takes on the character of any endeavour to achieve the collective goals of a large, latent group. A class in Marxist terms consists of a large group of individuals who have a common interest arising from the fact that they do or do not own productive property or capital. As in any large, latent group, each individual in the class will find it to his advantage if all of the costs or sacrifices necessary to achieve the common good are borne by others. 'Class legislation' by definition favours the class as a whole rather than particular individuals within the class and thus offers no incentive for individuals to take 'class-conscious' action.[40]

On the basis of a rational calculation, an individual belonging to an atomised society has therefore no reason to attach himself to a collective movement. We are concerned neither with a mass society nor with a class society; society consists, rather, of actors who tend in general to succeed by maximising their individual profits through collective non-action.[41] According to this view, the individuals composing a large-scale latent group have no interest in mobilising and coercion alone will win their support. This accounts for the coercive power enjoyed by the unions in the United States. Conversely, in small groups, where the action of each person counts and plays a crucial role, mobilisation is presented as the outcome of a rational calculation.

Ever since it was first published, Mancur Olson's study has been subject to numerous critiques. I would merely point out here that, as far as their personal self-interest is concerned, the individuals composing a very large latent group proposing to win joint public goods, such as fresh air, zero growth or equal rights, cannot help but act collectively. These goods cannot in fact be created in an individual manner; in addition, their production cannot by definition be monopolised by particular persons. In cases such as these, the actors do not mobilise in the hope of enjoying specific rewards, for individual and

collective gain are here the same.[42] As Harriet Tillock and Denton
Morrison point out, 'in the case of certain public goods, individual and
collective interests are logically merged both psychologically and
ideologically'.[43] Ethical commitment thus becomes mixed up with
personal self-interest, and it is indeed the aim of the ideology of social
movements to reinforce an isomorphism of this kind. In order to
prevent too high a proportion of persons from being tempted to win a
'free rider', and thus to opt out, one must therefore have recourse to
normative preoccupations and to ideology, inasmuch as they reinforce
the solidarity of the whole.

Bruce Fireman and William Gamson have produced their own
critique of the theory expounded by Mancur Olson, and have emphasised that the costlier a failure is (as, for example, in the case of a
strike), the less tolerable a utilitarian strategy will be for those who
participate in a social movement; in the case of a strike, failure would
depend upon the number of persons mobilised whereas, in other cases,
such as a demonstration, the consequences would not be so dramatic.[44]
Since, from this perspective, individual action is linked to collective
action, the group will be organised in such a way as to lower the cost of
participation and reinforce collective sentiments. This will increase
its efficacy and enhance the integration of the actors and, consequently, their own satisfaction – the individual as a person also needs
to be listened to by others. This is why, contrary to the hypothesis
advanced by Mancur Olson, not participating in such a group may be
costly from the actor's point of view, for it may undermine his
self-image and his self-esteem. It is therefore not merely the quest for
specific rewards (as the utilitarians believe) that drives the actor to
commit himself to a collective movement, nor is it irrelevant what size
the group which sets it in motion may be.[45] Well aware of these
difficulties, Mancur Olson acknowledges that purely social and non-
costly incitements to act, such as the attention an individual may enjoy
within a group, can hardly be accounted for in terms of pure interest.
However, he immediately goes on to add that this kind of incitement is
unlikely to emerge within a large-scale latent group (unless it can be
divided into a number of small groups), and he also stresses that many
small groups, especially in the United States, are profoundly heterogeneous and that, even in a more limited framework of this kind, purely
social incitement is also difficult.[46]

It seems at first as if Mancur Olson's theory, which is meant to account for the absence of collective mobilisation in a society with a generalised market in which individuals each adhere to a utilitarian moral position, may readily be reconciled with the model advanced by Albert Hirschman. As far as Hirschman is concerned, each individual, to maximise his own self-interest, can either 'exit' from a group (that is, 'defect', change state, religion, class, or even family), or use his 'voice' and protest or, finally, remain loyal. Fundamentally, in a market society, the individual acts in such a way as to make his personal 'exit' likely – from his class through social mobility, or from his territory through the kind of horizontal mobility which is peculiar to American society. Instead of committing himself to a strategy of collective protest, of mobilisation, the actor maximises his gains by opting for an individual exit.

It is already plain, however, that the more open a society remains, the easier defection is. As Albert Hirschman observes, 'in societies which inhibit passage from one social stratum to another, resort to the voice option is automatically strengthened: everyone has a strong motivation to defend the quality of life at his own station'.[47] Defection is also easier in a society in which the family, primary groups, or the various different kinds of membership group, play a less crucial role, through their non-imposition of an unrelenting loyalty, in social control.[48] Hirschman holds that, in the American political tradition, individualism encourages people to embark upon the march towards the West, reinforces the 'myth of the frontier', and explains why, both in the past and in the present, people prefer 'flight to combat'. In this respect, the hippies also belong fairly and squarely within the same tradition.[49]

The studies of Mancur Olson and Albert Hirschman put us in a better position to understand Sombart's interpretation of the absence of socialism in the United States.[50] Since a socialist movement requires collective mobilisation, it has little chance of spreading in a society where individual mobility favours the maximisation of personal self-interest. There is a sense in which Adam Smith's arguments, which lead logically to those of Mancur Olson (who does, however, set aside, at least by implication, the hypothesis of the invisible hand) and of Albert Hirschman, and which presuppose the generalisation of the market economy and an end to the differentiation between politics and economics, fit perfectly with English and American society, where the market has developed by itself while the state has not differentiated itself to the extent of having a genuinely institutionalised structure.[51] In Great Britain and in the United States, where individualism and Protestantism are readily combined with each other without giving rise to an atomised mass society, the early emergence of capitalism has led to *laissez-faire* and the state has remained weak.[52] Conversely, in France and in Germany, a highly independent, differentiated and institutionalised state has prevented the extension of the market economy, together with the associated spread of individualism. This accounts for the persistence of collective solidarities of a class or territorial nature which come into conflict with the state, and for the greater frequency of political mobilisation. It is also probably reasonable to infer that, in social systems with a highly institutionalised state and with substantial communal solidarities of a religious, territorial or class nature, the actors are more attached to the functions that they perform within institutions, to the roles connected with such institutions, or indeed to the collective values of their membership groups. In this sense, one can argue that the conception of 'over-socialisation', condemned at a more theoretical level by Denis Wrong,[53] is more applicable in circumstances such as those described above than it is in a context where the absence of a strong state and the relative openness of classes, groups and territories allows the actors to be more independent, so that they are the more able to direct their action towards private benefits and to abandon all forms of collective mobilisation.

These strategies in favour of private benefits appear, therefore, to be eminently individualist in nature, and the kind of protest to which an actor may have recourse, in preference to exiting, is itself sometimes still the outcome of a calculation resting upon the defence of personal interests.

A large number of manifestations of protest, however, do not derive from individual calculation, for protest may in fact be the result of failed 'exit'; it may also be the consequence of feelings of loyalty or of collective identification, or it may follow on, as in the case in Switzerland, from the actual organisation of the political system.[54] Calculations in terms of profit and loss can hardly be held to account for these types of collective behaviour. Aware of this difficulty, Hirschman has sought to ward off any comparison between his own approach and that of Olson and has advanced a cyclical theory which leads, from the quest for private happiness, beyond the disillusionment which necessarily follows on from that, to public commitment, with the actor[55] then deciding to enter the public domain. Hirschman's account of the demonstrations against the war in Vietnam, together with the conclusions he draws from May 1968, leads him to emphasise the benefit an actor may derive from participating in a collective action which improves his own self-image, so that an activity which is presumed to be costly may in reality turn out to be beneficial for the actor, no matter what collective results are obtained.[56] In the days immediately following the invasion of Cambodia, Hirschman acknowledged that in some situations, participation in collective protest may have become an essential end in itself.[57] Taking the argument still further, he admits that the decision to protest should not be assessed merely in terms of costs and benefits but also in terms of the risk of repression which may follow on from it.[58] More generally, Hirschman now places much emphasis upon the collective dimension of the 'exit' which may occur as a result of a state's decision to encourage emigration in order to avoid domestic protest (as, for example, in Cuba) or to bring down the socialist vote (as, for instance, in a number of Italian regions, where the socialist vote is high when emigration is low and vice versa); he even manages to demonstrate that the individual 'exit' towards the suburbs of American towns may, in some cases, lead to collective protests on the part of those already there, who refuse to make another 'exit'.[59] In such circumstances, both exit and protest are to be accounted for not so much in terms of a rational calculus developed by an actor as in terms of the political programmes advanced by various states or by more structural contradictions.

The model which Albert Hirschman had advanced and, as we have seen, subsequently revised, allows one to account for collective action; indeed, it acknowledges that such a thing as collective action is actually possible. Conversely, Mancur Olson admits that his theory does not really allow one to analyse such phenomena, phenomena which would moreover assume a dysfunctional and somewhat irrational character.[60] He argues that only small groups can be mobilised, since only there can each actor reasonably anticipate an increase in his personal benefits. The larger groups, on the other hand, are not mobilised, according to Olson, except where there is recourse to constraint or where there is pressure from élites which derive individual rewards from the collective movement. In such eventualities, a group is 'mobilised'[61] in spite of itself, without its therefore being previously endowed with associative or community structures.

The criticism which Claus Offe and Helmut Wiesenthal advance of Olson's model rests upon the reintroduction into the analysis of precisely the socio-economic dimension which all latent groups have, since none of them consists simply of wholly identical individuals. They emphasise that, whereas leaders of the business world can act as individuals, workers must necessarily unite in order to defend their personal interests collectively. They therefore hold that the logic of collective action is, in each case, quite dissimilar. For the time being, I would merely note that this observation does not in any way contradict Olson's model, for not only does he admit that only small groups can act, but he even shows how the business world manages to organise itself into trusts and other forms of monopoly which serve to restrict economic expansion.[62]

Those who have power are less numerous, are less often divided among themselves, have more resources at their disposal and have a clear understanding of their own real interests. According to Olson, they therefore constitute a group which is readily mobilised and organised because each actor finds some benefit in it. The workers, on the other hand, have first to gather together and organise themselves into huge unions, and the more developed the unions are, the more heterogeneous they become; the workers then find themselves obliged to build up a strong bureaucratic organisation, which is bound also to have dysfunctional effects.[63] Claus Offe and Helmut Wiesenthal next attempt to show how certain interests can be effectively defended within the existing framework of atomistic political practices, whereas those interests which presuppose some form of collective organisation come into collision with the political framework of liberalism.

The conflict between the two groups therefore unfolds within the framework of a particular kind of politics, namely liberalism; it also has its effect upon the nature of the political forms themselves. What Claus Offe and Helmut Wiesenthal maintain is that the first level of the conflict, at which costs and benefits constitute the fixed parameter of the action, is accounted for by the logic of collective action described by Olson, since it analyses the actors' behaviour and explains why some stand more chance than others of gain. But this logic is incomplete: it fails to account for the second level of the conflict, at which collective action bears on the redefinition of what is meant by 'costs' and 'benefits'. The aim of this second kind of conflict does not consist in 'obtaining something', but in finding out what it is one actually wants to obtain by getting rid of a deluded and false perception of one's real interests.[64] The liberal political order thus imposes on the working class a pressure group strategy which does not really suit it at all; it obliges it to separate political struggles from purely economic claims, with party and union activity being opposed to each other, and it hems it in within a juridical order of contracts and obligations which restricts its capacity to mobilise. Although this approach remains too generalised a one, and does not take into account, for example, the actual history of the capitalist societies in which these conflicts are enacted, on the basis of it one can try to analyse the problem of mobilisation not only in relation to the model of mass society, or indeed to that of methodological individualism, but also by concentrating upon the social organisation peculiar to each of the groups involved in the confrontation.

Political mobilisation therefore depends upon a previously constituted social organisation. In opposition to the theoreticians of mass society and writers who asserted a connection between the power of crowds and the scale of mobilisation, we are now in a position to show how mobilisation in fact requires the prior formation of close social ties. A return to Marx may prove helpful here, for his work contains original analyses of the ties which can be established between class and mass. In *The Communist Manifesto*, for example, Marx shows that the proletariat forms a mass which, through the development of industry, becomes more and more concentrated. In opposition to the bourgeoisie, the workers founded 'permanent associations in order to make provision beforehand for these revolts. Here and there the contest breaks out into riots.'[65] This conception of mobilisation presupposes the formation of organisations which place a limit upon society being structured as a mass.

Union is then helped on by 'the improved means of communication . . . that place the workers of different localities in contact with one another'.[66] Marx here formulates a theory of mobilisation which in many respects anticipates that advanced in our own time by Karl Deutsch,[67] which shows how atomisation must be overcome by organisation and how this in turn necessitates communisation. For Marx, insofar as industry 'concentrates in one place a crowd of people unknown to one another', and insofar as 'capital has created a common situation and common interests for this mass', it is therefore already 'a class as against capital but not yet for itself'. In struggle, this mass unites and constitutes itself as a class for itself.[68] Marx has also applied this analysis to the peasantry, in the classic text on small-holding peasants, who 'form an immense mass'; their 'isolation is strengthened by the wretched state of France's means of communication',[69] which prevents them from creating a community, national organisations and political parties. The class in itself therefore remains a mass; it can only become a class insofar as it organises itself, thereby making mobilisation possible.[70]

In contrast to the interpretation that Mancur Olson gives of the Marxist analysis of class, which would have it that classes, being latent groups, would be incapable of mobilising, I would draw the reader's attention to the manner in which Marx employs the notions of mass, crowd and class to establish, at least in theory, the possibility of a collective mobilisation dependent upon a form of organisation which would do away with isolation. In the last analysis, one could almost assert that Mancur Olson subscribes to Lenin's implicit criticism of Marx's theory, for Olson maintains, as does Lenin, that a latent group is not able to organise itself and must therefore be activated by a party élite, which may have recourse to all available means of constraint. Lenin employs the notion of 'mass' too, but for him the isolation of those constituting it means that it is necessarily apathetic; the masses will not spontaneously mobilise and their strikes are therefore, for Lenin, ineffectual. Whereas Marx holds that, in order to mobilise, 'the proletariat organises itself as a class and therefore as a [generalised] political party', for Lenin it is the party which structures the class mass from the outside,[71] keeping for itself, much as in Olson's account, particular rewards, thus making the professionalisation of its leaders easier to justify.

By contrast, Marx, together with the mass society theorists, maintained that the members of latent groups could mobilise by themselves, but for the mass society theorists mobilisation presupposed some kind of self-organisation, whereas for Marx collective action was still regarded as a consequence of atomisation. The modern theory of mass society has inherited this perspective and, taking its inspiration from de Tocqueville and the modern theory of pluralism – which rests upon the notion that there is an equilibrium between groups – affirms that organised groups are by their nature opposed to mobilisation. For William Kornhauser, it is precisely because intermediate groups would be under threat in a mass society that mobilisation and

Figure 1.1 *Collectivities classified along vertical and horizontal dimensions of integration*

Vertical dimension:	Horizontal dimension: links within the collectivity		
	Communal organization	Un- or weakly-organized	Associational organization
Links between collectivities			
Integrated	A	B	C
Segmented	D	E	F

extremist political behaviour become a real possibility.[72] In the light of Maurice Pinard's findings, it seems reasonable to suppose that the presence of powerful intermediate groups can also make the potential for mobilisation all the greater;[73] the atomised masses may also demonstrate their apathy by remaining depoliticised or, on the other hand, appear to be spontaneously loyal to society as a whole, while expressing no allegiance to an intermediate or peripheral social structure.[74] Each of these propositions would seem to vitiate the basic principles of the modern theory of mass society.

Anthony Oberschall rejects both those models which deduce mobilisation from atomisation and those which assume that mobilisation never affects latent groups. In their place, he suggests that mobilisation depends both upon a strong organisation inside the group and upon its separation from the society's other classes or collectivities.

Anthony Oberschall in fact distinguishes between two different variables (see Figure 1.1).[75] The first, which he terms horizontal, concerns the internal organisation of the social group: based on the *Gemeinschaft–Gesellschaft* distinction, it enables one to differentiate between community or associated structures and internal organisational networks.[76] Oberschall holds that the existence of such structures is an indispensable condition for the birth of a mobilising tendency which will enable social groups to defend their particular interests. In order to analyse the precise way in which these groups will act, Oberschall employs a second variable, which he terms vertical: considered as a function of this second variable, social collectivities may be either allied with the ruling classes or the authorities – this 'integration' enabling them to take advantage of a kind of representation which favours the defence of their own interests – or 'segmented', that is separated and isolated from these same classes and

authorities.[77] It is only in the latter case that mobilisation is
unleashed.[78] Since segmentation reduces social control and strengthens particularisms, the representative élites of these classes or ethnic
and cultural groups, finding that they have from now on been pushed
to one side, have everything to gain from a mobilisation of this kind,
inasmuch as they are now deprived of all access to these sites of power.
According to Anthony Oberschall, this interpretation of mobilisation
may readily be reconciled with the Marxist perspective.[79] Indeed,
whenever Oberschall presents an overview of his model, he invariably
employs a problematic which is organised in terms of social classes:[80]
the mobilisations which arise in D or in F, for example, occur within a
class. In D, 'The more segmented a collectivity is from the rest of the
society, and the more viable and extensive the communal ties within it,
the more rapid and easier it is to mobilize members of the collectivity
into an opposition movement.'[81] In F, 'In a segmented context, the
greater the number and variety of organisations in a collectivity, and
the higher the participation of members in this network, the more
rapidly and enduringly does mobilisation into conflict groups occur,
and the more likely it is that bloc recruitment, rather than individual
recruitment will take place.'[82] These two cases of mobilisation are
plain enough, for they arise in situations where there is segmentation
as a result of one type or other of social organisation within a class. The
intermediate situation, however, is a more ambiguous one: indeed, in
E, the collectivity is organised neither in a communal nor in an
associational manner; nevertheless, it is still segmented.[83] At first
glance, Oberschall's hypothesis seems to bear some resemblance to the
traditional theory of mass society. It cannot, however, be aligned with
it, both because this segmented and disorganised collectivity may arise
within a society in which other social classes have preserved their own
internal organisations and because the mobilisation which arises in E
presupposes, according to Oberschall, 'common feelings of oppression and similar enemies'.[84] Awareness of a common destiny here
bolsters internal organisation, thereby limiting disorganisation and
warding off atomisation. This being the case, and even though it is
vital to give a more exact account of the nature of the vertical variable
than Anthony Oberschall does,[85] logic demands that we take a deeper
interest in the two dimensions inherent in the horizontal variable. As
Sandor Halebsky has shown, this variable must be interpreted as
much in relation to the sentiment of identification felt by the actors as

Figure 1.2

	Intermediate group ties	
	High proportion	Low proportion
High degree Sensed integration (of individuals)	A Nonmass society, less likely to be qualified	B Nonmass society, possibly qualified
	Vigorous protest possible in both cells, more likely to be of a group interest nature; erratic character less likely.	
Low degree	D Leaning toward mass society	C Mass society
	Vigorous protest possible in both cells, less likely to be of a group interest nature; erratic character more likely.	

in terms of the organisational structures of the various groups. His model (presented in Figure 1.2) gives us an exhaustive account of the relations between the two dimensions of the 'horizontal' variable.[86] It is, however, as well to bear in mind that Halebsky does perhaps accord too much weight to the sentiment of integration as against social ties: he maintains, for instance, that one is dealing with a social system evolving towards mass society when the individuals' sentiment of identification with the group is weak, even if the ties internal to such groups are strong. One could equally well regard the opposite hypothesis as true. Furthermore, these two dimensions of the 'horizontal' variable ought to be correlated with the 'segmentation–integration' variable. Notwithstanding all these objections, I would stress that the model advanced by Halebsky enables one to reintroduce, in the general context of mobilisation theory, the traditional analysis, which tends at present to be neglected, of mass society: according to this theory, in this type of society a number of exceptional, collective movements, which depend neither upon communal organisations nor upon associative structures, may be unleashed. I would stress, however, that Nazism did not develop in a mass society of this kind but that it has tended to flourish, as we shall see below, where there are highly organised social structures.[87]

It was Charles Tilly who attempted a general survey of the different conditions favouring mobilisation, and his emphasis has been upon the resources available to the actual group which embarks upon a process of collective action of this kind. According to Tilly, a group's mobilisation is linked to the defence of a collective interest formed within the framework of relations of production and articulated by the actors themselves (the problem of 'true' and 'false' consciousness). This group must then organise itself, a process which Tilly defines in terms of the following proposition: the stronger the group's feeling of identity and the more intense its network of internal relations, the more organised the group is.[88] On this basis, since mobilisation is conceived as 'the process by which a group ceases to be a set of passive individuals and becomes an active element in public life',[89] it demands recourse to collective resources of various kinds (money, labour, publicity, time devoted to mobilisation, symbols).[90] This is why mobilisation results in a form of rational collective action 'insofar as it produces indivisible goods'[91] rather than individual goods. Action then becomes both collective and intentional, so that the sociology of mobilisation here turns its back both on traditional crowd psychology and upon individualist utilitarianism.

Collective action now assumes a more specifically political guise inasmuch as it constitutes itself against a power which it undermines or from which it attempts to extract concessions.[92] Collective mobilisation is therefore in itself laden with a political dimension, for it is formed in response to the state which it confronts.[93] Thus, in the Vendée, the mobilisation which occurred on the Mauges plateau against the revolutionary state was not so much a conservative reaction as a movement for the defence of a closely knit community. Since urbanisation had taken little hold there, the community had preserved its collective ties and, refusing to allow itself to be atomised into so many citizens, resisted the authorities.[94] In this sense,

revolutions and collective violence tend to flow directly out of a population's central political processes, instead of expressing diffuse strains and discontents within the population . . . specific claims and counter-claims being made on the existing government by various mobilized groups are more important than the general satisfaction or discontent of those groups and . . . claims for established places within the structure of power are crucial.[95]

Power is therefore a key issue for Charles Tilly. Nevertheless, being mainly concerned with France, his explanation of the birth and development of peripheral collective action does not really seem to take into account the type of state which has arisen there. To what extent would an identical mobilisation develop in relation to a state with quite

different structures and with strategies of its own differing markedly
from those considered above?

Mobilisation against the state

It would thus seem crucial that any analysis of collective mobilisation
should contain a more precise account of the state as variable.[96] As
Theda Skocpol observes, 'we can make sense of social-revolutionary
transformations only if we take the state seriously as a macro-
structure'.[97] It is therefore on the basis of her treatment of the type of
state as being itself an independent variable that Skocpol undertakes a
comparative study of revolutions and manages to establish a strict
relation between their outbreak and the specific types of state which
the social groups – in France (in 1789), in Russia (in 1917) or in China
(from 1911 on) – launching themselves into collective action, had to
confront. In all three cases, mobilisation was organised in societies
with agrarian structures in which particularly institutionalised and
independent bureaucratic[98] states had been established.

Theda Skocpol holds that it is the military conflicts between these
states and those societies which have undergone a faster economic
development that obliges the former to modernise themselves.
However, they encounter resistance from powerful aristocracies, and
this renders such transformation more difficult. This explains their
collapse and the mobilisation of the peasantry, over which the aristocracy has long since abandoned all political control, leaving this
function to states, which from then on are under threat. According to
Skocpol, in *States and Social Revolutions*, 'it was the breakdown of the
concerted repressive capacity of a previously unified and centralized
state that finally created conditions directly or ultimately favourable to
widespread and *irreversible* peasant revolts against landlords'.[99]

Considered in an international context, the mobilisation of the
peasantry therefore only occurs where a certain kind of state comes
under threat. According to Skocpol, other states, such as Prussia or
Japan, which have maintained other kinds of relation with the ruling
class, have managed to ward off the outbreak of revolution. There is no
need, in the framework of the present analysis, to embark upon a closer
study of this comparative account of the birth and development of
revolutions which were to lead, in the three cases in question, to the
formation of still more bureaucratised states. I would simply note here

that, while Theda Skocpol manages to introduce the state as a variable into her explanation for the rise of revolutionary mobilisation, one can nevertheless challenge her decision to describe, in much the same terms, as bureaucratic–revolutionary states, states which are in fact very different from each other: the French state at the end of the eighteenth century was perhaps more institutionalised than the Russian state, and its mode of operation differed still more from that of the Chinese Empire. Conversely, for Theda Skocpol, bureaucratised though the French or Chinese states may be, they are nevertheless still permeated by the dominant landed class, which prevents them from being modernised; as an example of the opposite case, she presents that of the Prussian state, which, in her view, because it succeeded in integrating the landed aristocracy into its own structures, managed to free itself from its influence.

It is a little startling, in a general sense, to find a state which was to continue to be dominated by the power of the aristocracy being described as a bureaucratic–absolutist state. Furthermore, one would be within one's rights if one chose to reject a number of Skocpol's classifications, such as that which posits an opposition between a less independent French state and a more independent Prussian one, and to argue that this proposition makes more sense if reversed. Finally, it is to be regretted that the British state, which has rightly been considered a non-bureaucratic one, is here aligned with the Prussian and Japanese ones.[100] Despite these reservations regarding the nature of the states under analysis, Theda Skocpol's work had the virtue of placing the emphasis upon the state as variable and upon its role in the outbreak of the revolutionary process.

It is worth noting, however, that Theda Skocpol tends to disregard the internal networks which structure, in many different ways, social groups embarking upon mobilisation, and to which authors such as Anthony Oberschall and Charles Tilly have, by contrast, drawn our attention. Whereas she does, for instance, accord some weight to the modes of sociability uniting French peasants within their own territory, modes which serve to increase their independence,[101] she does not present a systematic analysis of what is, as Oberschall and Tilly have shown, an undoubtedly crucial dimension of mobilisation. Nevertheless, Theda Skocpol does note the extent to which peasant collectivities that are prone to uprisings have managed, as much in France as in Russia or in China, to preserve their independence, whereas, in

Prussia or in Japan, they are wholly dominated by the central authorities.[102] Mobilisation does indeed depend upon the strength of the social ties woven between the various actors. We must, however, examine the manner in which it develops in relation to the other actors and, in particular, in relation to the state, which may in turn serve to limit its extension. In his latest study, Anthony Oberschall stresses how the state tends generally to be the favourite target of a social movement and he analyses, much as Gary Marx had done,[103] the manner in which it is liable to intervene in order to reduce the movement's resources (money, jobs and so on), by employing force, by altering the function of its leaders, by limiting the recruitment of new members so as to prevent those who are merely sympathisers from participating,[104] by promoting rival groups and, finally, by presenting a very negative image of the movement to public opinion. These sorts of intervention are meant to affect the efficacy of the organisations which unleash mobilisation, so as to cast a slur on their achievements and cause discouragement and a return to passivity. This perspective leads to mobilisation being presented as a dynamic movement which gives rise to many, shifting strategies on the part of all the actors involved.

One therefore has to cross the many variables which serve to organise the kind of social framework conducive to mobilisation with those which determine the nature of the many different types of state in existence, which must themselves be rigorously distinguished from each other. In this respect, although it is true that the particular logic of each state[105] imposes itself on all the social actors involved, with the latter finding themselves forced to adopt modes of behaviour which correspond to the kind of state which they are facing, they can nevertheless manage to commit themselves, this time because of their own structures and values, to strategies of mobilisation which are peculiarly their own.

If mobilisation is therefore organised within the framework of social structures favouring the permanence of closely knit collective relations, it is only transformed into a movement which brings social change when it confronts a specific type of state.[106] I want now to apply this interpretation of the conditions conducive to mobilisation to a number of historical examples. We would do well, I think, to begin with certain studies by Charles Tilly and by those who have adopted his position. In his study of movements of collective action in present-day France,

Tilly has come to take more account of the state as a variable; he never tires of emphasising the very centralised nature of the state which has been constructed in France, based as it is upon the power of the bureaucracy and upon the permanent hold it has over the social and territorial peripheries. For Tilly,

nineteenth-century centralization and nationalization of politics, as the state crushed its local rivals, incited widespread protest . . . the enormous centralization of power within the French system has probably defined more different kinds of struggles in France then elsewhere, as confrontations between the state and its enemies.[107]

Charles Tilly is here describing the action of a state which, in the absolutist tradition, strives to master the whole of the social system and thus unleashes, to a greater degree than in other countries, violent reactions which themselves repeatedly provoke the collapse of political authority.

The manner in which collective mobilisation alters is itself linked to some extent to increases in the power of the state. Charles Tilly thus distinguishes competitive mobilisation, which leads to the groups involved in the acquisition of disputed resources being opposed to each other, from defensive mobilisation, which occurs when a state's domination has become intolerable, his aim being, in the last analysis, to show that, in the middle of the nineteenth century, with the victory of democracy,[108] mobilisation was at last able to move on to the offensive, abandoning communal structures so as to cast itself in the form of associations, parties or unions. One thus progresses historically from competitive mobilisation, by way of reactive collective action, arriving in the end at proactive mobilisation. This may still be just as violent as the previous type,[109] for the strikes themselves, though shorter in duration than other forms of collective violence, also had a more determined leadership.[110] For all its different forms, mobilisation directed against the state therefore loses nothing of its intensity.

In a highly original chapter, Charles Tilly even undertakes an analysis of strikes in a number of different countries, comparing Great Britain and Germany with France. This being his aim, he establishes a relation between the type of strike – its form, duration and extent – and the type of political power which each of the working classes had to confront.[111] He thus shows that, during the period 1900–29, the strikes occurring in France and in Great Britain were quite different in nature. In France, they tended to last a short time (15 days' work lost by each striker), they mobilised relatively few workers (300 per strike), and they were relatively common (6 to 12 conflicts for every 100,000 workers each year). Conversely, in Great Britain, strikes lasted longer (27 days), mobilised more workers (1,100 workers, on average, per strike) but were less frequent (4 strikes for every 100,000 workers each year). In order to account for these differences, Charles Tilly places the emphasis upon the reformist tradition of the British unions, which had impressive resources at their disposal and knew how to mobilise when necessary, so that their point of view could, by a genuine process of bargaining, be heard.

In his study of the subsequent period (1945–68), Tilly notes the emergence of further differences in the structure of strikes in the two countries. Whereas, in Great Britain as in France, strikes in this period last approximately the same length of time and occur as often, in France they now mobilise large sectors of the working class, which at last manage to take their place in the political market, while in Great Britain participation in strikes drops ever lower because, in the context of a system of representation of multiple social or even territorial interests, the representatives of the working class not only manage to have their voices heard but, in addition, repeatedly accede to political power. The nature of the political system therefore accounts for the relative integration of the working class, as represented by the Labour Party, explains demobilisation and, as a recoil effect, the appearance of small-scale wildcat strikes. As Charles Tilly observes, the British example allows us to answer the question: 'what happens to strikes after the workers have won political representation?'[112]

Charles Tilly does not, however, subject the nature of each state to a genuine critical examination, even if he is aware of the differences between the two political systems. Nevertheless, he outlines a perspective which other authors were later to flesh out more fully.[113] Emphasising quite properly the need for a comparative analysis of mobilisations, and of the transformations which they undergo in different countries, Charles Tilly takes full account of the rhythms evident as the political market is extended through political reforms, but he does not study, for example, the features which are peculiar to the British state when he focuses upon the struggles which oppose the English authorities to the various social movements mobilized against them.[114] Finally, I would add that it is also crucial to consider to what extent the three kinds of mobilisation follow on from each other, irrespective of the type of state with which they are confronted.

Relinquishing a comparative perspective of this kind, to which the sociology of mobilisation will undoubtedly have to return if it aspires to master the crucial problem of the relations between types of state and the nature of mobilisation, Charles Tilly's pupils have shown how the perspective outlined in *The Vendée* can serve to inspire the analysis of collective movements in nineteenth-century France and, in particular, those which arose in opposition to the *coup d'état* of 1851. Ted Margadent shows how the regions which mobilised were both highly organised collectively and divided off from the rest of the social system. Indeed, mobilisation occurred in rural communes faced with urbanisation and with integration into the national market and into a wider political context. The persistence of communal links did, however, guarantee a greater internal solidarity. Mobilisation against 'the centralised bureaucracy'[115] was based upon the solidity of local volunteer associations, youth groups and so on; the cafés ensured that the groups' lines of communication were never broken.[116] In France, local integration was thus achieved through circles or cafés, which made sure that sociability endured.[117] This function was also performed by all the other forms of communal structure thanks to which mobilisation was propagated.[118] Charles Tilly's general model[119] suggests that, alongside these more communal forms of solidarity, there arose voluntary associations which also served to reinforce sociability;[120] 'secondary groups' like primary groups were thus able, contrary to Cooley's objections, to serve as a basis for solidarity. Thus mobilisation is unleashed both by segmentation and by an internal organisation which depends upon communal organisation but which may also have an associative character. Margadent is thus able to conclude: 'the townsmen and villagers who rebelled in 1851 shared both proactive and reactive orientations to the nation-state, and they mobilized manpower on both an associational and a communal basis'.[121] I would further point out that this mobilisation develops, according to Margadent, in opposition to a particular kind of state, which he describes in much the same way as Charles Tilly does. In France, Margadent observes, the historical growth of the state 'has involved the elaboration of complex bureaucratic and military hierarchies . . . [and] the . . . destruction of localized systems of authority'.[122] In this respect, there was a mobilisation 'of villages in arms against the state',[123] which was trying to increase its hold still further over both the countryside and the big towns, where mobilisation was also occurring in this period through the political clubs, the cafés and the mutual aid societies, that is through the whole of the working class's social network.[124]

The Nazi collective movement and the Prussian state

In order to assess the crucial role played by different kinds of group in the process of mobilisation which is realised against particular kinds of state, I shall now consider the Nazi movement, for the advocates of the theory of mass society have always accorded it a special place, as it seems to them to demonstrate the validity of the relation established by them between atomisation and mobilisation. Today we are in a better position to assess these authors' presentation of their theory, thanks to a number of recent studies that offer us a deeper understanding of German society of the period; the perspectives outlined by Oberschall and Tilly likewise enable us to arrive at a better appreciation of their model. My purpose in examining this extreme case is also to pay more attention to the values and ideologies which lead the actors involved towards mobilisation. Even nowadays, the theoreticians of mobilisation still tend too often to neglect this dimension, which is nevertheless inherent in social action, the ideologies developed by social groups being reducible neither to communal values alone nor to projects emanating from organisations of the associative type. Mobilisation does indeed, as is the case with all kinds of social change, depend upon the resources that are available and upon the ties woven between the various actors, but it also testifies to the power of more or less developed world views, of ideologies and of utopias which are sometimes messianic in nature.[125]

Many writers subscribing to the unsociological perspective of crowd psychology interpret the crisis of the Weimar Republic and the success of the Nazi movement as the consequence of the complete atomisation of society, a process which gives rise to individual actions of a purely psychological nature; juxtaposed individuals, separated from all social ties, would thus constitute a crowd, would adopt all the extremist and illogical forms of behaviour and would make all the most extremist ideologies their own. Mobilisation would thus not result from the intentional calculus peculiar to each actor, nor would it be aided by close social ties. Latent groups would, in the last analysis, be fitted for mobilisation because of the emotion which had taken hold of them.[126] Much as in Le Bon's studies, the atomised Nazi crowds would be attracted by the charisma of the leader; they would tend to be women, emotional, and fascinated by the words that modern means of communication transmit in such quantities. Individuals would be 'sleepwalkers', behaving as if hypnotised, and the 'nationalisation of the masses'[127] would be achieved with the help of a romantic symbolism, with torch-lit parades reminding their audience of the ancient deities of the German people. Once atomised, the crowd would form a community once again; with *völkisch* ideology favouring the revival of a *bündisch* type of solidarity unifying hearts and minds,[128] the Nazi crowd, brought together in shared celebration of common myths, would be easily mobilised.

According to Hannah Arendt, 'the masses grew out of the fragments of a highly atomised society whose competitive structure and concomitant loneliness of the individual had been held in check only through membership in a class'.[129] Already present before the régime was established, atomisation was deliberately intensified by 'the totalitarian regime which always transforms classes into masses'.[130] Class solidarities vanished along with allegiances to the nation-state; the era of irrational crowds was thus born, which led necessarily to totalitarianism. Hannah Arendt gives no clue as to the causes of the atomisation which existed prior to the advent of totalitarianism and which the latter used in order to bolster itself; in addition, the individuals who constitute the mass seem sometimes to originate in 'all of the different political parties', sometimes solely in those who are marginal and in the lumpenproletariat.

Emile Lederer and Sigmund Neumann are in agreement with Hannah Arendt in seeing atomisation as the essential condition for the birth of fascist power. Lederer also emphasises the way in which the Nazis deliberately destroyed pre-existing organisations and so acknowledges that they had not yet disappeared. Sigmund Neumann, while keeping a little closer to Hannah Arendt's analysis, differs from her in that he maintains that the proletariat, which had for a long time remained outside the national community and had enjoyed a strong culture of its own, managed to resist the attractions of Nazism, so that it did not dissolve into the atomised crowd and therefore did not adopt its traditional forms of behaviour.[131] Taking precisely the opposite view to that developed by Emile Lederer and the theoreticians of mass society, Franz Neumann begins by bringing out the existence of strong collective, social ties in Weimar Germany, in which groups were, he maintains, both numerous and well organised. It was in fact Nazism, he argues, which undertook to destroy them, through 'the atomisation of the individual. Such groups as the family and the Church, the solidarity arising from common working plants, shops, and offices are deliberately broken down ... There must be no social intercourse outside the prescribed totalitarian organisation.'[132] Atomisation is thus, in Neumann's view, the result of Nazism rather than the other way round.

Studies by modern historians have in fact shown how German society was far from undergoing a process of radical atomisation. Not only was the solidarity of the ruling class maintained, with the latter dividing itself off still more from the rest of the social body, but numerous other social groups managed to preserve their own organisational structures. And it was these latter, far more than atomised individuals, who were mobilised, at any rate as far as electoral behaviour was concerned, in support of Nazism.

Contrary to what has been argued by Kornhauser, the existence of groups therefore does not guarantee stability. Indeed, it is quite the other way round, inasmuch as groups with strongly communal links joined the Nazi movement. In Schleswig-Holstein, for example, Rudolf Heberle has shown that the part of the rural population which gave its support to Nazism belonged to 'homogeneous communities with a strong sentiment of solidarity'.[133] As Bernt Hagtvet has quite rightly observed, it was not despair or, indeed, a lack of 'voice' which prompted some to rejoin the Nazi movement: 'Joining the NSDAP was a conscious political decision ... the farmers' transfer to Nazism was a *collective* action.'[134] Following in the wake of the middle classes, the peasants quite consciously gave their support to Nazism. Far from seeming to be a hypnotised crowd, the Nazi movement turns out to be a collective action whose meaning was endorsed by all involved. Mobilisation, based here upon communal ties, was in no sense irrational; indeed, the Nazi Party served as a new integrating structure.

In this sense, the Nazi movement is the outcome not of atomisation but of opposition, of the separation between social groups which had preserved their internal solidarity. Furthermore, it is worth pointing out that the groups which were aligned with Nazism were highly organised and, at the same time, remote from the central authorities; they were in a state of 'segmentation', as is the case, for example, with the middle classes, which also wanted to protect their 'interests', their particularism, with respect to other social groups: 'Contrary to the claims of mass theory, it was the *high level of participation in secondary associations under conditions of superimposed segmentation which made for the rapid mobilization of people into the Nazi movement*.'[135]

Thalburg, a small German town in a rural context, was socially very cohesive and loyalty to one's membership group was very pronounced there. Its population was essentially a middle-class one and the proverb 'Two Germans, a discussion; three Germans, a club' was readily applicable to it. There was an infinite number of local societies, ranging from the hunters' club to the choral society: 'The many clubs and societies cemented individual citizens together. Without them Northeim would have been an amorphous society. Yet few of them cut across class lines.'[136] Through its rejection of the German Social Democratic Party, the town was to topple over, in a matter of a few years, into Nazism and, from 1933 on, Hitler's movement, having enjoyed a runaway success in the elections, was to embark upon the systematic atomisation of local society.[137] It destroyed and reorganised all those groups which had originally enabled it to make inroads into the social system. This example shows yet again how Nazi mobilisation depended upon communal structures and was carried out in a wholly deliberate manner. I would therefore assert that a reactionary mobilisation follows the same path as a progressive collective movement. Furthermore, I would note that those militants who were integrated into communal structures played in Germany, as in the France of 1851, a crucial role; in addition, they received what Olson would term 'selective incitement'.[138]

The mainly Protestant rural areas seem to have been cut off, relatively speaking, from the mainstream of society and were lacking any of the associations which might have represented them to the outside, in the *Gesellschaft*. According to Oberschall's own typology, they were in a state of high segmentation. By contrast, the Catholic rural areas were in a position to make inroads into the *Gesellschaft* through the mediations of the *Zentrum*. Their solid organisations, their strong internal integration, which gave rise to an effective socialisation and their regular representation in national terms in the upper echelons of the state, meant that they were not in a state of segmentation and were therefore able to resist Nazi mobilisation. The economic crisis tended to spread confusion in the rural areas, which still had an organisation of the *Gemeinschaft* type, and this favoured the advance of the Nazis, whose ideology was wholly directed towards a return to this type of natural community. The predominantly Catholic rural areas were better equipped to put up an effective resistance to Nazism,[139] relying as they did upon their own modern organisations in order to preserve their own representation.

Rainer Lepsius maintains that much the same explanation may be advanced of the resistance of the working class, which was also highly structured, with communal organisations, with a strong awareness of its own separate identity and enjoying, thanks to the German Social Democratic Party, an effective representation at the national level.[140] In the heavily industrialised urban areas, such as the Ruhr, the Rhine or central Berlin, the socialist vote restricted the Nazi mobilisation. The National Socialist vote was denser in the country than in the town and, the smaller the collectivity that was involved, the higher this vote was.[141] If, however, it is now established that mobilisation in a Protestant environment in the countryside, or in small towns in the rural areas, was based upon solid communal links or upon organisations of the associative type, we still do not seem to be able to call upon analyses which will account for the structure of the Protestant milieu in the large towns. Yet data of this latter kind would seem to be all the more indispensable given that, in the large towns, the Protestant *petite bourgeoisie* appears to have kept its distance from Nazism whereas the Catholic *petite bourgeoisie* rallied to it.[142] Considered all in all, the middle classes, which were heavily represented in the Nazi ranks and lent the movement a crucial degree of support, would seem in turn to have been solidly organised groups rather than atomised ensembles. Their 'central extremism', as Lipset has called it, which emerges in this context is therefore the outcome not of a sudden panic but rather of an intentional behaviour developed within secondary organisations still more highly organised than those of the working class.[143]

The middle classes therefore cannot be considered to be an emotion-dominated mass lending itself to any and every manipulation or mobilisation; the middle classes, and the upper middle classes in particular,[144] gravitated towards Nazism in the wake of the upper class by abandoning the conservative parties and by following the strategies adopted by their associations.

The various kinds of mobilisation can therefore never be accounted for in terms of the isolation and destruction of primary or secondary groups. Although influenced by religious allegiances and by context (over half of the Nazi votes of July 1932 derived from collectivities of less than 25,000 inhabitants, whereas the large cities, such as Berlin or Hamburg, further emphasised their support for the parties of the left and never gave more than 26% of their votes to Hitler's party), the vote for Hitler thus had a class basis also. While the workers were still relatively untouched (apart from the small proportion of conservative ones) and the unemployed voted more and more for the left, and the new electors did not in any systematic sense rally around Nazism,[145] it was above all the peasants, the middle classes and the upper classes which were prepared to follow Hitler,[146] each of these categories being highly organised into associations or groupings.

The theory of mass society is therefore particularly ill-suited to explaining the Nazi vote. Furthermore, it is also vitiated by the various studies made of Nazi militants, almost half of whom always remained in their place of birth. These militants were neither isolated nor mobile and, far from seeming to be professional agitators, the militants supporting Hitler's cause, especially in the countryside and in the small towns, where they were most entrenched, were highly integrated into the local community and thus succeeded in having an impact upon the electoral behaviour of their fellow citizens.[147]

Mobilisation therefore does not in general result from the atomisation of society. As those authors who have 'rediscovered' the presence of primary groups in modern industrial societies have already demonstrated,[148] such groups continue to mould the personality of the social actors and to determine their behaviour. It is groups, rather than individuals or crowds, which serve as vectors for the mobilisation of Protestants in the countryside, of the middle classes in towns or, again, of the Catholic and working-class collectivities which put up an effective resistance to Nazism. It is thus plain that, in the last analysis, many different kinds of mobilisation may operate in competition with each other at one and the same time. Mobilisation, in such a situation of generalised crisis,[149] follows several different paths at once, so that sometimes action is offensive in nature, being effected through communal rather than associational forms and in opposition to a particularly highly institutionalised state, action with which the Nazi movement, for example, would clash;[150] sometimes other sorts of mobilisation emerge in defence of social groups which are organised both in a communal manner and around associational structures;

sometimes, again, mobilisation may arise within middle classes consciously concerned to protect their own social status and, in this case, they tend to be mobilised more on an associational basis or in response to the greater atomisation to which they are vulnerable.

These different kinds of mobilisation arise in the name of opposed ideologies and world views (whose particular influence must be examined), with religious divisions sometimes being superimposed upon social ones or, conversely, sometimes remaining distinct from them; they assume, in addition, different degrees of intensity, ranging from simple electoral mobilisation to participation in demonstrations of protest in the street or to physical confrontation. They are supervised in varying degrees by the common man and by the militant, the professional of politics, who derives personal rewards from his involvement in it. They produce 'exits', enacted under duress, both of individuals and of a more dramatic nature, which represent forms of collective rejection and which sometimes re-create effaced loyalties of a class, religious, cultural or territorial nature, growing in strength on the periphery and thereby undermining the loyalty owed to the central authorities. Caught up in this whirlwind, in which it is also a key actor, the state confronts several different kinds of mobilisation in turn and itself supports still others, but, being highly institutionalised, it succeeds in preserving its own independence, so that other, totalitarian political institutions result from these warring mobilisations.

2 ❧ States, free riders and collective movements

Analysis of the state and of collective action requires, to put it succinctly, a thoroughgoing discussion of methodology, for social facts of this order can in fact be analysed just as effectively in terms of a structural perspective, which gives the whole precedence over its component parts, as in terms of the function of the action of individual actors, who perform on the basis of the roles they have in each of these structured ensembles. The opposition between holism and individualism may therefore be applied just as readily to a study of the state as to social movements. For Durkheim, 'the whole does not equal the sum of its parts', and therefore 'the group thinks, feels, and acts entirely differently from the way its members would if they were isolated. If therefore we begin by studying these members separately, we will understand nothing about what is taking place in the group.'[1] Which is why, as far as Durkheim is concerned, these social facts 'consist of manners of acting, thinking, and feeling, external to the individual, which are invested with a coercive power by virtue of which they exercise control over him'.[2] If one adopts a structural perspective of this kind, action depends upon the function which the actor exercises within the whole, upon the roles which are connected to that function, and upon the values and norms which are peculiar to the group and which exercise a kind of social control over each of the actors who are members of it. Many paradigms within modern sociological theory, whether functionalist, structuralist, or any one of their many combinations (Parsons) or revisions (Merton, Gouldner and so on), tend therefore to give precedence to the whole in their understanding of the action of an actor who has been socialised within that whole and whose values depend quite strictly upon the roles that he plays there. This kind of sociological theory is applied to all sorts of social fact, as much to those derived from primitive societies as to those with which the sociologists of modern society are concerned.

Max Weber, on the other hand, holds that an 'action is "social" insofar as its subjective meaning takes account of the behaviour of others and is thereby oriented in its course',[3] which is why 'any form of functional analysis which proceeds from the whole to the parts can accomplish only a preliminary preparation for this investigation', it being possible to deduce human action not so much from the functions performed by the actor as from the values to which he subscribes.[4] Weber thus felt able to declare: 'I became a sociologist . . . to put a stop to the spectre of collective conceptions. Sociology rests upon the study of the action of one or more separate individuals and must consequently adopt a strictly individualist method.'[5] Structural or structural–functionalist perspectives and individualist approaches are thus barely compatible with each other, and it would seem an arduous undertaking to attempt to reconcile them.[6] Declaring his opposition to the holistic conceptions of 'closed' societies, Karl Popper asserted that 'all social phenomena, and particularly the functioning of all social institutions, should always be studied as the result of the decisions, actions, attitudes, etc. of individuals . . . one must never be satisfied with explanations of a collective nature'.[7] Whether it takes as its starting-point the work of someone like Weber, who maintains that a 'state' no longer 'exists' whenever there is no longer a probability that certain kinds of meaningfully oriented social action will take place,[8] or that of a writer like Simmel, who claims that 'strictly speaking, it must be admitted that only individuals exist . . . It is therefore in terms of method that we speak of the state, or of law . . . as if these were undivided entities',[9] the aim of methodological individualism, in its study of, for example, the state, will always be to base its argument upon actions intentionally performed by actors operating within the framework of a given system of roles, with it being in no way permissible to deduce those actions from the functions which they assume there. We know, on the other hand, that for Durkheim, for example, the state 'is a genuine organ of reflection',[10] endowed with a 'clear' consciousness. There is therefore a profound divergence between structural and individualist perspectives as regards their treatment of the state or of collective action.

A number of theorists have sought to reject this opposition within sociological method by locating the particular domain of each approach at a different stage in the history of human society. Putting it simply, the substantivist and holistic method would serve for an account of primitive or highly communal societies, whereas a methodological-individualist perspective would in the main be applicable to societies in which modernisation, the development of the market, industrialisation, urbanisation and so on have given rise to a high degree of individualism. This opposition calls to mind a large number of classical sociological theories of the dichotomising kind, such as those of Tönnies, Cooley, Redfield, and so on. One therefore needs to be in a position to date the emergence of individualism.

In *Trade and Market in the Early Empires*, Karl Polanyi claimed that the, in many respects tragic, spread of individualism occurred at the end of the eighteenth century, with the generalisation of the market giving rise to concern to maximise one's personal self-interest.[11] Polanyi's analysis is somewhat reminiscent of the criticisms which Macaulay addressed to James Mill,[12] or indeed those which Marx made of Bentham. In the modern period, Louis Dumont likewise concluded that 'the problem of the origin of individualism is that of knowing how, starting out from the general type of holistic societies, a new type, which was in fundamental contradiction to the common conception, was able to develop'.[13] According to Dumont, individualism is therefore the 'modern ideology' which should not, strictly speaking, be applied 'to other societies'.[14] For him, too, as for Polanyi, it was essentially in the eighteenth century that the 'individual-in-the-world' became the only reality. Authors such as de Bonald, de Maistre and de Tocqueville had already, regrettably, asserted as much, and Macpherson gives a similar interpretation of the birth of possessive individualism[15] which, according to Robert Nisbet,[16] was supposed to have brought about the definitive destruction of the 'community' in which the parts were still tied together in a coherent whole. More recently, a number of other authors have rejected this dating of the first appearance of individualism, arguing rather that, in England, peasant societies in existence long before the birth of capitalism were already based upon an individualism unknown to the peasant societies of continental Europe. Alan Macfarlane thus rejects Polanyi's conclusions outright, together with those arrived at by Louis Dumont in his earlier works, and chooses rather to emphasise features peculiar to English society, in which, from the twelfth and thirteenth centuries on, agriculture itself became individualist, whereas French rural society and, more generally, continental Europe as a whole, remained communal. In his opposition to the arguments of both Marx and Weber,

Macfarlane maintains that English individualism therefore preceded both capitalism and Protestantism.[17] These divergent models of individualism thus locate its birth at various stages of modern society, some arguing that individualism supplants holism towards the end of the eighteenth century while, conversely, others maintain that these types of society can coexist at one and the same time in different regions of Western Europe. In spite of their divergences, it is possible to argue that, in either case, the methods employed in the analysis of the real (holism and methodological individualism) only have explanatory power for a limited number of specific societies with a communal structure or, conversely, with an individualist basis. As far as historical time is concerned, holism would enable one to account for primitive societies, or indeed for societies of a traditional kind, in terms of both their social structures and their power relations, whereas methodological individualism would seem to be a more adequate tool for analysing the social structures and types of state present in modern societies. As regards space, holism would enable one to examine a number of collective social structures in the present day and of a type of particularly institutionalised state, whereas methodological individualism could be employed for the study of atomised social structures and for less highly structured types of state.[18] Furthermore, one could well imagine also that particular spaces within one and the same society, together with fragments of the type of state constructed there, require a holistic approach, while others, within the same society, might be analysed in terms of methodological individualism. Whether it is applied to a historically specific society, to one modern society as opposed to another, or indeed to different sites within one and the same society, research into the state, or into the social structures conducive to collective action, would in each case require its own appropriate, and therefore unique, method.

Those theories which depend upon methodological individualism, from the prisoner's dilemma to the models of K. Arrow, or indeed of Olson himself, presuppose the definitive establishment of a fundamental individualism, on the basis of which the actors proceed rationally, or at any rate intentionally, to their choices, in order to maximise their personal profits. Other authors, by contrast, concerned to deny the fruitfulness of methodological individualism, stress the enduring nature of the communal structures which serve as a framework within which the actors together decide upon their actions.

Whether these structures are of the collective or of the associative kind,[19] on their own they enabled resistance to the French Revolution to occur in certain parts of the Vendée,[20] they provided a basis for the mobilisation of revolutionary groups through clubs[21] or local sections,[22] and they made general mobilisation against the enemies of the Revolution[23] or collective resistance to Napoleon III's *coup d'état* possible.[24] They would provide a general explanation for the success of peasant movements involving collective action,[25] a form of mobilisation occurring in France, Russia, and China, where highly structured peasant communities threw themselves into revolutionary activity,[26] and in the modern period in South-East Asia.[27]

In various different periods – the Nazi example, as we have already noted, being a perfect illustration of this – mobilisation therefore occurs as a function of varying degrees of integration into collective structures: it can in no sense be said to be the result either of the irrationalism of the atomised masses nor of an intentional choice of actors seeking individually to maximise their own particular interests since, for these authors, the whole – in such collectivities – controls the action of the parts. Methodological individualism would not allow one to study these collective social structures, for the fusion of the group would be such as to endow it with a consciousness of its own, so that it would enjoy a complete hold over the values of each actor: a free-rider strategy would therefore be unimaginable. A common culture would thus prevail here over individual choice, and the face-to-face relations which are the rule in such primary groups[28] would guarantee the integration of the whole and a mutual dependence. As Craig Calhoun observes – on the basis of his analysis of communities of artisans at the very beginning of the nineteenth century – in order to conserve their former status, such communities show no hesitation in launching themselves into violent, mobilising actions, so that, within these small, highly structured groups, 'it is far easier . . . to identify free riders and exercise some form of internal discipline'.[29] Later on, with the workers organised in a more universalist manner, 'Class action was costly, its success uncertain, and being a "free rider" easy'[30] and better adapted to individual actions, actions which the English artisans, just like the peasants of South-East Asia, who feel themselves to be bound by an ethic of reciprocity and of loyalty,[31] for their part, refused to condone. This line of argument suggests that holistic structures would prevent any recourse to the free-rider strategy with which theorists such as

Mancur Olson, on account of their commitment to methodological individualism, have been preoccupied, for this kind of theory presupposes an individualist behaviour governed by a calculation in terms of profits and losses, a calculation which each worker may more readily adopt in *industrialised* societies. In this respect, the possibility of free riders would account for the reformism of the working class and would again enable one to frame an answer to Sombart's question regarding the absence of socialism in the United States. In an individualist society of this kind, a worker believes himself capable of benefiting more from a strategy solely in line with his own interests than from a hypothetical, and very costly and risky, collective strategy involving a thoroughgoing structural change.[32] One would therefore assess the efficacy of a theoretical approach on the basis of the nature of the facts it is supposed to account for. When the reality involved is communal or even highly associative in nature, methodological individualism would not be the appropriate method, and attempts at individual 'exiting' (Hirschman) and free riding (Olson) would continue to be little developed; both of these would, on the other hand, predominate in individualistic societies, thereby preventing the birth of any movement of collective action.

More recently, however, some have sought to reject an interpretation of this kind, deeming it excessively evolutionist, and have identified individualist strategies within social groups which are as highly structured and organised, collectively speaking, as any. As Michael Hechter claims, 'What process intrinsic to a structural conception can exist that would prevent an actor from opting for a free-rider strategy? The answer is plain: there is none.'[33] Hechter thus holds that a group's solidarity is not the outcome of a phenomenon of social or cultural control but depends throughout on the individual choices of each actor. This highly innovatory reinterpretation of the explanatory power of methodological individualism, which would actually entail applying it to supposedly holistic structures as well as to individualist societies, may also draw support from the original research conducted by Samuel Popkin. Popkin sets out quite deliberately to challenge the studies of authors who, in the wake of James Scott or Eric Wolf, argue that social relations in integrated pre-capitalist societies are governed by moral rules which guarantee a form of collective justice; he rejects this romantic view, which implies a holistic conception of the villages involved, and asserts that, in a collective context of this kind, peasants do nevertheless entertain individual strategies. They decide to invest in their families, in animals or in land, to manage their stock on an individual basis, and to negotiate patron–client relations, in the same way as they would seek to maximise their own profits in a market structure. Furthermore, they profit in many ways from a great number of indivisible collective goods, whether or not they play any part in producing them. This explains why the free-rider strategy is always a temptation to them.

Samuel Popkin thus maintains that Mancur Olson's theory may also be applied to peasant societies and that its usefulness is not limited to modern, individualist, market societies. In his study of rural societies in Tonkin, he maintains, like Olson, that in these small groups collective action 'requires conditions under which peasants will find it in their individual interests to allocate resources to a collective movement – and not be free riders'.[34] Being 'rational peasants', they prefer, where such conditions do not obtain, to adopt a free-rider strategy or even to 'exit'. Peasants in traditional societies, like workers in modern societies,[35] are therefore only prepared to mobilise if they believe that they can derive a greater advantage from their action, in terms of profits and losses, from following leaders who urge them to commit themselves to collective action.

The great merit of Popkin's approach is that it severs the mechanical relation, which so many writers take for granted, between a method for the analysis of the real and a particular stage in the evolution of societies. He resolves this difficulty by applying methodological individualism, as Michael Hechter argues one should, to all forms of society, regardless of the types of social relation or internal networks involved. One can, on the other hand, argue that it is crucial to employ at one and the same time both those theories which hold that mobilisation depends upon communal or narrowly associative networks (Oberschall, Tilly, Agulhon and so on) and those which link it to the maximal search for the realisation of individual interests. Mobilisation does indeed presuppose that each actor committing himself to collective action has an intentionality, but the bases for, and the mastery of, a calculation of this kind are perhaps not the same in highly structured societies where strong social control is the rule as in societies where individualism is given free rein. It follows, therefore, that the employment of a free-rider or 'exit' strategy is undoubtedly not so easy in the first case as in the second.

It would therefore be wholly artificial to apply the prisoner's dilemma to a highly structured society or to a primary group, for one would first have to shatter the affective and face-to-face ties which predominate there, and then to isolate the actors one from another, in order to encourage them to calculate solely in terms of the maximisation of individual choices, whilst remaining less concerned for the collective good which had previously been produced through highly interdependent social relations. Conversely, in a society of an individualist type, one could avoid these same dilemmas and, more broadly, the consequences of the perspective outlined by Mancur Olson, by taking into consideration the duration and repetition of individual actions, both of which allow an exchange of information to occur and, consequently, a cooperation that gives rise to collective goods.[36]

I would like, in passing, to transfer the same line of argument from collective action to the state itself. Some kinds of particularly differentiated and institutionalised state give the appearance of being bureaucratic structures to which one may be tempted to apply a method of holistic analysis, so great a hold does the role system seem to have over the actors. In this type of state (France, for example, or Prussia), together with societies in a semi-fused condition, the whole seems different from the sum of its parts and the structure appears to determine the behaviour of the actors. The impersonal rules are so strictly applied that the agents of the state cannot help but submit to them. Administrative law holds sway over the actions of civil servants and stipulates what their obligations are. At its most extreme, this obligation may even extend so far, in the case of France, for example, as to cover what certain senior civil servants do in their own private lives. Being thus purely functionaries, the agents of such a state seem to have no freedom of action whatsoever. But if the nature of the élite which had control over the upper echelons of the state is of relatively little importance, it is not so much because the functions which it serves to guarantee are determined by the roles it plays in a state – which acts, when all is said and done, more readily in the interests of a hegemonic class because, as a state, it has a degree of dependence – but rather because this élite really is identified with this highly institutionalised state.

If the agents of a state of this kind seem to lack a will of their own, it is because a socialisation into the state is achieved by the state's own training schools, which transmit its own values. The identification of the agents of the state with this structure, which controls their actions down to the smallest detail, is also reinforced by a meritocratic and universalist mode of recruitment, which excludes all intruders and prevents actors who emerge from the leading categories of civil society from infiltrating the state apparatus.[37] The civil servants then become the spokesmen for the general good and for the public interest. They are also prepared to change their own values when appointed to other roles within the state; indeed, so weighty do these roles appear that they may even compel agents to accept shifts in values of this nature.[38] More generally, the logic of this kind of state would seem to control the behaviour of the bureaucratic élite, regardless of its social origins or of its particular ideologies. It is therefore all the easier to understand how so highly structured a state might more readily undertake mobilising actions 'from above',[39] thanks to which it strengthens both its hold on society and its own legitimacy, through establishing a direct relation with all of its citizens.

Conversely, in a weak state, bureaucratisation is not taken so far, state socialisation is less developed, there is more circulation between the various élites, and the state's space is less firmly defended by statutory boundaries, administrative law being virtually non-existent. This is why people identify less with their roles, and the agents of the state can no longer be treated simply as functions in action. In a weak state (Great Britain, for example, or the United States), as we have seen in the discussion above of societies of an individualist type, the actors' values do not follow so purely institutional a logic, for the control exerted over them emanates from infinitely less constraining collective norms. Individualist strategies are therefore the more readily available, people may put a greater distance between themselves and their roles, and a free-rider strategy, more imaginable here than in the context of a strong state, may perhaps be adopted. However, in this case too, one can venture to question yet again the use of a holistic perspective adapted to a single type of state and of the use of an approach based upon methodological individualism serving for other types of state. Just as Samuel Popkin, along with various others, seeks to apply the individualist method to societies assumed to be highly structured as collective ensembles, so, too, one can show that even a strong state does not manage altogether to control its agents' actions, for agents succeed in preserving their own values and lose no opportunity to maximise their individual interests. This observation is obviously applicable to the simple strategy adopted by those actors who, in moving from one corps to another, from one grade to another, from one central administration to another, from one ministry to another, or from one regional or departmental prefecture to another, manage their own careers as best they can; they are always careful to take into account the amount offered in the bonuses granted by each ministry and to assess the advantage that they might derive from their appointment to a particular prefecture, run, perhaps, by a powerful politician who might help them to get back all the quicker to Paris; they weigh up the possible gain to be had from passing through a cabinet post in order to arrive more quickly at a political function, or to secure the top job in a large nationalised enterprise, or to achieve a position in which they can operate in the most effective manner possible in a particular large enterprise in the private sector. Even in a strong state, in which the ideology of public service weighs heavily on everyone, civil servants are, nevertheless, ordinary mortals and, as such, they calculate and seek to maximise their own advantages without interfering with those of the state. Moreover, research conducted at the Centre de Sociologie des Organisations, and that of Pierre Grémion, Jean-Pierre Worms and Jean-Claude Thoenig in particular,[40] has shown that the most prestigious agents of this strong state, namely the prefects, are not above forging special ties with local dignitaries and bending rules and institutionalised procedures in order to profit from their support, support which is crucial to the success of a prefect's action at the local level and favourable, in the longer term, to the advance of his own career. In a context such as this, in which the obligations of each are determined by the specific structure of each corps, a top civil servant may nevertheless try to opt out and adopt a free-rider strategy, choosing not to commit himself to a collective action which is, however, institutionally determined.

Conversely, if in a weak state the relatively low degree of institutionalisation of state structures makes individualist strategies all the easier to adopt, with a free-rider strategy seeming to be more functional and 'exiting' still a possible outcome, it is nevertheless plain that, in Great Britain, for example, social control organises individual strategies and restricts choice, as is evident from British cultures of deference, which do much to mould the perception of roles and identities within English political circles. Stephen Krasner likewise emphasises that, in the United States, the State Department seems to be a highly structured institution, which thus is in a position to impose its own political line on the government of the day.[41] In much the same vein, Theda Skocpol and Kenneth Finegold stress how, since the American Civil War, the American Ministry of Agriculture has constituted 'an island of strong state in a sea of weakness',[42] which is to say that some top civil servants in a weak state will nevertheless adopt types of action determined by the highly institutionalised roles of these very structured partial institutions. This may thus help the mobilising action effected by certain state institutions 'from above'.

If all social actors, both in primitive and in urbanised and industrialised societies, base their actions upon an intentional approach and are never, save in the extreme case of there being absolute external control, simple vectors of a structural causality being imposed upon them, their margin for manoeuvre, both in social structures through which collective movements may be unleashed and in the state institutions which are confronted with or, conversely, strive to provoke a mobilisation 'from above', will vary in response to these different contexts. A native of a highly integrated primitive society, a peasant from a rigid rural society, a worker living in a very homogeneous district, or any actor belonging to primary groups, is subject, just like a chief whose actions are controlled by traditions,[43] or indeed a top civil servant in a strong state (or even, on occasion, in a weak one), to very constraining pressures which serve to limit his/her freedom of action, so that it is much less than that enjoyed in a society of the individualist type. Nevertheless, in all these cases, the actors involved will preserve, even in a more coercive context, an independence which alone gives some meaning to their action and accounts for either their commitment or for their adoption of a free-rider strategy, both in collective and in state action. If, on the other hand, actors in contemporary societies marked by individualism will not deny themselves recourse to free-rider strategies which result in demobilisation, neither will they hesitate to commit themselves quite frequently to movements of collective action, despite being aware that they will not make any profit measurable in Olsonian terms. Motives of an ethical or ideological nature may encourage them to undertake actions which are liable to interfere with their own interests. As Douglas North observes, 'any successful ideology must overcome the free rider problem. Its fundamental aim is to energise groups to behave contrary to a simple, hedonistic, individual calculus of costs and benefits.'[44] Methodological individualism in the strict sense is not able, in these conditions, to account for such mobilisations as occur in the modern societies most deeply marked by individualism.

In order to understand the phenomenon of collective mobilisation, it is therefore crucial to examine the values of the actors who commit themselves to such a movement, together with those of the agents of the particular state against which the mobilisation is directed. To grasp the nature, meaning and possibility of a collective action, it therefore seems crucial to use the opposed methodologies of both the holistic perspective and the approach resting upon methodological individualism, applying them simultaneously both to the social networks through which mobilisation is realised (the utilitarian and demobilising strategy of the free rider always remains a possibility, its realisation simply being easier in industrial societies than in highly structured social groups) and to the type of state against which it is realised, a mobilisation which provokes, by recoil effect, multiple reactions depending as much on the values of the agents of this state as on the logic of its particular way of working.

3 ✥ The state and mobilisation for war: the case of the French Revolution

The French Revolution brought about the rise of the nation, gave the people a role in the forefront of things and also did much to reinforce the power of the state. The claims that were made about equality, together with assertions respecting the meaning of fraternity, served to establish a new kind of community, one resting upon the commitment of citizens. This was a community which had lost its organic character, so that the orders and the estates were shattered, the guilds disappeared and regional and provincial identities were worn away. Citizenship and universalism reflected one and the same shift; both of them bore witness to the emergence of a community of citizens who were from now on obliged to repudiate their peripheral allegiances. The construction of the state depends upon the creation in modern times of such a community of citizens. As Reinhard Bendix observes, 'In the nation-state each citizen stands in a direct relation to the sovereign authority of the country in contrast with the medieval polity in which that direct relation is enjoyed only by the great men of the realm. Therefore, a core element of nation-building is the codification of the rights and duties of all adults who are classified as citizens.'[1] The passage from the 'civil' to the 'civic'[2] implies that the state has become independent. Now, a crucial aspect of the formation of the state – as political and administrative locus – is the strengthening of a public force. The construction of the state and the emergence of a citizen army would seem to be intrinsically connected; the *levée en masse* during the French Revolution appears to be an essential moment in the institutionalisation of the state.

Strangely enough, however, historians of the French Revolution have often failed to produce a detailed analysis of the role of the army in what one might call the 'transformation' of the nation into a state. Alexis de Tocqueville, who was the first to insist that attempts to construct a state were a continuous feature of French history, and who emphasised the extent to which the French Revolution brought about a still greater centralisation of the administration, had almost nothing to say about the role of the revolutionary armies.[3] A number of historians or philosophers have admittedly acknowledged that their role was an important one. Some have been persuaded that the actions of the soldiers in Year II represented the war that the people would wage on all the aristocracies;[4] others, by contrast, have preferred to regard this war as an expression of a Jacobin and totalitarian Messianism.[5]

Opposed though these analyses may be, they both fail to comment upon the actual nature of military events. They merely employ the *levée en masse* as a means of bolstering up their respective visions of the French Revolution. Theda Skocpol, on the other hand, in her reflections upon the comparative analysis of the construction of the state, deliberately places the role of war and of the army well to the fore. She thereby seeks to shed some light upon the function played by the army in reinforcing certain states which, though already bureaucratised, have lost, through the very fact of having won their independence, all real control of local society.[6]

From one form of mobilisation to the next

Michelet was one of the few historians before Jaurès to take into account the role of the army in the unfolding of the French Revolution. He wrote as follows:

These armies, which were peoples' armies or, to be more accurate still, the fatherland itself, in all its ardour, would ask to go together and fight as a mass, friends with friends, as a soldier once put it. Friends with friends, kinfolk with kinfolk, neighbours with neighbours, Frenchmen with Frenchmen, they would all shake each other by the hand as they left, and the difficulty was not so much to keep them together but rather to separate them. To isolate them was in effect to deprive them of the best part of their strength. These great, popular legions were like living organisms; to have refused to allow them to act in the mass would have been in effect to dismember them. And these masses were not unruly crowds; the more numerous one allowed them to be, the more orderly their behaviour was. Popular wisdom had it that the more one was with one's friends, the better things went. The generals felt all the bolder, once they had observed that this was the case. They saw that, where these highly sociable people were involved, where everyone electrified everyone else – and more markedly the more people there were – it was necessary to fight with huge masses of men. For the first time the world was faced with the spectacle of bodies of men hundreds of thousands strong, which marched as with one breath, as with the same spirit, as if to the beating of a single heart. This was the real origin of modern war. There was at first neither art nor system in it. It emerged from the very heart of France, from its sociability . . . when one sees a whole canton, sometimes a whole department, in arms, around the altar, it is not hard to imagine the future demi-brigades of the Republic.[7]

In this text, Michelet employs two theories of mobilisation, similar to those usually distinguished by modern sociologists. He shows convincingly how the soldiers' units were like 'living bodies', so strong were the bonds of 'sociability' linking the soldiers one to another, inasmuch as they were kinsmen or friends originating in the same canton. In this case, mobilisation is a consequence of the strength of community ties. However, Michelet goes on to add that these groups formed 'masses' of several hundreds of thousands of men. The soldiers 'marched as with one breath, as with the same spirit, as if to the beating of a single heart'. It is perfectly plain that small, organically linked communities cannot at the same time constitute a unified mass. Mobilisation is achieved by the formation of a mass which, to Michelet's mind, presents itself as a juxtaposition of structured collectivities but which, in reality, presupposes rather the very separation from kin and friends which is ostensibly refused.

The sociological theory of mobilisation has undergone profound alterations in recent times. It has been a longstanding claim that the destruction of primary groups leads ineluctably to the formation of a mass society tending to favour the emergence of a whole number of extremist mobilisations. William Kornhauser was responsible for the classic formulation of this thesis; he maintained, in fact, that primary groups had disappeared from modern societies, leaving the door open to every kind of radicalism.[8] In the nineteenth century, this thesis had already been advanced by Alexis de Tocqueville or, somewhat later, by Ortega y Gasset. In the twentieth century, it was also used to account for Nazism (Neumann), for specific forms of communism (Allardt) or for poujadism (Stanley Hoffman). For Hannah Arendt, 'totalitarian movements are massive organisations of atomised and isolated individuals', whose loyalty is all the more total given that 'the completely isolated human being, with no other social ties with family, friends, comrades or simple acquaintances, derives all of his feelings of usefulness wholly from his belonging to a movement, to a party'.[9] In the interpretations of Hannah Arendt and J. L. Talmon, the French Revolution features as a totalitarian movement; it arises out of one of the first mobilisations of the atomised masses.

Other sociologists have sought to give a wholly opposite interpretation of the conditions conducive to mobilisation. For Anthony Oberschall, for example, mobilisation only becomes real when the primary groups succeed in preserving their specificity. The more deeply rooted the community links are, the stronger resistance and mobilisation will be.[10] Mobilisation would therefore no longer result from atomisation, but, on the contrary, from the intensity of collective structures, from the coherence of primary groups. This conclusion is borne out both by Charles Tilly's studies of the Vendée and by those of Maurice Agulhon of the Var. I would also point out, as Charles Tilly does, that this form of mobilisation through community structures attains its height in 1848. In the subsequent period, with the dissolution of such structures and the emergence of the political market, mobilisation was in the main effected through associations and political parties. With the advent of industrialisation, mobilisation would also assume the form of markedly political strikes.[11]

Whatever difference there may be between them, these mobilisations are all directed against the state. However, during the French Revolution, we come across the opposite phenomenon, what one might term mobilisation from above.[12] With this distinction in mind, I shall seek to show how the revolutionary state first of all tried to mobilise, for itself, the primary groups, and how it then attempted to provoke a mobilisation through atomisation.

Mobilisation through primary groups is clearly evident in article 20 of the draft decree on the organisation of the national guards, voted on 27 July 1791, which stipulates that the officers elected 'will ensure that citizens from the same communes (in the case of the countryside) and from the same quarters (in the case of the towns) are drafted together'.[13] As Jean-Paul Bertaud takes pains to emphasize, the fact that the tactical unit chosen, the battalion, is a unit restricted to 500 men originating in the same region, proves that it is an organisation of primary groups, chosen as such, on the basis of the same criteria as sociologists would later emphasise.[14] This type of mobilisation is quite plainly one of the two which Michelet had in mind in the text quoted above. This is also what Beauharnais asserts on 30 July 1790, when he stresses that each regiment, consisting of individuals domiciled in a province, represents the 'basis for an excellent organisation, for a fellowship which [. . .] is the most certain bulwark of public liberty'.[15] Likewise, for Lemontey, 'since the battalions of volunteer guards are being formed out of the inhabitants of the same department, the choices will be less random. Since all those who have enrolled will know each other, they will exercise a most useful censorship on opinion.'[16] In modern times, the rediscovery of the importance of primary groups had also occurred in the context of the army. Edward Shils and Morris Janowitz have thus emphasised that 'political, social and moral values hardly had any influence at all upon the determination' of the ordinary German soldier of the Third Reich for, 'so long as he felt himself to be a member of his elementary group and thereby linked to the expectations and demands of the other members of the group, his military conduct had every chance of being good'.[17] Primary groups thus play a crucial role in the German army, the American army (Stouffer), and indeed in the army of the French Revolution, that is to say in a locus which would seem to be a profoundly atomised one.[18] The mobilisation of the nation in 1791 did not imply any commitment, on the part of the soldiers, to revolutionary values. With not a thought for Rousseau, Reason or Justice, this mobilisation was effected through territorial solidarities, which helped to increase the singleness of purpose of the actors involved. The soldiers may well have justified their participation in the armed struggle in terms of their commitment to the values of the Revolution, but mobilisation did not depend solely upon revolutionary values; it was in fact organised on the basis of collective solidarities.

As Charles Tilly has also, quite correctly, observed, up until the *levée en masse* of 1793, the voluntariate at department level expressed a particular relation binding the communes to the state, for it was the former which provided the latter with soldiers. This crucial role played by the local authorities may also have helped to ensure the resistance of these collective structures.[19] The *levée en masse* destroyed this privileged relationship; from that time on, the state tended to address itself to the citizens themselves.

As early as January 1792, Jean Debry is recorded as asserting that 'to recruit an army by making every department responsible for providing a contingent is actually to revive a militia régime',[20] and Mathieu Dumas, who was chairman of the military committee, in the course of the same discussion emphasised that 'each citizen only responded to this call to arms because of the depth of his individual commitment or because of the contribution he felt he might make, and certainly not because of his readiness to fulfil his obligations towards the state'.[21] From this time on, mobilisation was effected in terms of the direct allegiance of each individual to the state. On 20 July 1792, the fatherland was declared to be in danger; in order to combat the enemy forces, it was decided to 'marshal against them a military force so imposing in terms of its mass alone' that it would succeed in destroying them. Instead of having recourse to the primary groups, it became necessary to proceed with a more ideological mobilisation, which necessitated an appeal to the masses. We must, Carnot declared, 'lay the foundation for a new military system which, by turning every citizen into a soldier, will deal a mortal blow to the spirit of distinction through the annihilation of that last and most terrible of guilds, known as the army of the line'.[22] Invoking the inspiration of Rousseau, who held that every citizen should be a soldier, Carnot showed how all citizens 'would end up by uniting as one in this great and single common interest, the salvation of the fatherland'.[23] The volunteers of 1792 are supposed to make a unity out of the Republic; particularisms, regional solidarities and peripheral community structures are all set aside. Mass mobilisation is from now on national and explicitly ideological. Citizens no longer commit themselves simply to their collective bonds but rather to the defence of an idea.

The *levée* of 1793, involving 300,000 men, which was prompted by military setbacks, was clearly conceived of in such terms. For Saint-Just, 'the unity of the Republic requires unity in the army; the fatherland has but one heart'.[24] Likewise, according to Albitte the elder, it is the *esprit* which must be made national, and it is this *esprit* which will lead the nation to victory. Hence the decree of 24 February 1793, which proclaimed: 'All French citizens, from the age of 18 to those who have reached 40, and who are unmarried or widowed, are to regard themselves as being in a state of permanent requisition.' The state now reached all citizens, who had to give proof of their new allegiance. The construction of the state was not, however, yet complete. On the one hand, conscription was still carried out at the departmental level, with each of them having to supply a given number of soldiers; on the other, the manner in which these soldiers were nominated was still very vague and, in practice, alongside the volunteers, recourse was also had to election, to the drawing of lots and even to substitution (the last method being explicitly stipulated in article 17 of the decree of 24 February 1793).

Faced with the quite impossible task of obtaining 300,000 new soldiers, the Convention resolved, on 23 August 1793, to introduce the *levée en masse*. The chairman who presided over the drafting of this decree, Bertrand Barère, gave the reasons for it:

What would you have us do? Supply a contingent from each departmental and territorial division? Let us leave the venal use of this seigneurial or federalist method to the Germanic corps, to the confederacies of Germany and to the imperial edicts. To ensure its liberty, France's contingent comprises the whole of its population, the whole of its industry, the whole of its labours and the whole of its genius.[25]

From this time on, 'every citizen is a soldier' and it is no longer a question of assembling in the capital of each department, for that would be to 'federalise'. In its article 8, the decree of 23 August 1793 declares: 'The *levée* will be general.' This mobilisation from above disrupted the arrangements with the local authorities and dealt a severe blow to regionalism. For Marcel Reinhard,

the mass is a much more striking expression than 'the people', serving as it does to invoke, in terms of numbers, the great majority of citizens who, precisely insofar as they are neither former nobles, nor bourgeois, nor educated people, nor the rich, cannot be distinguished one from the other and are conscious of being on approximately the same level, of having common interests and at the same time common habits, traditions and language. It is a kind of class sentiment, but it differs from that of belonging to the Third Estate; it is, rather, a favourable coefficient, a kind of consciousness, a pride even, for this mass has in its favour the strength of its numbers and of its impulse. It is a mass in movement.[26]

Even if, as things actually stood, the departments still played some part in the new mobilisation, Jean-Paul Bertaud emphasises the concern shown to unsettle as many soldiers as possible, by shifting them, quite systematically, from their native regions. He gives examples of the reservations that were expressed regarding this deliberate atomisation, and quotes the observation of a head of a battalion: 'We would prefer to serve together for when you know and like each other, setbacks are less harsh and successes more encouraging.' For other requisitioned men, 'the interests of the Republic will simply be served with all the more ardour by citizens fighting alongside their friends and their kin'.[27] These reservations were soon to be swept aside, for mobilisation by means of atomisation would seem in fact to be a necessary condition for the transformation of the nation into a state, a process which presupposes the end of peripheral allegiances and requires, by the same token, still more ideological unity than the earlier form of mobilisation.

The transformation of nation into state was, moreover, greatly

reinforced by the increasing professionalisation which the army underwent in the course of the French Revolution. This professionalisation
appears to have been a crucial factor in the differentiation of the state
from the many social or regional peripheries, serving to organise the
people and the nation at arms – the central image of democracy
triumphant – and guaranteeing its ultimate ascendancy.

Although it is true that de Tocqueville all but ignored the role of the
army in his analysis of the French Revolution, the only text which he
devotes to it does nevertheless emphasise that

the army organises itself, goes to war, wins fame for itself; great generals get their
training there. A common goal and common passions are preserved there, when the
nation no longer has any. In a word, citizens and soldiers constitute, within the same
stretch of time and within the same people, two wholly different societies. The bond
formed by the one slackens as that of the other tightens.[28]

A number of modern sociologists have also stressed the importance of
this process of professionalisation. Samuel Finer, for example, shows
that the army, during the French Revolution, appears to be, for the
first time in Europe, an independent organisation which serves to
reinforce the centralisation of authority; conversely, he holds the
discourse on fraternity to be purely 'ephemeral'.[29] Similarly, S. F.
Scott acknowledges that 'the Revolution . . . created a professional
officer corps' which was a part of 'the general bureaucratisation of
French political and social institutions'.[30] Marcel Reinhard, a historian of the French Revolution, also observes that in 1794 'the army from
now on registers fluctuations in the political situation without seeming
to favour one side or the other. It has more *esprit de corps* and forms a
group that is separate from the nation . . . military spirit prevails over
the civic'.[31]

The professionalisation of the army therefore reinforces the institutionalisation of the state. This was a process, moreover, which had to a
large extent been begun under the *ancien régime*. The reader may recall
that the venality of the various ranks of officer, from sublieutenant to
general, had been abolished, rank by rank: from the reforms set up by
Choiseul to those carried out by the Comte de Saint-Germain, we find
the gradual establishment of a career based on talent and seniority,
and the imposition of a form of discipline inspired by the Prussian
example which little by little transformed the French army into a
'machinery',[32] a system of highly regulated roles. Likewise, Ségur's
reform, which restricted entrance to the military training schools to

those who held four quarterings of nobility, should be interpreted less as an attempt at reaction on the part of the nobility than as a stage in a process of professionalisation, the *nouveau riche* bourgeoisie being excluded from the upper ranks of the army, primarily because they did not satisfy the rules of professionalisation;[33] promotion was to be in terms of seniority within each rank, an army career becoming ever more institutionalised the more the pay was increased. Crucial factors in this professionalisation, such as the great military training schools at La Fère and Mézières, together with the Académie des Sciences or even the various state corps (Engineering, Bridges and Roads, Mines, and so on), attained from the time of the *ancien régime* a level of technical excellence unrivalled in Europe.[34] During this period, a theoretician like Guibert was already insisting how crucial it was to have a citizen army that was professional: 'What a simple matter it is to have invincible armies in a state whose subjects are citizens'.[35] Clausewitz, pursuing Guibert's train of thought in the course of his meditations upon the armies of the French Revolution, was later to assert that 'from now on . . . every war in Europe [will] be waged with the full resources of the state, and therefore [will] have to be fought only over major issues that affect the people'.[36] Furthermore, it is of interest to note that the concept of the state is employed by the two theoreticians (Guibert, Clausewitz) who are attempting to reconcile the emergence of a professional army with the necessary *levée* of citizens; at the time most preferred to speak in terms of the fatherland or the nation.[37] Those, however, who were calling for the transformation of the nation into a state through the professionalisation of the army could not help but speak in terms of the state.

The Declaration of the Rights of Man itself implies the idea of a meritocracy. Thus article 6 stipulates that 'all citizens are equally admissible to all honours and public positions, according to their capacities and without any other distinction but that of their virtues and their talents'. We know, however, that the national guard was to be recruited solely from among active citizens, that its members had to provide their own equipment and that they did not really follow a specific career; in these respects, it ran counter to any genuine professionalisation. Robespierre was also opposed to professionalisation: the national guards were to be prevented from 'forming a corps and from adopting any particular spirit resembling *esprit de corps*'. He went on to add: 'Consider to what degree the spirit of despotism and domination comes naturally to the military men of every country; how readily they separate the quality of citizen from that of soldier'; it was his opinion that 'one should do one's utmost to merge, among [the national guards], the quality of soldier with that of citizen'.[38] Soldiers should be recruited from among the whole citizen body; professionalisation could be set aside.

At the time, however, the process of professionalisation seemed to be ineluctable. Increasingly, arms and uniforms came to be provided by the state; this was the first stage in the army's advance towards independence and differentiation. Buttons then became standard (decree of 5 September 1790), regiments were called by numbers rather than by names (decree of 1 January 1791), and the old regimental flags were burnt (decree of 30 June 1791). Most important of all, discipline became identical throughout the army (decrees of 14 and 15 September 1790), and one could no longer leave service of one's own accord, as soldiers were still doing after Valmy and Jemappes; the agreement of the authorities was now indispensable and without it one ran the risk of being charged with desertion (decree of 13 September 1792).

In addition, a genuine career was gradually established. As early as February 1790, the Count of Montmorency emphasised that a soldier entered upon a 'career', and that the speed with which he rose in that career depended solely on his talents and his merit. As Buzot stressed, on 11 February 1793, a 'profession of arms' was finally being created. From 19 September 1790 on, appointment to the post of non-commissioned officer and officer depended both on seniority and upon the judgement of the officers already established, only a third of whom owed their new office to election by soldiers. Without going into a detailed analysis of the often shifting rules regarding the appointment of officers, I will merely note here that they tended to favour professionalisation. In 1793, we therefore find that 85% of the colonels had more than 25 years' experience; the same could also be said of two-thirds of the lieutenant-colonels. Even if a number of them had won promotion through the Revolution, they were all genuine professionals in the service of the state and the nation.[39]

These statistics, which refer to the army of the line in particular, could also be applied to the volunteers, among whom were in fact numerous officers of the line. The amalgamation which was supposed to unite two battalions of volunteers with one battalion of the line, within the context of the *levée en masse*, served in this sense to ensure not so much the triumph of armed democracy as that of professionalisation and, as a consequence, the transformation of nation into state.

A close study of Dubois-Crancé's report, presented in the name of the Committee of War, in February 1793, shows that this text, which served to organise the amalgamation, gave a lot of room to the idea of professionalisation. The battalions of the line, which were 'the most practised in the profession of arms', should, the chairman declared, be preserved in their entirety; in the mixing of each of them with two battalions of volunteers one would thus succeed in giving 'examples of training and discipline to some, of pure civic spirit and devotion to the fatherland to the others'. For Dubois-Crancé, 'our volunteers themselves, whose errors are often only due to their inexperience, have need of principles, of tactics, of order and of administration, such as are established in the armies of the line; this mixture therefore cannot help but be useful'.[40]

The picture is, from now on, quite clear: 'An army, no matter how brave or how numerous it is, is only imposing or terrible to the enemy to the degree that all the corresponding threads of its mechanism, from the corporal up to the general, lead through a hierarchical and uninterrupted succession of powers, to a centre that governs the whole.'[41] Victory could not be achieved without a punctilious respect for the division of labour. For Barère, each person had to occupy his 'post' and carry out his 'function':

Here each shows solidarity with the other, be he metal-worker or legislator, doctor or blacksmith, scholar or day labourer, gunsmith or colonel, arms manufacturer or general, patriot or banker, the artisan of slender means or the rich landowner, the artist or the smelter of cannon, the fortifications engineer or the maker of pikes, the countrydweller or the townsman; one and all are brought together, all are brothers, all are useful.[42]

The *enragés* challenged the prevailing spirit of meritocracy; Claire Lacombe, on 26 August 1793, spoke as follows to the Convention: 'Don't try to tell us that a volunteer army would harm our military organisation by depriving us of experienced leaders. The more talent they have, the more dangerous they are.'[43] Jean Jaurès, who is one of very few of the historians of the French Revolution to have analysed in fine detail the part played by the army in these events, also emphasises the extent to which the Convention 'was preoccupied with giving as many guarantees as possible to merit, knowledge and enlightened and effective commitment'. He saw the amalgamation as consisting of the 'construction of an army which was extraordinarily powerful as much in numbers as in organisation, and as much in the impetus instilled in it by popular energy as in method and science'.[44] Carnot was to be responsible for the organisation of this army, which involved the application of a 'technocratic ideal'; in this respect he gives the impression of being a 'Saint-Simonian *avant la lettre*' for he maintained that 'power should revert to the learned'.[45] As under the *ancien régime*, the great military training schools and the state corps continued to play a crucial role in the improvement of this increasing professionalisation.[46]

This professionalisation could nevertheless have been thwarted by the maintenance of election procedures respecting a significant proportion of the officers. One would then have been faced with the classical opposition, to be described subsequently by Max Weber, between functional or bureaucratic organisation and democracy. However, insofar as the elected officers were almost always professionals also, such a contradiction did not really arise. Through mobilisation, professionalisation, and also through the rapid development of military administration itself,[47] a topic which I have chosen not to analyse here, it is indeed the state which guarantees its ever greater hold over the nation, whilst at the same time it reinforces its own institutionalisation.

4 🐎 Ideology, collective action and the state: Germany, England, France

The sociology of knowledge establishes various kinds of links between ideologies and social settings. It endeavours to reveal a correlative or causal relationship between knowledge, in the general sense of the term, and the social system. Whether its inspiration is Marxist (from Marx to Lukács), Weberian (including the relationism of Mannheim) or functionalist or ethnomethodological, the sociology of knowledge interprets ideologies, world views or, indeed, values according as they are produced by a social class, a group or, again, an aggregate of interacting individuals. It never takes into account the specificity of politics, though this may revolutionise the conditions in which knowledge is produced. Marx, for example, saw the social classes as the only begetters of the ideologies which expressed their interests. In his view the representations, thought and intellectual commerce of men appeared here again as a direct emanation from their material behaviour.[1] Similarly, according to the model that predominates in the works of Marx and Engels, the state is the state of the most powerful class, that which is economically dominant and which, by means of the state, becomes the politically dominant class as well.[2] Marx never attempted, instead of linking forms of knowledge to social classes, to link them to the different types of states, although he did occasionally acknowledge their existence when, for example, he contrasted the French or Prussian state with the British or Swiss state.[3]

By placing the emphasis, as he occasionally did, on the specificity of states, Marx could have snapped the connection he ceaselessly forged between ideologies and social classes, and conceived of correlations between ideologies and types of states. Since he did not try, he was led to consider intellectuals solely in terms of their membership of a class and never according to their relationship with states. Hence, according to Marx, intellectuals could be regarded only as the political and literary representatives of the social classes whose interests they expressed. Having stated the problem in these terms, therefore, Marx ignored the ties which, in some cases, bound intellectuals to certain particularly institutionalised types of states – such as France or Prussia – with the result that the theories they developed and the ideologies that sprang up in such a setting were a function of the state and not of the social class. It may then be postulated that other theories and ideologies would come into being in the presence of a minimal state such as Great Britain. Although social relations in these countries were identical in nature, the difference in the type of state called into being contrasting world views and determined the particular roles played by the intellectuals in each case.

Within the Marxist tradition, the question of intellectuals and the role of ideologies were given particular attention by Gramsci. In his view 'they correspond . . . to the function of "hegemony" which the dominant group exercises throughout society and . . . to that of "direct domination" or command exercised through the state and juridical government.'[4] Going even further than Marx, Gramsci considered that intellectuals were the agents of the dominant class, and that they enabled it to exercise its hegemony both over society and over the state. Once again, the specific intellectual/state relationship was effaced. Yet in contrasting the states of the East with those of the West, Gramsci emphasised that in the East 'the state is everything', whereas in the West the state was the 'moat' of the fortress of civil society which, unlike the 'primitive and gelatinous' society of the East, was seen as a 'sturdy structure'. On the basis of this distinction, Gramsci could have shed light on the different roles played by intellectuals not only in relation to social classes but also according to the different types of states. Unfortunately he did not take that course. Perry Anderson sums up Gramsci's thought in the following model:[5]

East	West
State	Civil society
Civil society	State
Coercion	Consent
Domination	Hegemony
Movement	Position

He takes the view that, according to Gramsci, 'the preponderance of civil society over the state in the West can be equated with the predominance of "hegemony" over "coercion" ".[6] This model has the merit of outlining a comparative and differentiated sociological approach to intellectuals and ideologies. However, it remains inadequate. The fact is that, in his interpretation of Gramsci, Perry Anderson maintains his own East–West antithesis, which does not enable him to account for the substantial differences that separate Western societies themselves from one another.[7] In the same way, he sees them as having been equally aristocratic societies in the seventeenth century but ignores the phenomenon of institutionalisation of the state in France and relegates to the background the factors that make the French absolute monarchy, where the state became autonomous and differentiated itself from the nobility, distinct from the English aristocratic system where, in contrast, the state remained minimal and non-differentiated.

Marx, Gramsci and Perry Anderson aside, therefore, it is essential to recognise the diversity of the modes of political centralisation which operated in the West if we are then to attempt to study the emergence of ideologies according to the type of state they encounter, if it is true that in the West domination is not only exercised through civil society but sometimes, on the contrary, transmitted essentially by the state.[8] Here we would like to employ a sociology of knowledge which depends not on socio-economic settings but *inter alia* on socio-political settings, and then to see how relationships develop between ideologies and types of states, taking as a first example Western Europe at the end of the nineteenth century. In so doing we aim to challenge both the developmentalist and evolutionist view, which ties the advent of a particular kind of ideology, such as communism, closely to a particular moment in industrialisation,[9] and those models which deny the diversity of historical political processes and claim that identical sets of state ideological apparatus perform, to the profit of the bourgeoisie, similar activities in all Western countries.[10]

The French model

As we have seen, highly institutionalised, differentiated and autonomised states – of which France is the ideal example – can be distinguished from those that have undergone a process of political centralisation leading to a minimal state. On the basis of this distinction, which makes politics the independent variable, we must take into

Table 4.1 *Relationships between state and dominant class in Western Europe*

France	Germany	United Kingdom
E+	E+	E−[a]
F−	F+	F+
I+	I+	I−
M+	M−	M+

Note: E+ or E− Differentiated or non-differentiated state (centre).
  F+ or F− Fusion or absence of fusion of state with ruling class.
  I+ or I− Industrialisation from above or industrialisation from below.
  M+ or M− Open political bargain or closed political bargain.
[a] In the case of the United Kingdom, as we shall see, given the fact that there is no truly differentiated state, the problem of its possible fusion with the ruling class does not arise. The political area is occupied by an Establishment. In this case, therefore, the F+ represents a social fusion without real differentiation of political roles.

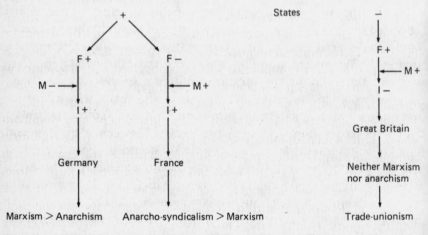

Figure 4.1. Ideologies and socio-political settings in Europe at the end of the nineteenth century

consideration those relationships that exist, in each case, between the state and the dominant class; in some cases a fusion may be observed and in others a differentiation. But beyond this first political variable – state or non-state – which raises the question of fusion with the ruling class, we must also take into account another political variable, independent of the first because it is of entirely different origin: that of the political bargain through which, at different rates, democracy is attained. In order to account for the emergence of ideologies, therefore (and here we shall deal only with the ideologies which structure the collective action of the working class), it is essential to use both these political variables in order to analyse the results of their many combinations.

Among the highly institutionalised states, the German state was unable to differentiate itself from the aristocracy. In this case, the result was a fusion of state with dominant class which, as Barrington Moore observed, was responsible for the revolution 'from above'[11] and favourable to change and to rapid industrialisation pursued with the active participation of the state.[12] In such a context it is easy to understand the rapid development of a Marxist social democracy that expressed the direct antagonism between the working class and a dominant class in close osmosis with the state. The rise of Marxism corresponded to the formation of a sturdy working class born of the rapid industrialisation and dominated by an alliance of the aristocracy and the bourgeoisie. Lassalle's version, in contrast, points to the weight carried by the state in the organisation of the dominant classes.[13] German social democracy was organised in the very image of the state it hoped to conquer; it was as centralised and disciplined as the state itself, and it is understandable that R. Hilferding spoke of 'Bismarckianism'. The state, however highly developed or institutionalised, none the less emerged as the instrument of a dominant class. Thus social domination was clearly visible through political domination. It is thus understandable that the trade-union was subordinate to the party. The factor that separated Kautsky from Bernstein, and which ultimately became the essential issue in the great theoretical debate that stirred German social democracy at the time, was the question of the state. The revisionists wanted to implement an indirect strategy for gaining power through the economy (which in our model represents an adequate action in the presence of a weak state) and to transform the party into a democratic party, trade-unionist version. For Kautsky and the majority, on the other hand, the working-class party must make 'the state its own'.[14]

This situation accounts both for the vigorous development of Marxism and for the weak development of anarchism.[15] The workers' movement, then, was struggling not so much against the state *per se* – in accordance with the anarchists' programme – as against the state of the dominant class.

In France, in contrast, the institutionalisation of the state was accompanied by marked differentiation from the dominant class. The absolute state, or the bureaucratised state, presented itself as a machine for dominating civil society and not as the instrument of the dominant class. Domination was thus experienced first in its political dimension, which perhaps explains the initial upsurge of anarchist theories and the subsequent spread of anarcho-syndicalism.

In the second half of the nineteenth century anarchism spread in France, parallel with the great strengthening of the state.[16] The vast influence exerted by Proudhon over the workers' movement up to the beginning of the twentieth century testifies to the weight carried by anarchism. According to Proudhon, the state was far from being a mere tool of the dominant class; it was a differentiated machine that had to be fought as such. In his analysis of Napoleon III's *coup d'état*, he emphasised the specificity of the resultant state.[17] Confronted with the French state – whose originality, incidentally, he failed to perceive – Proudhon developed analyses identical with those advanced, from opposite ideological horizons, by both de Tocqueville and Marx. In Proudhon's view, 'centralisation being by nature expansive and intrusive, the purview of the state constantly grows at the expense of corporative, communal and social initiative'.[18] Marx, analysing the Second Empire in his turn, took up Proudhon's analyses only to refute them systematically; in his opinion the state hems in, controls, regulates, oversees civil society and holds it in tutelage; he saw it as a 'frightful parasitic body which surrounds the body of French society like a caul, and stops up all its pores'.[19] Faced with the French state, Marx abandoned his traditional analysis in terms of social class to acknowledge, like Proudhon, the specificity of the political domination exercised in this context. He also agreed with de Tocqueville, who emphasised that 'under the old regime, as in our time, not one city, town, village or tiny hamlet in France, not one hospital, factory, convent or school could dispose independently of its own property. Then as now the administration thus kept all Frenchmen in its tutelage.'[20] The fact that liberal thought, Marxist theory and anarchist analysis, despite their incompatibility, agreed in recognising the particularity of the French state reveals the profound influence exerted on ideologies by socio-political settings.

As Pierre Ansart rightly observes,[21] a structural homology can be perceived between the practice of mutualism among the workers, which flourished in France in Proudhon's day, and its theoretical creation, which also developed, in the image of the workers' friendly societies, by rejecting the state in favour of independent economic action. This being so it must also be recognised that the activity of the movement was perhaps determined primarily by the type of state to which it was opposed. A slower rate of industrialisation and the maintenance of an economic structure in which, as a result, small producers and craftsmen acted only as an intervening variable admittedly favoured the acceptance of anarchist theories, but were nevertheless overdetermined by the specificity of the state. We should also mention, with Yves Lequin, that anarchism was equally successful at the time in infiltrating the large-scale industrial sector.[22]

In these circumstances it is not surprising that, unlike what occurred in Germany, anarchism long held the upper hand over Marxism. As Edouard Droz observes: 'Through his own work and that of his followers, Proudhon did most to create the Confédération Générale du Travail [General Confederation of Labour].'[23] Similarly Jacques Julliard and Annie Kriegel both draw attention to the strong influence exerted by Proudhon, through Pelloutier, over revolutionary syndicalism.[24] The organisation of labour exchanges and the acceptance of the idea of the general strike[25] illustrate the working class's attempts at self-organisation. Pelloutier considered that it was in the workers' interest 'to unite, and to look upon the trade-union and the co-operative society, not as an employment bureau and a compulsory savings bank, but as schools of revolution, production and self-government'.[26] It is striking to find in Pelloutier's writings the British concept of self-government; in both cases it expresses rejection of the state. However, whereas in the United Kingdom the limited character of the state was highly unfavourable to the development of anarchism or anarcho-syndicalism, in France the strength of the state was accountable for their rise.

In opposition to the development of a socialist party which would set out to conquer the state, and in opposition to Marxism and its Guesdist expression, Pelloutier, developing the labour exchanges, subscribed to the view which speaks of 'mutualism, co-operation, credit and association, and declares that the proletariat possesses in itself the instrument of its emancipation'.[27]

In these various forms − individualist and terrorist, mutualist, collectivist and syndicalist[28] − anarchism consequently developed on a tremendous scale in France, corresponding to the power enjoyed by the state in that country. From this standpoint, the antithesis between French anarchism and the Marxism which developed in Germany was attributable – in the opinion of both Bakunin and Kropotkin – less to a difference between the 'Latin mind' and the 'German mind' than to the type of state built up in each of those two countries and to its greater or lesser differentiation from the dominant class. It is thus understandable that at that time the attitude of the strikers reflected, in Michelle Perrot's view, 'a belief in the primacy and omnipotence of political factors'.[29]

It is true that at the Marseilles Congress in 1879 Guesdism triumphed over the corporatist and mutualist movement.[30] Nevertheless anarcho-syndicalism long maintained its control over the workers' movement, and the Amiens Charter of 1905 still reflected its influence.[31] In addition 'Guesdism, which claimed kinship with Marx, in fact retained at the outset a strong anarchist or Blanquist influence'.[32] Whatever their differences in approach, these three movements sought to define themselves in relation to the state by fighting it or by organising themselves outside it and against it. Guesdism, the French version of Marxism, concentrated on action against the state: 'Let us say and repeat to the proletariat', declared Guesde, 'that unless the working-class party seizes the state there can be no transformation of society and no emancipation of labour.'[33] The French socialist movement gradually rejected co-operative organisations, friendly societies and anarchist trends, and the exclusion of anarchism became final in London in 1906 with the temporary backing of Jaurès, who cannot after all be regarded as a statist.[34] However, the French section of the Workers' International (Section Française de l'Internationale Ouvrière or SFIO) which was formed in 1905, while rejecting revolutionary syndicalism, long retained traces of Proudhonian influence[35] and was infinitely less structured than German social democracy.

The birth of the Communist Party at Tours in 1920 was to accelerate the organisation of the French workers' movement on state-like lines. As Annie Kriegel aptly observes: 'Each party constitutes itself as the negative of the state which, within its territorial sphere, it sets out to destroy – on the model of the German Social Democratic Party, whose design as the negative of the Prussian state so captured the attention of Lenin . . . The French Communist Party rediscovered what gives the French political system its coherence and unity – the concept of absolutism.'[36] There could be no clearer demonstration of the weight carried by the 'state' variable in the organisation of the social system, of political parties, and of the ideologies sponsored by different social or political movements. Like anarchism, which found particularly favourable soil in France, Marxism, as it developed later, at a time when industrialisation was further advanced, adhered in its turn to state determinism. The successor to anarchism, the answer to the formidable French state, the Communist Party, which planned to take over the state and not to destroy it, constituted itself in its image: 'The Communist Party functions like a state because it is modelled on the state.'[37]

The British model

If we turn now to the British model of a political centralisation which took place without any true differentiation of state structures, we find that the installation of the machinery of representation – whatever the real difficulties of making it work, especially in relation to the working class – made possible some degree of self-government for civil society as a whole. Although Great Britain was ruled by a dominant class – an Establishment which absorbed new arrivals from the middle classes – the working class did not embrace Marxism as it did in Germany, which had likewise experienced fusion of the ruling class with the state and fairly rapid industrialisation. The British working class did not go to war with the dominant class but negotiated, often violently, with the employers to improve its living conditions and its standing in society as a whole. It almost invariably rejected any recourse to the state and any growth of the state, preferring to strengthen itself, the better to assert its rights. Just as it did not embrace Marxism, the working class did not accept the anarchist or anarcho-syndicalist model which had been such a success in state-structured France. The works of Godwin and William Morris notwithstanding, anarchism never became acclimatised in Great Britain for the state itself remained weak. The state was not the main issue to be opposed or utilised.

As G. D. H. Cole observes, anarchism managed to entrench itself firmly only in countries ruled by a strongly dominant state, such as France, Italy or Spain; it had no *raison d'être* in Great Britain.[38] Literary anarchism apart, such anarchist groups as arose in Great Britain were most often led by foreigners – at the end of the nineteenth century, Kropotkin; at the turn of the century, Jewish workers from Russia,

Germany or Poland – all of them from countries where domination was maintained, often brutally, through state institutions or the use of force by a powerful empire. But anarchism remained negligible: 'Where state tyranny is little felt, for lack of experience of centralisation and bureaucracy, it is much more difficult for revolt to start spontaneously, or for slogans like "neither God nor master" to find an echo.'[39]

Lastly, as George Woodcock notes, anarchism remained virtually non-existent in the Netherlands, the United Kingdom and the United States. All these are countries where the state is only slightly differentiated. The first type of state may be explained by the model of consociational democracy, in which respect for schisms is accompanied by an accommodation between élites to avoid building up the state; the other states are social systems in which civil society manages more or less to regulate itself, likewise avoiding differentiation of state structures.[40] The only form of anarchism which came to light in those societies was a peaceful one influenced by Tolstoy and remained within civil society.[41]

Anarchism remained an anarchism of civil society which was not directed against the state, and its theorists were more often poets or writers than movement organisers.[42]

According to David Apter, the new anarchism making its appearance in the English-speaking countries is a reaction against the system of roles in civil society and not the expression of a struggle against a state. The young people's counter-culture attacks the social identity of the protagonists; violence is directed against oneself and not against political authority.[43]

In the United States, as in the United Kingdom or again in the Netherlands, the type of anarchism which finds expression today may thus be seen as evidence of the absence of a truly institutionalised state. Here once again, in a negative sense, politics appears as the independent variable that determines the kind of ideology emerging.[44]

Thus Great Britain, unlike Germany or France, never really welcomed either Marxism or anarchism. As Henry Pelling observes, British trade-unionism from the nineteenth century onwards was infinitely stronger than that of other European countries; highly self-organised and aware of its strength, 'the British movement was neither very Marxist nor clearly oriented towards party politics'.[45] Preferring economic action to political struggle, the leaders of the British workers' movement even refused to take part in the Second

International which met in London in 1896. The 1880s witnessed attempts to organise several Marxist movements, such as the Social Democratic Federation around Hyndman, which sought to subordinate trade-union action to political action, and to assign a vital role to the state. These movements, extremely hostile to trade-unionism, remained outside the popular culture of the British workers who, for their part, opted most often for a purely economic struggle.[46]

In the face of economic difficulties and employers' reactions, however, the trade unions themselves, as we know, gradually entered the political arena in order to defend their own rights. It should be remembered that this process led to the formation in 1900 of the Labour Representation Committee, which was broadly dominated by the trade unions; the representatives of the socialist movement were in the minority. In 1906 this committee became the Labour Party, which was to set itself the task of giving expression, on the political scene, to the workers' demands for improvements in wages and working conditions. Even though this parliamentary socialism triggered reactions of rejection, and gave birth to a revolutionary socialism that was sometimes Marxist in inspiration and to a direct-action trade-unionism closely resembling French anarcho-syndicalism, it took lasting hold as the mode of representation of the British working class.

In contrast to the situation which prevailed in Germany, where the workers' movement confronted a state undifferentiated from the dominant class, the British working class, save in unusual times, has on the whole ignored Marxism. It has refused to subordinate the trade union to the party. Integrated into the political system and able to be 'heard' by representatives whom it controls, it has scorned French-style anarcho-syndicalism and its struggle against the state, and has never known separation and rivalry between union and party.[47] Through the payment of compulsory dues by unionised workers to the Labour Party, the practice of almost inevitable unionisation and the predominant position of the unions in the Party, the working class has subjugated the political apparatus and communicated to it its own pragmatist and reformist ethos, the expression of its full participation in civil society. Hence the Labour Party does not betray the working class (Miliband), but speaks for it.[48] Marxism, anti-statism, and an economic pragmatism allergic to ideology – such are the three ideological responses in close correlation with the type of state which emerges, in the majority of cases, in each of the systems studied. Let us add that, whereas in France 'revolutionary syndicalism equals trade-unionism plus direct action',[49] conversely it may be contended that in the United Kingdom trade-unionism equals revolutionary-inspired syndicalism, in so far as it seeks to cause civil society to evolve, minus direct action. Up to the First World War French syndicalism had its similarities to trade-unionism; but while the British trade unions were subsequently to succeed in taking control of the Labour Party, in France they were to yield pride of place to the parties for a long time to come. The logic of the state or centre thus weighs heavily on the union/party relationship and on the ideologies through which it is expressed.

We may briefly note that this purely political logic also determines the methods of settling labour disputes. Trade unions in the United Kingdom and the United States always prefer to reach agreement directly with the employers in a contractual setting because, 'in contrast to French Jacobinism, Anglo-Saxon liberalism leads to a curbing of the state's power to intervene, even at the cost of a trade union monopoly'.[50] In France, on the other hand, collective agreements do not exist, and recourse to the state and the courts is often the result. This Jacobin tradition is reflected in the very conception of the right to form and join trade unions, which the Waldeck-Rousseau Act raised to the status of a public freedom on the same footing as freedom of opinion; the state was thus to act as an arbitrator, with most disputes being settled in court.

In Great Britain, on the other hand, the situation was practically the reverse. Since the 1870s the law has developed negatively, intervening only rarely in collective relations in order that the state should not be called upon to rule in disputes. As a result, such disputes came to be treated mainly as matters of equity. Hence the 'voluntarism' characteristic of industrial relations in Great Britain, where free collective bargaining was for a long time the corollary of the absence of legislation.[51] A product of the 'weakness' of the state and the self-regulation of British civil society, this voluntarism, as we know, was gradually worn away, from the 1960s onwards, by the Industrial Relations Act (1971), the incomes policy and the social contract; whereas in France, in contrast, the state was trying during the same period to encourage collective bargaining[52] – a transformation which is perhaps indicative of the diminishing role of a state in France today as it turns towards liberalism. The differences between the two models nevertheless remain striking and continue to depend on the nature and role of the state. A further indication of the extent of these differences is the almost total absence of political strikes in Great Britain up to the 1960s, whereas in countries like France lacking a route of access to the state, the working class uses the strike as an alternative means of exerting collective pressure. The strike served in this case as an extra-parliamentary channel for political participation by the working class.[53] In contrast, with voluntarism in decline, the British labour movement managed to integrate itself into the machinery of the state in order to limit its action.

Rather than find itself regulated from above, the trade-union hierarchy preferred to legislate for itself. Hence the participation of the unions in the political centre, the rise of corporatism and the often violent reactions it provoked at the base.[54] From the difference in the impact of Marxism and anarchism in France and Great Britain respectively at the end of the nineteenth century to the contrasts which persist today in the matter of industrial relations, and, for example, the more or less effective application of corporatism, it is clear that, as time goes on, the 'state' variable continues to have its specific effect.[55]

As we have tried to show, the state emerges as the true independent variable, industrialisation being only an intervening variable in countries which are all capitalist in structure. The relationship between these variables explains why Great Britain and Germany, two countries where industrialisation was fairly rapid, produced profoundly different ideologies because their states were radically dissimilar. The same relationship accounts for the conflicting ideologies which flourished in France and Germany respectively – countries whose state structures were comparable. However, while Marxism spread in Germany, where the state was tied to the dominant class, anarcho-syndicalism developed in France, where domination mainly took a political form. The fact remains that, once industrialisation was widespread in France, anarcho-syndicalism gave way to variants of Marxist-inspired socialism.

This potency of the state seems to us an essential factor. In conclusion we may point out that it even influences the manner in which an ideology takes shape. Just as Proudhon, de Tocqueville and Marx agreed in recognising the distinctive character of the French state, so today Robert Dahl, Wright Mills, David Easton and James O'Connor, despite their conflicting theoretical approaches, accord little importance to the state itself in their analyses of American society. Again, within the contemporary Marxist movement, James O'Connor in the United States and Ralph Miliband in the United Kingdom concentrate mainly on the contradictions of capitalism or the homogeneity of the ruling class, thus ignoring the problems of the state, whereas Nicos Poulantzas and Claus Offe in France and the Federal Republic of Germany, in spite of their differences, agree in recognising its essential character as a constituted public area. This means that even the theoretical models thrown up within a single school of thought, e.g. Marxism, should not be interpreted solely in terms of their internal logic and that the controversy they arouse is not confined to the cognitive level but perhaps depends more upon the type of state in whose presence they have been constructed.

5 🐎 Individual action, collective action and workers' strategy: the United States, Great Britain and France

Paradoxical though it may seem, the perspectives outlined by Lenin and Mancur Olson respectively, on the basis of radically opposed theoretical positions, do in fact agree on one specific point, namely that the working class tends not to commit itself to a movement of collective mobilisation. Admittedly, quite contrary reasons may be held to explain this theoretical convergence. According to Lenin, it is the dominant ideology which, in serving the interests of the bourgeoisie, leads the workers spontaneously to prefer to improve their standard of living; likewise – and this is quite a different argument – it is this same ideology which, through its alienation of the workers, diverts them from any genuine consciousness and therefore makes it necessary for a party of professional revolutionaries to be formed, in capitalist as well as in other countries, which, operating 'from the outside', is the only agency which will manage to provoke an otherwise quite improbable mobilisation of the working class. Lenin, in *What Is To Be Done?*, thus maintains that spontaneously the working class prefers to adopt a trade unionist strategy, that is an action leading to the collective maximisation of its interests rather than committing itself to a revolutionary action. In these circumstances, action would remain instrumentalist and utilitarian; it would unfold in a pragmatic manner and would not give rise to any collective mobilisation, but, in Lenin's eyes, it would still nevertheless exist.

In Mancur Olson's treatment of the problem, the overall judgement is the same, but it rests upon quite different analyses. It is indeed, he argues, because each worker as actor attempts to maximise his own interest that he refuses to commit himself to a collective movement, for he knows full well that the additional cost in money, in time and so on that he would have to sustain would always be higher than the marginal gain he might make from his collective commitment with other workers. Since each worker reasons in this manner, no action ought logically to follow. One ought therefore to be witness neither to the birth of a revolutionary movement nor even to the formation of a trade unionist collective action of the kind which Lenin deplored. Collective inaction is here the consequence of a rational behaviour rather than of an alienated form of conduct. To put a stop to this refusal to commit oneself, professional trade unionists, or in Lenin's case professional revolutionaries, would have to exercise some constraint over the workers so that they would feel obliged to participate in the collective movement. In both cases, a theory of the absence of voluntary mobilisation would serve to justify the attribution of a motivating role to a professional élite, which would be the only grouping to derive any specific advantage from such mobilisation. Those involved professionally in politics may thus develop their own partisan organisations, control seats in parliament, local appointments, newspaper editorials and so on, and thereby enjoy a power on the public stage, which the mass media amplify still more, and a crucial role in the organisation of society. Those involved professionally in trade unionism may likewise perform certain functions within the unions themselves, either nationally or at branch level, in a word live for and by unionism in much the same way as professional politicians, as Weber puts it, live for and by politics. It is worth noting that Lenin's and Mancur Olson's observations concern in both cases such societies as England and the United States, that is social systems deeply marked by individualism, in which the market was created very early on and the state remained a weak one, in which the ideology of Social Darwinism and of equality of opportunity gave rise to a genuine belief in social mobility, in which utilitarianism and pragmatism were imposed as social philosophies, and in which socialism and, *a fortiori*, Marxism had very little resonance, in the workers' movement in particular. In societies of this kind, systematic and closed ideologies have had, generally speaking, hardly any impact, and belief in social mobility has actually been transformed into a collective myth destructive of collective solidarities. In the United States, Darwin has proved more influential than Marx, and the model of the 'struggle for existence' or of the 'survival of the fittest' – the fairy stories of the Horatio Alger type – serves to show what faith there is in the possibility of an individual ascending the social scale.[1] Insofar as society there has been transformed into something wholly permeated by the economic, individual strategies have been preferred to collective action.

In terms of Albert Hirschman's theoretical framework,[2] the workers, like any other American citizens, prefer 'exit' strategies to the more costly 'voice' actions. In a society in which social boundaries are less crystallised (Lenski), in which the frontier for a long time made horizontal mobility possible (Turner), and in which Protestantism serves to legitimise actions of an individualist kind, the functional quality of 'exit' strategies accounts for the weakness of the collective action of the working class. Indeed, the American working class has found its sociability networks being more and more damaged by the separation between workplace and residential areas,[3] which undermines still more seriously any possibility of mobilisation, reduces collective identification and limits to an even greater degree the influence of a universalising perspective such as socialism. In such a deeply individualist society, utilitarian behaviour aimed at the maximisation of gain, through the adoption of strategies particular to each actor, is common. Given such conditions, one can readily grasp just why it is that the majority of contemporary models of political theory, inspired by a utilitarian economic science, have seen the light of day. Of these various theories, that developed by Mancur Olson is especially deserving of critical attention, inasmuch as he attempts to demonstrate how improbable it is that any collective action will occur in large-scale social groupings (latent groups, in his terminology) within a society built upon individualism. Utilitarianism and collective ethics or action would hardly seem to be compatible with each other. Furthermore, this is precisely the claim that is made by a number of American authors with Marxist sympathies, who maintain that a rational calculation leads each worker to prefer an individual strategy to the hypothetical results of a socialist collective action which, through the upheavals which it is bound to produce (flight of capital, fall in the standard of living, a possible use of violence), may well turn out to be more costly.[4] Thus, for a number of advocates of 'analytic Marxism', in a society built upon utilitarianism it is more rational to turn away from socialism.

Some critics of Olson's perspective have felt that his model cannot really be applied to social groups whose structure depends upon high levels of sociability and rests upon the solidity of internal networks, networks which provide a framework within which actors would act, being themselves governed by the solidarity which binds them to their respective groups and by the psychological ties which are woven there and which fashion their personalities.[5] This criticism seems to me to be a misdirected one, inasmuch as such collective ties of the primary type are the very thing that has disappeared from within the American working class, which is increasingly wanting in communal structures and which therefore provides a context in which each worker may well regard an individualist strategy as being more effective. Again, I would argue that, instead of accusing the leaders of the American workers' movement of betrayal,[6] much as others have levelled a similar accusation at the leaders of the British Labour Party, we would do better to develop a more rational interpretation of the behaviour of American workers. We stand a better chance, I believe, of understanding just why it is that socialism is so weak in the United States, or why labourism is so strong in Great Britain, if we set aside explanations which invoke conspiracy, or indeed alienation, and pay proper attention to the actual intentions of the actors involved. In this respect, methodological individualism is an approach which is peculiarly well-suited to the analysis of the ways of acting of American workers, inasmuch as the latter would seem to be much less integrated into sociability networks than their British and French counterparts have long been.

The power of the market and of individualism therefore accounts for the weakness of socialism within the working class. Furthermore, it is well known that a rapid expansion of the market may often be correlated with a state that remains weak. Marx himself observed that the state 'changes with each country's border. It differs between the Prusso-German empire and Switzerland, between England and the United States. "*The* present state" is thus a fiction.'[7] Since in the United States, 'bourgeois society did not develop on the foundation of the feudal system, but developed rather out of itself . . . the state, in contrast to all earlier national formations, was from the beginning subordinate to bourgeois society, to its production, and never could make the pretence of being an end-in-itself'.[8] Marx is therefore at pains to emphasise the determinant role played by feudalism in the creation of a state which succeeds in differentiating itself, in constituting itself as an independent agent, and against which the workers' movement will, in France for example, as I have already observed, marshall its forces. Conversely, Marx concludes that no collective movement will emerge in a country in which the state is unable to achieve a real structure for itself and in which there is, within the framework of a liberal democracy, so thoroughgoing a subordination of society to economic criteria.[9] This interpretation has been a constant feature of the Marxist current throughout the twentieth century, as it has sought to understand the reasons underlying the exceptional character of the United States, which is the most industrialised country in the world and yet has never had a truly wide-ranging socialist movement.[10] This hypothesis has also been frequently advanced in the United States itself, where theorists have applied it in the main to the nature of the political régime, and have argued that, if socialism is absent there, it is because political rights were won early on in the country's history. Authors as diverse as John Laslett and Robert Dahl have adopted this argument.[11]

At the opposite end of the spectrum, Louis Hartz wrote a classic study, in the 1950s, *The Liberal Tradition in America*, which is wholly unconcerned with explanations in terms of economics. Hartz declared: 'It is not accidental that America which has uniquely lacked a feudal tradition has uniquely lacked also a socialist tradition.'[12] Since American society was, during this period, both profoundly individualist and liberal (if one excepts, of course, the race question), any mention of a possible reinforcement of the state was met with hostility; in doing this, it staved off the formation of a socialist movement, such as might have arisen in response to a stronger state. Too little perhaps has been made of the fact that Sombart himself had formulated this same thesis many years before. Setting aside the question of the frontier and of social mobility, Sombart's celebrated study included a treatment of the political factor, and he in fact reckoned that 'among American workers one therefore finds none of the opposition to the state that is to be found in continental-European socialism'.[13] This was because the American workers' movement had not had to set itself up in opposition to the state, for the state was not a highly differentiated one; it attempted instead, much as other groups did, to make its voice heard, to enter into negotiations and to bargain so as to win decisions that went in its favour. In this sense, the fact that the American state has remained 'incomplete'[14] has had crucial consequences for the mode of action of the working class, for it has given rise to a type of political régime which does not favour the expression of collective interests of the universalist kind. This accounts for the decentralised nature of political life in the United States, for the particular structure of a party system which involves the forming of coalitions of heterogeneous interests, for their adjustment to such conditions in the shape of political machines designed to win votes wherever possible ('catchall' parties, as Kirschheimer puts it), and for the dominant role of the local bosses, whose job it is to weave a clientship network out of a set of quite diverse interests, which never find expression as a highly structured universalist ideology. American political science, from V. O. Key to Robert Merton, has shown how 'the political machine does not function through a generalised appeal to broad political concerns but through direct and quasi-feudal relations between the local representatives of the machine and the electors of the neighbourhood. Politics is transformed into personal ties.'[15] So local and clientelist a framework does not provide the best setting for intellectuals, and it is they who have often played a key role in the building of a socialist movement.[16]

Types of state therefore have a profound influence, through particular political régimes and the party systems associated with them, upon the conditions governing the emergence or otherwise of a socialist movement. As I have already observed, the type of state to be found in France, Great Britain or America is one of the crucial factors affecting the appearance of socialism. This is also very much the conclusion that Seymour Lipset comes to, although he is not so much concerned with the type of state as with its sympathetic or hostile treatment of the working class, in countries as diverse as the United States, Australia, Germany, France, Spain and Italy; he demonstrates how, in the last three countries, 'trade union organisations were harassed by state institutions that claimed to represent the electorate democratically. Because the unions were weak . . . intellectuals or other upper-class radicals came to dominate the labour movement.'[17]

If we turn our attention to another country in North America, namely Canada, we find that a socialist movement has emerged there, in response to a state which is highly structured and has a longstanding tradition of interventionism,[18] which effectively means that the political specificity of the United States is not réducible to the nature of the régime, with its presidential and non-parliamentary character giving rise to particular electoral strategies, or to its federalism, which, it is sometimes claimed, results in conflicts being fragmented and produces a general crumbling and heterogeneity which is hardly compatible with universalising ideologies such as socialism.[19] In reality, as Ted Lowi has observed, it is because 'no rational system of law, legitimation or of repression existed, such as could have rendered a socialist critique more convincing', that a critique of this sort never became fully fledged and never gave rise to a collective movement, for, 'in the American context, it is Madison rather than Marx who seems to have the last word'.[20] The weakness of the state and the fortune enjoyed by individualism as a collective representation therefore accounts for the virtual absence of socialism in the United States. This is why sociologists tend to argue more in terms of strata than of classes. From Warner to Lipset to Bendix, one finds American social structure being treated as if it were a huge stairway connecting superimposed strata,[21] and it is thus emphasised that an individual can change strata, that mobility is individual rather than collective, and that an actor's, and more particularly, a worker's 'exit' is achieved through his personal strategy rather than through involvement in a collective movement. The strata do not therefore constitute holistic ensembles, with a nature and will of their own and a part to play in history, nor is there a struggle between strata that is analogous to the class struggle.

One can readily grasp just why, under these circumstances, Weberian sociology of class, which is nominalist in inspiration and emphasises individual action above all else, should have proved so appealing. For Weber, 'classes are not communities', which is why 'one is mistaken if one regards them as communities', for 'movement from one class situation is common, easily done and diverse, and "class unity" is a highly relative notion'.[22] Because Weber rejects all collective psychology of class, as a thoroughgoing nominalist he has to refuse to regard a class as a real whole, with its own will and specific history. It may be worth recalling at this point the influence enjoyed in the United States by the thinking of Schumpeter, who taught there from 1913 on and ended up by making it his home during the inter-war period. After having admittedly stressed that 'class is something more than an aggregation of class members . . . which is aware of its identity as a whole, and sublimates itself as such',[23] and having insisted that relations between social classes may in fact remain constant, Schumpeter reverts to the notion of permanent 'circulation'. In the last analysis, for Schumpeter, 'for the duration of its collective life, or the time during which its identity may be assumed, each class resembles a hotel or an omnibus, always full, but always of different people'.[24]

Schumpeter also uses the image of the lift to bring out the importance of the mobility of individuals who, 'in the sphere of their real interests', which do not include politics, adopt a mode of behaviour which makes it possible for them to circulate from one class to another, from the very fact that the line of demarcation between classes is neither 'rigid' nor 'broad'.[25] These interpretations of social classes are particularly well-suited to the analysis of American society and any number of sociologists have employed, within an individualist framework of this kind, the notions of stratum and of social mobility, and have therefore jettisoned the notion of class in its holistic sense. All of these factors would seem to encourage social actors to prefer the quest for 'private happiness' over the improvement of the 'public good' through, for instance, involvement in a collective action.

It is nevertheless the case that, even if for a whole number of reasons American workers are deeply divided,[26] the United States has throughout its history seen a large number of strikes. In this sense, there would seem to be a flaw in Olson's argument. Comparative analysis of strikes shows that they have always been particularly drawn-out there, that they have not usually had an explicitly political dimension and that they have also constituted a stage in the process of negotiation, of bargaining, which is so characteristic a feature of American society.[27] In order to account for the specific features of strikes in the United States, which have always lasted longer there than in other Western industrialised countries, and which seem not to vary in length, whilst in France and in Great Britain strikes have altered in length from the nineteenth century up until the present day, many authors invoke the decentralised character of the American political system, thus reintroducing a political variable.[28] As P. K. Edwards observes, 'there is a virtually automatic tendency for strike frequency to be lower in centralised than in decentralised bargaining systems'.[29] In a society of this kind, with its weak state, the workers, too, adopt a pressure group strategy and make determined use in their action of the resources available to them. An action of this kind is not meant to destroy the system, and does not presuppose a strong class consciousness; there is instead a framework which enables one to conduct strikes at the local level whose nature may be accounted for in terms of 'costs and benefits'.[30] This is effectively to underline the fact that, in such a context, when collective action arises, it does nevertheless preserve a utilitarian dimension.

In the British system, which has a weak state too, we encounter a large number of the traits I have outlined with respect to the United States. In Great Britain, strikes tend also to lack any explicit political dimension, the workers do not confront a strong state, and industrial relations pit the workers against management instead.[31] This institutionalisation of conflicts and the high level of unionisation here, too, confers a crucial role upon the unions, which seem to be effective organisations enabling the workers' interests to be represented. Olson's theory would seem to give one a better chance of understanding the workers' strategies than Lenin's, for their display of indifference towards Marxism and towards various other ideologies accounts for their commitment to trade unionism, which favours loyalty over any strategy of collective 'exit'. Furthermore, 'Labour in Parliament was not merely a political party; it was the parliamentary emanation of the Labour Movement.'[32] Admittedly, the situation differs from that in the United States, inasmuch as the workers are organised in a party and not simply in pressure groups, yet in that context, too, their perspective remains a deliberately gradualist one and cannot be explained simply in terms of alienation.[33] British workers, in contrast to American ones, feel themselves to be to a greater degree members of a social class with a collective dimension and they have preserved, over a long period of time, forms of communal existence which, broadly speaking, favour collective action. Their strikes nevertheless remain highly deferential in spirit and tend not to result in any political mobilisation.

Strikes have, admittedly, been frequent and often intense; resistance in defence of, and for control over, factories have also been an enduring feature, giving rise to a high level of militancy at the base, and to a resurgence of conflicts, which often have the appearance of being a rejection of the trade union activities of the workers' organisations.[34] Yet this kind of resistance within particular enterprises does not undermine Lenin's argument that working-class spontaneity 'has fitted well with the dominant cultural (and institutional) traditions in Britain',[35] so much so that one might interpret it not as simply the result of alienating mechanisms but as a reaction better adapted to the British political system itself. It is therefore the case that, even if British workers have a strong consciousness of constituting a particular kind of social grouping, they tend in general ·to remain 'loyal' and are less radical than French workers.[36] Even where they have a real conscious-

ness of their own social identity, British workers do not set themselves
up in opposition, as a quasi-holistic reality, to other social groups or to
the authorities, and English sociologists and historians, in their
attempts to account for British working-class political action, have
quite logically been drawn increasingly towards autobiographical
studies, narratives of working-class life which can hardly be said to be
compatible with the structuralist perspectives so widespread on the
Continent.[37] They have also become interested, usually in the course of
rejecting a structuralist Marxism, in theoretical perspectives which
place the emphasis upon social mobility and upon social hierarchies
conceived in terms of status and prestige;[38] classes are then conceived,
as is the case with someone like Anthony Giddens, as an aggregate of
individuals, a lack of social mobility being regarded as the necessary
condition for any structuring of a class.[39] A perspective of this kind
rests upon a recognition of the crucial role played by classes, but this is
simply because such a recognition accords with the underlying realities
of British society. Since, in the last analysis, social mobility seems to be
considerably 'underestimated' and since the thesis of closure seems
disputable, given the existence of processes from which the British
workers also derive some benefit,[40] a purely holistic approach to the
working class would appear, here too, as in the United States, to be less
and less feasible.

In France, by contrast, the working class has often been regarded as
a unified agent with a will and specific values of its own, which could
all be examined in their own right, which is why a more structural
Marxist interpretation has had such an influence upon peoples'
perception of the working class. Contemporary French Marxist
authors have tended to spurn the handful of texts in which Marx insists
that class consciousness has a crucial role to play, and have tended to
argue instead in purely structural and virtually holistic terms, an
approach which would seem to be perfectly correlated with a particular kind of socio-historical vision of reality. This vision permits no
hesitation in speaking of state, nation, people, or indeed of the working
class and of the Revolution, as so many entities which throng the
history of a society which has never proved favourably disposed
towards the individualism of the market.

It is undoubtedly true that, from the eighteenth century up until our
own day, ideologists have played a central role in French history,
precisely because, whether on the right (de Bonald, Taine, Renan,

Maurras) or on the left (Rousseau, Robespierre, Michelet, Jaurès, Sartre), they have invariably argued in holistic terms, with people, army, state and working class confronting each other as if they were so many bodies endowed with their own wills. These generalising world views, which have shown the utmost contempt for all utilitarian interpretations of a Benthamite kind or for theories whose preoccupation is with individual psychology, and which have preferred instead to indulge in reflections upon the soul of a people, the destiny of a nation, the will of a state or of the working class, seem at first glance better adapted to the peculiarities of French society, in which, from feudalism up until the modern period, allegiances to peripheral structures, both of a territorial and of a class nature, have remained very firm and have repeatedly run foul of a state which claims to enjoy a monopoly over legitimacy. This accounts for the constant conflicts which have arisen between these multiple entities, which tend of their nature to favour closed and systematic ideologies, for strikes which, because they are directed against the state, have an explicitly political content, for the crucial role played by political parties, for the weakness of the unions and for the rejection of voluntarism.[41] Since they have invariably been apprehended as densely knit communities, the people, or again the working class, have almost always been presented in the literature as if they spoke with a single voice and as if an agent were simply the living expression of a social grouping in motion.[42] One can therefore understand just why it is that French sociologists have been so opposed to what they regard as psychologism, namely the analysis of workers' values, of their consciousness and, a fortiori, of their individual projects. At the risk of caricature, one could put it that for a long time now French sociologists of the working class have simply felt entitled to disregard the questions raised by Lenin and by Olson, on the grounds that social reality seemed to them to be totally different from that which prevailed in England and in the United States. The working class has thus often been presented as a single agent, organised collectively through its parties and its unions, with its role being determined by its place in the relations of production. As André Gorz observes, 'the political imperatives of the class struggle have thus prevented the labour movement from examining the desire for autonomy as a specifically existential demand . . . proletarian militants have generally opposed the yearning for individual autonomy and dismissed it as a residual sign of petty-bourgeois individualism. Autonomy is not a proletarian value.'[43] Nevertheless, for some, even today, saying 'farewell to the working class' is a way of continuing to imagine it as an agent, a unique and holistic entity. It then becomes possible, if the occasion arises, to carry over such generalising interpretations on to the 'new working class',[44] the presumed spearhead of change.

Without wishing to linger over this point, and produce a sociology of the sociology of the working class, useful though it might be, I shall simply give a brief comparison of the thought of two contemporary French sociologists, representing wholly different intellectual currents. Nicos Poulantzas condemns the 'problematic of the subject', according to which

the agents of a social formation, 'men', are not considered to be, as Marx regards them, the supports of objective instances acting upon them through the class struggle, but as the genetic principle of the levels of the social whole in their guise as 'concrete individuals'. This is the conception of social actors, as individuals regarded as the origin of 'social action'. Research is thus not directed towards the study of the objective coordinates which distribute agents among the various social classes and towards the modes of action of the class struggle, but towards finalist explanations based upon the motivations underlying the behaviour of individuals–actors.[45]

Poulantzas thus condemns the 'anthropologism of the subject'[46] and reckons, like Althusser, that the agents of production occupy their respective places 'insofar as they are the "supports" (*Träger*) of these functions' integrated within the relations of production.[47] Adopting much the same line of argument, Manuel Castells proposes that one should 'speak of sites rather than of individuals', for 'the kind of analysis which sets out from concrete actors and their strategies is necessarily caught up in a dead end'.[48] In the last analysis, for Nicos Poulantzas, 'social classes are not empirical groups of individuals', for the 'sites . . . are independent of the will of these agents'.[49] This being his point of view, one can understand why he should condemn 'the stupidity of the bourgeois problematic of social mobility', strategies involving social climbing bearing witness merely to the persistence of 'petty bourgeois individualism'.[50] From this perspective, as from that of Lenin, any trace of individualism remaining in workers can only be a sign of their alienation. However, in the case of Poulantzas, in contrast to Lenin's conclusions, individualism seems to have little influence if one takes into account the structural character of the determination of the position and action of the working class as a whole, inasmuch as its movement and collective action is held to depend no longer upon an external agency.

The Marxist interpretation of the French working class thus claims the right to dispense with any account of the values belonging to the workers themselves; it analyses the structures and not the actors and, this being the case, never tires of criticising the more empirical kind of research conducted in England or in the United States. It is thus surprising, and all the more unexpected, to find in the work of Alain Touraine, whose theoretical concerns are wholly different, a language which is often just as generalising and virtually holistic. For Touraine, it actually is a question of studying the transformations of the 'working-class consciousness' and of the 'workers' movement'. The workers' movement is 'that aspect of working-class action which undermines the relations of production in the name of production itself. The workers' movement is not just a class movement; it is the working class in action.'[51] Distinguishing a number of stages which the working class passes through as a function of its insertion into a more or less developed technological framework and division of labour, Alain Touraine has emphasised how the working class has come to adopt different values in, for example, the construction industry, steel and, finally, in gas and electricity, where the workers have become white-collar supervisors. For Touraine, the working class had a class consciousness only during the establishment of the big factories at the end of the nineteenth century, in which Taylorism prevailed. When this moment had passed, the working class no longer had class consciousness even if working-class consciousness persisted. This explains why Touraine sets out to investigate the development of the workers' movement in post-industrial society: 'After this moment of crisis, working-class consciousness became located within the work system, not so much to bury its sense of discontent and its prepared-ness to advance claims as to lose there every absolute principle of opposition'.[52] Consequently, 'class consciousness stands at the gateway to industrial society; it is the peal of thunder serving to mark its birth'.[53] The workers' movement did of course continue to be active, but it no longer depended upon class consciousness and it no longer occupied so central a position in a society.[54] What concerns Alain Touraine is thus the problem of the transformation of collective consciousness. He acknowledges that studies of 'personal satisfaction' or of 'the assessment of life chances' are important but, as far as he is concerned, such perspectives only have a bearing upon 'the individual' and his 'strategies' and are therefore marginal to his own sociological analysis.[55] He acknowledges the 'usefulness' of an 'economistic' approach, where the workers, too, 'operate in a so-called rational manner, that is to say seek to maximise their individual advantages', but wishes himself to pass 'from the point of view of the individual to that of organisation or of the system of social relations'.[56] Alain Touraine's studies of the French working class do in fact bring out very forcefully the crucial role of values and of consciousness, without which one would have little chance of understanding workers' strategies. I would, however, tentatively observe that these studies are nevertheless structural in their inspiration insofar as they make the state of collective consciousness of the workers depend upon the nature of the organisation of the work system and that, as a consequence, they too readily skirt around the problems raised by Olson at the level of the organisation of that system. For Alain Touraine, 'unionism is not just an alliance set up for the purpose of obtaining "collective goods", as Mancur Olson or Anthony Oberschall suppose, but a movement defined by its position within the relations of production of industrial society'.[57] Since, in France, the working class seems to appear in the guise of a collective actor who shows no hesitation in mobilising, Olson's conclusion is presumed to be mistaken, for it cannot account for this action 'of a category which contests the relations of domination'.[58] One cannot help but wonder, however, whether this specificity of the French working class ought not to be first examined in a comparative manner. Given a perspective of this kind, Olson would manage to throw some light upon the behaviour of American workers in an individualist, market society with a weak state, whereas Lenin, or from a very different angle contemporary English sociologists, would succeed in identifying the reasons for the functional character of a reformist trade unionism. Conversely, French sociologists of the working class would bring out the supposedly more collective character of a working class, because it is there organised in a more structured manner and because the parties and unions which are aligned with it are prepared, given their virtually holistic conception of it as a social grouping, to provoke collective acts of mobilisation against both management and, above all, against the state, which is presented equally holistically.[59]

There would thus seem to be a close fit between sociologists, the societies to which they belong and the types of state which are operative there. One can, however, question the value of such correlations, insofar as they encourage us yet again to identify a particular method for the analysis of reality (either methodological individualism or holism) with the type of object being subjected to analysis. I would wish, rather, to cross methods with objects, so as to apply methodological individualism to the actions of French workers, and I would also hope, in order to ward off any excessive simplifications, to employ a more holistic approach in shedding light on other aspects of the American working-class world than those described by Olson.

Do French workers, as social actors, also employ strategies for the maximisation of their individual interests which thereby distance them from any participation in a collective action? Does the analytic grid of methodological individualism enable one, insofar as it avoids turning it into a holistic reality, to see the working-class world through different eyes? I would begin by observing that, at opposite ends of its history, namely the middle of the nineteenth century and during the present period, individual strategies appear to be so strong that they would seem to affect class solidarity. One only has to read accounts of the lives of French workers to appreciate the extent to which they resorted to strategies of individual 'exit', which undermined 'loyalty' and by the same token reduced collective 'voice' and mobilisation. Martin Nadaud thus describes how important it had been to him to rise both professionally and socially: 'a sort of vaingloriousness arose in my mind. It was a healthy symptom of a nascent ambition, a kind of inner lever capable of stirring a young man's conscience.'[60] As a specific social actor, Nadaud wished 'to climb'[61] and, once his 'fortune' was made, this future leader of the working class had only one 'worry': 'where', he exclaimed, 'can I hide my pile?'[62] Although he did take part in popular struggles, he never therefore forgot to employ a strategy which would bring about his own rise in the social scale and which put him at odds with the other workers for, as he observes, 'jealousy and hatred' separated them from him.[63] As Efrahem, a shoemaker during this same period, observed, the workers were 'isolated, scattered'. 'Let us keep quiet', he said, 'about our absurd jealousies . . . let us bottle up our hatreds . . . let us establish friendly, cordial and fraternal relations with each other', let us not sink ourselves in 'the individualism and egotism of isolation'; all in all, the workers should constitute a 'corps' so as to affirm their 'solidarity'.[64] What Efrahem quite explicitly identifies is the power of individualism; what he cries out for is the establishment of a holistic structure, as his use of organicist metaphors makes quite plain. A tract of this period reads as follows: 'No longer cast us from your bosom, o worthy bourgeois . . . if it is a bad thing for the worker to free himself and become a bourgeois in his turn, whose fault is it?'[65] However, in the thick of the political mobilisations of 1848, the *Journal des travailleurs*, founded by the workers delegated to the Luxembourg, declared: 'The task which we have in hand today is absolutely not, and never shall become, an individual task . . . Individual tasks only bring disappointment and shipwreck. Collective tasks are inexhaustible.'[66] This is a perfect illustration of Albert Hirschman's arguments, since there is disappointment here with both purely individual projects and with collective commitment.[67] These workers want at one and the same time individual success, which is however felt to end up in 'disappointment and shipwreck', and the success of a movement of collective solidarity, whose fragile basis they are familiar with but whose capacity to bring about still other disappointments they refuse to acknowledge. As Jules Leroux observes, 'the class does not exist; there are only individuals'.[68] To set up an enduring 'fraternity' among them was therefore no easy matter, more especially given that a wish for 'independence', a need 'for a self-image' held such sway that, as the printer Vasbenter declared in a letter to Flora Tristan, 'one must appeal to peoples' material interests for if our appeal was only to their devotion to the cause, it would be sure to fall on deaf ears; let us appeal to the egoism' that is so commonly a quality of 'genuine workers':[69] 'the genuine worker rarely spends time with his workmates from the workshop, he has few friends and finds it hard to form lasting attachments . . . there are many workers who want to settle down . . . and these will have the just, legitimate aspiration of all labourers, namely ownership'.[70] I would add that, during this period, there were a large number of workers' guilds which entered into competition with each other, which defended their respective privileges, by force if need be, and which presented themselves as structures which one may regard as resulting from individual choices which quite deliberately allowed for a degree of protection and withdrawal into oneself. Since this community of professionals was open to all those who constituted a part of a structure of collective defence, there is a transition from what was corporatism in an objective sense to corporatism in a subjective sense.[71]

But how is one to reconcile collective action and a calculated degree of fraternity with 'egotism'? This is in fact a crucial question, for it allows one to glimpse the difficulties, but also the possibility, of a collective mobilisation on the basis of a multiplicity of individual 'egotistical' decisions. But the passage from one to the other – where, in the latter case, mobilisation depends upon individual interests and not upon the reified will of a holistic social structure – does not occur automatically. This remarkable text from the *Atelier* makes this very plain:

We are well aware that the communists say that there is a very real moral happiness in sacrificing oneself. This is not our view. There is undoubtedly great moral satisfaction to be had from having made an act of self-sacrifice; but the pain involved almost always outweighs the pleasure; and one needs a more powerful motive than that of moral happiness to be prepared to sacrifice oneself.[72]

The French worker whose views are expressed here would seem to have penned an exact replica of the materialist and utilitarian critique which Bentham made of Rousseau. The egotistical pleasure of the French workers derived from the satisfaction of their own interests and not from the kind of moral pursuit of happiness advocated by a man such as Saint-Just. French workers in the nineteenth century, without ever having read Bentham, calculated 'pleasures' and 'pains' in much the same manner as the British founder of utilitarianism (and, subsequently, writers like Mancur Olson) had stipulated. As I have already observed, liberals such as Bentham, or indeed James Mill, entertain a purely individualist conception of interest and disallow any notion of a collective interest, such as social groups, and *a fortiori* social classes, might be able to defend. It is the individual who must calculate rationally just where his interest lies; given these conditions, one cannot speak of the interests of the working class, still less of its happiness. Happiness does not derive from the public domain, as it does for Rousseau or for Saint-Just, but from the private one.[73] Workers would therefore not be likely to be tempted by an entrance, even if a provisional one, into the public domain. As convinced utilitarians, French (and British) workers would therefore be unacquainted with the Hirschmanian cycle, unless they were to let themselves be tempted by the deceitful sirens of idealism, which invariably distract them from their own best interests.

The pursuit of private happiness seems to be a constant feature of the nineteenth century and it is something of a paradox to observe the purchase enjoyed by this individualist strategy in a society where the holistic representation of social structures would seem to predominate. One could readily compile a long list of workers' memoirs which, throughout the nineteenth century, bear witness to the power of this utilitarian and individualist attitude.[74] In our own day, if we turn to the other end of working-class history, individualist motivation seems fairly often to lie behind the action of workers, who thus become ever more different from each other. It is tempting to claim, as Pierre Dubois does, that ' "the working class" is a mobilisatory myth to which reference is made in particular phases of struggle, and which enables one temporarily to mask internal differences; it is nothing but a myth'.[75] This would nevertheless be tantamount to admitting that, even as a myth, this notion aids mobilisation and, as a consequence, the latter still occurs on mythical, and therefore quasi-holistic bases, and not as the result of an accumulation of individual and rational choices. Now, given the logic of my own argument here, it seems preferable to examine once more the values of the workers themselves rather than the weight of mythologies. Just as in the early part of the nineteenth century, so too nowadays, the individual quest for an 'exit' strategy seems to be playing an ever greater role. This is largely due to the existence of an increasing, and by no means negligible, inter- and intra-generational mobility in the French working class. As Claude Thélot has shown, in 1977 31% of the sons of workers were, at 40–59 years, in work or else on the sicklist; in 1953, only 21% of them were.[76] Intra-generational mobility is likewise quite a significant feature of working-class life: almost 12% of workers in 1965 were practising a different trade five years later, 2.5% of whom had become small businessmen.[77] In the years 1960–70, there was also a large increase 'in working-class households where a fall in the number of children was correlated with an increase in the educational success of the children'.[78]

Thus, just as in the nineteenth century, French workers can live in the hope of bringing a strategy of mobility to a successful conclusion, of achieving an increase in personal satisfaction without relying upon the hypothetical results of collective action. This explains the relatively pronounced adherence to Benthamite values: if one compares, for example, the two SOFRES polls regarding a possible banning of the right to set up in business, to go it alone, we find that if, in 1976, 58% of workers took a dim view of this, by 1983, some 72% felt the same way.[79] On the other hand, these polls suggest that, between these same two dates, there was little change in the percentage of workers seriously concerned about the possible banning of political parties (from 27% to 32%) or of the unions (from 46% to 44%). This suggests that French workers are very deeply attached to individual strategies, such as the setting-up of businesses, which is the most telling instance of a logic of the market rather than of class, and that they are far less preoccupied with the idea of a suppression of the actual instruments of collective mobilisation. The workers' attachment to liberalism is, furthermore, quite explicit: 57% of them in 1985 were in favour of it, 69% favoured competition and only 16% wanted a command economy, and 39% wanted nationalisation.[80]

Our own period, like the nineteenth century, has seen the logic of the market, strategies for individual enrichment, advancement in one's chosen career, hopes of setting up in business and of 'going it alone' wield a powerful attraction over a broad section of French workers, of whom a number, as we have seen, manage to turn these hopes into reality. Similarly, 58% of workers see nothing wrong in profiting from any surplus value that may accrue from rises in land and house prices;[81] 62% of them aspire to move into a house of their own, a development which will make the working-class household still less central than it was before.[82]

French workers are not highly unionised and do not put union action at the top of their list of priorities; 53% of them even go so far as to describe the general strike as a 'bad means' of changing society,[83] and only 12% (falling to 9% in 1983) consider that, 'to be a good citizen', one should join a union. Similarly, only 6% regard membership of a political party as a criterion of citizenship. I would further observe that, between 1976 and 1983, the proportion of workers who felt that it was necessary to join a party fell from 6% to 2%.[84] This bears out the supposition that workers, generally speaking, favour individual action and turn their backs on collective action. Even though the French working class is still a deeply exploited one, French workers, in their capacity as individual actors, seem by and large to subscribe to liberal and individualist ideology and conceive of their working or even educational future[85] solely in terms of the maximisation of their opportunities within a system which they know to be particularly unjust, a system which is a highly structured social hierarchy consisting of a large number of somewhat forbidding 'barriers'. Conservative workers are therefore not the only ones to reject all commitment to collective action:[86] the majority of members of the French working class still, admittedly, have a strong class consciousness but they prefer to try and link their fortunes, as much as possible, with those at the top rather than hope to change their situation through an act of collective mobilisation.[87] Having established that the attitude of the present-day French worker may be described in terms of a will to 'escape' from a social group which has for so long preserved in its own culture and defining characteristics, Andrée Andrieux and Jean Lignon emphasise that 'the worker who seeks escape gives himself up, in his own life, to an activity in the strict sense of the term; but the kind of activity that is involved is a purely personal one, the pursuit of a means of escape. It does not tie the worker to other workers in the context of a given cause; on the contrary, it isolates him.'[88] In the present period, numerous 'elements serving to erode class consciousness' have therefore emerged, and workers seem to find it less easy to participate in collective actions; indeed, the number of disputes has dropped for several years running, with the number of days lost in strikes having decreased more drastically still.[89] Furthermore, in the heartland of the French working class, Lorraine, the steelworkers themselves seem to have opted for isolation; there, too, 'individualism has come out on top'.[90] In Lorraine, the birthplace of a supposedly united working class, which is organised, capable of acting collectively and conscious of its own identity, Gérard Noiriel has highlighted the importance of 'strategies of individualisation', which have spread as the present crisis worsens, with the possibilities for climbing in job terms being 'means for mobilising, on an individual basis, the energy of those who are not satisfied with their lot'.[91] This is clearly to admit that, insofar as mobilisation exists, it is individual and not collective. And even when a genuine mobilisation occurred, as in May 1968, at Bulledor, in the region around Paris:

solidarity cannot be taken for granted since it is no longer the natural expression of a specific social class, as was the case with the traditional workers' parties, but has to be justified as effective in relation to 'individual needs'; as one worker stressed on this particular occasion, 'I've come out on strike . . . it's the masses that prevail; one man on his own does not win a war.' It is therefore because he knows that collective commitment will maximise his 'benefits' that each worker may decide to participate in a collective action which is not the consequence of the holistic will of a class that is supposedly united and has a clear sense of its strategy. In cases such as these, there truly is 'a utilitarian conception of a strike'.[92]

In the last analysis, whether it is purely individual or whether it is the outcome of the commitment of a plurality of individuals to a collective action liable to work to the advantage of one and all, mobilisation nowadays turns out very often to have a utilitarian character.[93]

Thus, in the present period, workers sometimes try to escape on an individual basis, that is to 'exit', and sometimes they all decide to participate in an action which might be described as communal rather than collective, such is the extent to which it is the outcome of the addition of individualist and utilitarian modes of behaviour. One can therefore readily grasp how numerous actors might have been tempted to come to terms with the 'embourgeoisement' of the French working class and thus turn themselves into latter-day Benthams, adapting themselves to the ever more pronounced dominance of the laws of the market and, by the same token, abandoning a supposedly more collective commitment, such as had previously been directed for the most part against the state. At a time when anti-statism is dominant, the increasing individualism of French workers seems itself to imply that holistic models have become less convincing, whether they refer to the state or to the working class. I see no need to linger here over the precise terms of the debate regarding the 'embourgeoisement' of the working class; it is simply that the actual use of the category 'embourgeoisement' would seem to suggest that the English and American model has triumphed over the supposedly more collective traditions of the French working class. I would note instead that if the 'new workers' baulk at the idea of committing themselves collectively, the same must be *a fortiori* the case with all the workers who are employed in the spaces created by the 'bypassing of the strongholds of the working class'.[94] In areas like Normandy, where new industries have been established and where the culture and traditions usual in the older industrialised zones, such as Lorraine or the Nord, are lacking, the working population is recruited above all from among the women, the young and immigrants, with each wage-earner, often employed by temporary enterprises, working in several of them at once: 'the wage-earners are highly individualised, only know each other as members of work teams, and have no collective dimension enabling a collective defence to be established'.[95] Once one has brought home the fact that the 'iron man', the white, male Ford worker, the very incarnation of the values of the heroic episodes in the workers' struggles of the turn of the century, has been replaced by other categories of worker, one can more readily understand why it is that the working-class communities which are supposedly firmly welded together by their history and interests are falling apart at an ever faster pace. The 'loneliness' of this new working class may also be related to the fact that the new generation of waged workers will have had, since the 1960s, more of a 'self-consciousness' than a 'class consciousness'.[96] The picture seems clear enough: now that we stand at the other end of the history of the French working class, individualist strategies – combined with a new emphasis upon the actor – seem to be the rule, so that the old solidarities are eroded and the will to commit oneself to a collective movement is undermined. This tendency is further exacerbated by the fact that workers are more and more divided[97] into a large number of distinct categories with different interests, ranging from the skilled, white-collar 'new working class' to the temporary 'new working class'.

The workers' movement would thus often seem to be faced, both in the nineteenth century and in the present day, irrespective of the successive stages in the division of labour, by individualist strategies on the part of a significant number of workers. Moreover, there is no guarantee that such workers will have any memory of the history of their own class.[98] Those who have analysed these two crucial moments in workers' history have often been led to compare them to the intermediate stage, that of the end of the nineteenth century and the early years of the twentieth, which the workers' movement has tended to represent as a community committed to action and prepared to mobilise collectively in the defence of its interests as a group. The historians of the working class have, admittedly, presented an image of this social group at this moment in its existence which makes it virtually impossible, given the research perspective involved, to arrive at an accurate idea of behaviour of an individualist type.[99] At this period, in the great steelworks and car factories, a working class seemed to constitute itself, protected by its unions and represented by its political parties. As Michelle Perrot shows, in such circumstances a strike is often 'a collective gesture, a passionate cry of protest . . . the workers constitute themselves as a group, advance their claims as if with one voice, en masse, so as to avoid all reprisals'.[100] As a collective act, the strike 'crystallised' the workers into a unified whole and the intervention of the police served 'to give the group a still greater sense of unanimity; the strike seemed to be a collective festival: hence the processions, the chants, which were ways of denouncing people that almost came instinctively, ways of sticking together and of making a din'.[101] The 'concerted action' of the proletariat was in the main planned in cafés, taprooms and eating-houses, the nerve centres of working-class social life,[102] all of which served to strengthen social ties favouring collective mobilisation.[103] In Lorraine, where, hand in hand with the development of heavy industry, there emerged a working class which epitomised the traditional conception of what an authentic working class should be, in the shadow of the tall blast furnaces, the strikers' solidarity and political consciousness was indeed bolstered in the cafés. As Serge Bonnet observes, 'city cafés had inherited the role of village taverns'; they helped to preserve communal ties; processions, festivals and dances were, in one form or another, connected to the cafés, which were thus the source of an 'elementary social life'.[104] In the region of Toulouse,[105] just as, a little later, in the area around Lyons, 'the mobilisation of the working masses', the spread of strikes, resulted, in the 1890s, in a mass strike movement of quite unprecedented proportions.[106] The history of the Confédération Générale du Travail (CGT) is closely bound up with this type of mobilisation, which was the most effective expression of the steelworkers' action, and involved forms of solidarity based upon workplace structures which gave rise to highly integrated communities.[107] However, even in a context of this sort, which is especially conducive to collective mobilisation and which seems at first to undermine, as far as this particular period and the history of the workers' movement is concerned, the usefulness of any approach based upon methodological individualism, and, in addition, to rule out any utilitarian activity on the part of the workers' themselves, one can quite legitimately question the value of so unnuanced a presentation of the strategy of the workers, who are presumed always to operate within the framework of the community to which they belong. As Denis Segrestin observes:

the approach taken is essentially unitary, though it tends to be based upon majority decisions and may indeed be unanimous; the approach taken is also pitched at the level of the most direct solidarities, in the context of a quite genuine personal commitment. This is an approach which is not, psychologically, very costly nor is it very marketable; someone who takes out membership neither alters nor improves his standing in the community; someone who either has no membership card or who chooses not to renew it, does not endanger his status within the community.[108]

It is undoubtedly this 'not very costly' and 'not very marketable' quality of commitment to trade unions which accounts for their low levels of membership, even in a period in which communal or workplace solidarities are still strong. If one accepts a proposition of this kind, one could well end up by concluding, much as Olson does but this time within the framework of a 'community', that each worker who is a member of this solidarity network may be tempted to apply a free-rider strategy and 'travel free', inasmuch as the overall price of the collective action is paid by others, who also belong to the workplace community. A research perspective of this kind would seem not to have attracted historians of the working class of the end of the nineteenth and beginning of the twentieth century, so attached have they been to their quasi-holistic vision of a united working class, imbued with a deep sense of solidarity and prepared to mobilise in collective action. There is no material to hand that would serve to illustrate the reality, at this crucial moment in the history of the workers' movement, of a 'cost–benefits' calculus of a very utilitarian kind. Now, if one really can point to the existence of individualist strategies in the context of a peasant village, which cannot therefore be regarded simply as a reality of a holistic kind,[109] there is all the more reason to suppose that such behaviour was a feature of a historical period in which workers together formed a workplace community welded together by a common culture. The true object of our enquiry must be to discover what it is that guarantees the solidarity of workers, without therefore treating such solidarity as a natural datum, as if the sharing of a socio-economic position invariably gave rise to a social community. It is therefore vital that we take account of the issues raised by Michael Hechter's iconoclastic question: 'what process inherent in a structural conception could exist such as to prevent an actor from opting for a free rider strategy?' As far as Hechter is concerned, 'the answer is quite clear, there is no such process'.[110]

In methodological terms, the crucial thing is perhaps to break once and for all with every form of research which binds a method to an object, so that we may then establish an evolutionary sequence, with each stage in the history of a social fact being analysed by means of a specific method.[111] It has in the end to be admitted that, even where one is dealing with a workplace community which seems to be the embodiment of the myth of a united working class, Olson's enquiry is still of real value. Whether a caste or a class is involved, the observer must assume that the actors always have a point of view of their own; they may simply feel that loyalty in this type of structure, given the choices on offer in a society relatively lacking in fluidity, appears to be a functionally less costly behaviour whereas, as members of a stratum, they would probably have no hesitation in 'exiting'. This perspective would seem, furthermore, to be a crucial one if one is to explain the solidarity which may exist between the members of a working-class collectivity at a given moment in its history: instead of always having recourse to interpretations which rest upon notions such as social control, reproduction of norms, or 'working-class culture', which may indeed sometimes have a part to play, one can also regard solidarity as the outcome of a commitment on the part of those who are willing to declare their solidarity. I hope that such an approach might usefully be employed in analysing this crucial moment in the history of the working class. On the other hand, it is just as indispensable that, in a period such as the present one, when workers seem committed to a more individualist and utilitarian point of view, we should cultivate a deeper understanding of what the behaviour of different workers has in common. Studies by Guy Michelat and Michel Simon do, for instance, show how a communist culture may be preserved within the party of a working class which has undergone 'embourgeoisement' but which emerged, as far as intergenerational mobility is concerned, from a communist workers' milieu.[112] In other words, the sons of workers in an 'exit' situation often prefer, despite the hypotheses of Olson and Lenin, to remain loyal to their original milieux. This does not mean that one should always try to grasp the connection between the nature of the milieu, the more or less communal or individualist context, and the choices made by actors. I would further add that the behaviour of the workers also varies as a function of their placing within a public or nationalised sector or, again, their participation in the private sector in general: in the private sector one finds that class-based unionism is in fact more common, in part because of the more explicitly political character of the workplace milieu.[113] This is as much as to say that one can correlate the more manifestly collective forms of behaviour with highly institutionalised states, where the public sector has been greatly extended. If the state does play such a crucial role in determining workers' mobilisation, it is likely that in the future one will find workers in the United States becoming mobilised to the same extent as in France, as aspects of the strong state begin to emerge. This is Ted Lowi's perspective also, as the following passage suggests: 'In the American context, it is Madison, not Marx, who seems to be having the last word. This, of course, can change. As the American national state has expanded and federalism in the economic domain has all but disappeared, one of the conditions that seems to have systematically inhibited socialism is no longer present.'[114]

6 ✥ The state versus corporatism: France and England

I

We must distinguish between the birth of democracy and the creation of the state. The state results from a division of political labour that does not take place in all societies. All societies, of course, experience a division of social labour, but only some experience that basic division of political labour that leads to state differentiation. Among Western countries, it is when they emerged from feudalism that such differentiation did or did not take place. To this first variable, state or no state, one must add a second, namely, democracy. Democracy first appears in its representative form and then blossoms all the more easily if it does not confront the obstacle of the state. Democratic representation and state development thus appear almost antithetical. In England, centralisation and representation seem particularly compatible, whereas in France, state development and representation seem almost incompatible. Later on, democracy expresses itself through universal suffrage. From this point of view, however, countries with states do not seem more opposed to the expansion of suffrage than countries with centralisation.[1]

One might note that, historically, the revolutionary French state preceded English democracy. However, because of the many regimes that France experienced during the nineteenth century, expansion of suffrage remained threatened and chaotic. This multiplicity of regimes indicates how difficult it is to reconcile democracy, in all its forms, and the state, which pretends, by itself, to represent the general interest of the people. A change of regime (for example, in France, the passage from the July Monarchy to the Second Empire, to the Third and Fourth Republics, and, finally, to Gaullism) does not bring about a transformation of the state, which, quite independently, manages to institutionalise itself even further. Rather, it expresses the strength of representative or direct democratic demands. Thus, the various types

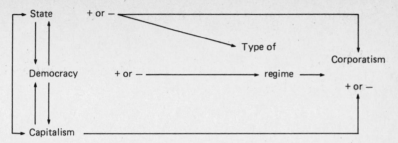

of states – which are independent from capitalism, since they precede it – are themselves more or less compatible with the development of democracy and with the appearance of particular political regimes.

Here I would like to suggest that the current debate on the appearance and fate of corporatism in contemporary Western societies cannot advance if it does not consider the distinctions enumerated above. The state, democracy, and capitalism are independent variables with multiple relationships; all contribute, each in its own way, to the creation or the absence of corporatism.

II

In a recent article, Leo Panitch has shed light upon the heterogeneity of present research on corporatism. According to him, corporatism sometimes refers to a distinct economic system, one that differs, for example, from feudalism, from capitalism, or from socialism; sometimes to a 'state form', one that differs, for example, from fascism or from parliamentarianism; and sometimes refers to a particular system of interest representation, one that differs from pluralism or from syndicalism.[2] The theory of corporatism does indeed take into consideration the political regime (what Panitch calls the 'State form'). However, it does not take into account the type of state itself, whose existence precedes the particular regime associated with it at one moment or another in its history.

According to Philippe Schmitter, 'corporatism can be defined as a system of interest representation in which the constituent units are organised into a limited number of singular, compulsory, noncompetitive, hierarchically ordered and functionally differentiated categories, recognised or licensed (if not created) by the State and granted a deliberate representational monopoly within their respective categories in exchange for observing certain controls on their selection of leaders and articulation of demands and supports'.[3] By this definition, it would seem that the state is at the centre of the corporatist system. However, the notion of 'state' is not defined, and it seems to be used without regard to the particular history of the concerned societies.[4] It may seem surprising that while we turn more and more often to historical sociology, we can still talk, in this manner, of the state 'in general' and not reflect on the relationship that a specific state, born in particular circumstances, cultivates with the corporatist process.

Philippe Schmitter admits, furthermore, that it is indispensable to distinguish societal corporatism from state corporatism:

Societal corporatism is found imbedded in political systems with relatively autonomous, multilayered territorial units; open, competitive electoral processes and party systems; ideologically varied, coalitionally based executive authorities – even with highly 'layered' or 'pillared' political subcultures . . . State corporatism tends to be associated with political systems in which territorial subunits are tightly subordinated to central bureaucratic power; elections are non-existent or plebiscitary; party systems are dominated or monopolized by a weak single party; executive authorities are ideologically exclusive and more narrowly recruited and are such that political subcultures based on class, ethnicity, language, or regionalism are repressed.[5]

This time the author uses the concept *political system* to analyse the unexpected arrival of societal corporatism, and he reserves the notion of state for the second type of corporatism, modifying in that manner the first general definition of the state.

However, this distinction presents a great number of difficulties when we examine the lists of countries that are supposed to represent the two types of corporatism. On the side of societal corporatism appear Sweden, Switzerland, the Netherlands, Norway, Denmark, Great Britain, West Germany, and the United States – all sharing common characteristics of corporatism.[6] On the side of state corporatism appear Portugal, Brazil, Spain, Greece, Mexico, Peru, Fascist Italy, the France of Pétain, National Socialist Germany, and the Austria of Dollfuss. This kind of corporatism, according to Schmitter, corresponds to the necessity of putting in place 'a stable and bourgeois-dominant regime' that responds to the concentrated means of production. Critics have already pointed out that Schmitter thus introduces in his theory of group representation a rather different perspective of Marxist inspiration. He resorts to notions of political system and regime and is thus generally silent about the type of state in which societal corporatism can be established. By doing this he places in the same category: (1) countries that have a state – the product of a historical differentiation linked to the crisis of feudalism and to the resistance of peripheries, which has encouraged the state's autonomy and institutionalisation (for example, France); (2) countries that maintained processes of fusion and that have not experienced the emergence of differentiated structures because the centre assures, without major crisis, the representation of interests (for example, Great Britain); and (3) consociational democracies, which for a long time have avoided both the state and any true centre (for example, Switzerland).[7]

These profoundly different types of state simply cannot in the same manner lend themselves to societal corporatism. Also, each type of state generates specific mechanisms for managing social conflicts and directs the action of the working class into specific channels. By not taking into account the multiplicity of state types, each with a particular history, Schmitter uses the concept of state to describe systems with state corporatism that are, in fact, authoritarian or totalitarian *regimes*. In such regimes, according to our own more restrictive definition of the state, a state cannot truly exist because differentiation – an essential attribute of the state – remains absent.

How can the state variable be measured? The state can indeed remain constant while the regime transforms itself radically. From the Third to the Fourth Republic through Vichy, the state was not essentially transformed; it was the regime that profoundly modified itself. In the same way, political systems with relatively identical corporatism have completely opposite state types (for example, Switzerland and Austria), and, as has often been noted, the representation of some interests, like those of agriculture, are almost always unified no matter what the state type or regime type.

Furthermore, a country that has neither a true state nor a real centre (Switzerland) may develop centralised interest groups, whereas a country with a very differentiated state may develop centralised interest groups (France). The relationship between the type of state, the type of regime, the structure of interest groups, and the kind of corporatism is thus far from clear.[8] These difficulties will be reconsidered later on when I discuss how the formation of a differentiated state affects the mechanisms of representation.

It should be noted, however, that until now most of the theories of corporatism remain silent on this question. This is especially true of the theory presented by J. T. Winkler, according to whom 'corporatism is an economic system in which the State controls and directs private interests right down to their internal policy'.[9] It is highly significant that the author neglects the question of the nature of the state in his long essay, referring to it nonchalantly in a short appendix. Since corporatism is conceived as an economic system, the state is presented in a universal manner. It is deprived of any particular history in each of the countries where it comes into existence. Without institutional reality, it benefits only from a certain functional autonomy, which enables it to better control the world of business. Thus, the problem of the state – of its origin and of its nature – remains ignored.

Panitch is highly critical of the economistic perspective of Winkler and of corporatism viewed as a system of interest representation, such as in Schmitter's proposal. His approach to the corporatist model is in terms of social classes. In his opinion, contrary to Winkler's, corporatism does constitute a political structure that has as its sole function the integration of the working class into the capitalist state. This view does have the merit of taking into account the political dimension of corporatism. However, Panitch approaches the state as a capitalistic entity that during the sixties and seventies reinforced its 'coercion' toward trade unions with the active collaboration of the Labour party.[10]

Furthermore, although Panitch insists on the role of the state more than Schmitter does, he nevertheless does not consider the historical dimension of this social fact and does not distinguish between the different types of state at the heart of capitalist societies. According to him, the countries that experience, in a limited manner, a corporatist representation are the Netherlands, Sweden, and Great Britain, countries where social democracy has dominated the trade-union movement. He feels that France and Italy have escaped corporatism thanks to the existence of a strong Communist current and in spite of state intervention.[11] The state seems always to remain the same; it is only the resistance to its action that changes. I would argue, however, that some countries have not had great Communist movements among the working class because that class had access to the centre and was not combating a state. France saw the development of a statist-oriented Communist movement and, earlier, an anarcho-syndicalist movement because the working class was combating a particular type of state.[12]

Again, while Panitch (drawing inspiration directly from the works of

Nicos Poulantzas) recognises the autonomy that the state possesses
a capitalist society, this autonomy remains only functional, no matt
which capitalist society is in question. The state still does not exist as a
specific space, differentiated and institutionalised, and a result of an
original history. In his most recent works, the position adopted by
Panitch is more complex. While he still maintains political corporatist
structures are 'a form of capitalist domination', he also stresses that, by
itself, monopolistic capitalism is not a sufficient condition for their
appearance. He demonstrates that in the United States monopolistic
capitalism is very highly developed whereas corporatist structures are
not. According to him, it is always the pressure groups that play an
essential role in this political system; the trade unions are like interest
groups and remain exterior to power.

Panitch equally insists that parliament continues to exercise a vital
function in countries where corporatism has flourished, for it alone
promotes the expression of interests not directly linked to a class.[13] But
he does not move away from an economistic explanation of corporatism to ponder the distinctive influence of the type of state or the
particular role of politics. To him, the decisive factor in the development of contemporary corporatism is the level of employment: in a
period of unemployment the trade unions are weak, and the state can
do without them; in a period of expansion the trade unions are strong,
and the state tries hard to solicit their cooperation.

Moving even further away from an economistic theory of the state,
and thus, of corporatism, some, like Claus Offe, underscore the
indispensable 'distance' that has to be established between capital and
its state, the latter having to be in the position to manage social
interests as it pleases, by selecting the demands it chooses to answer.[14]

By rejecting outright the theories of R. Hilferding, Offe brings to
light the existence of two systems that interact upon each other: the
marketplace (economy) and the state (politics). The latter does not
have as such any capitalistic nature, which might account for how it
maintains the order of capitalism. Offe rediscovers, quite naturally,
the vocabulary of systems analysis in analysing the guidance role that
the state assumes when it selects contradictory demands. Close also to
the theses of James O'Connor on the fiscal crisis of the state, Offe's
thesis sees in the state a system capable of reconciling demands geared
to the accumulation of capital with those of assuring its legitimacy by
increasing the loyalty of citizens. But, in the same way that O'Connor

refers to a political system when he analyses the role of the capitalist state in the administration of a fiscal crisis (a political system without any institutional base, without historical dimension, and without distinctive personnel linked to a system of particular roles), Offe, too, reduces the state to a political system, one with a functional autonomy favourable to the survival of capitalism.[15] With different metaphors and contrary courses of theoretical inspiration, we find again – despite everything – distinctions close to those proposed by Poulantzas, who differentiates the reigning class (*classe régnante*) from the hegemonic class in order to establish between them relations of functional autonomy based on their separate autonomies.[16]

This difficulty is equally present in the more recent works of Jürgen Habermas, who is inspired by the analyses of O'Connor and Offe. Habermas examines exchange relations in the economic, socio-cultural, and politico-administrative systems by analysing the operations of regulation, the fiscal appropriations, and the social allowances that reinforce the loyalty of the masses.[17] There again, the adaptation of systems analysis to the Marxist perspective enables us to discover specific crises at the entrance and exit of the politico-administrative system, crises that systems analysis by itself would not unveil. Nevertheless, this approach does not address the question of the origins of the state. Nor does it explain particular state types appearing in diverse capitalist societies, each of which is linked to a specific type of crisis.

Still today, Habermas, like Offe, chooses not to take into account recent work in historical sociology on the state. Thus, we are left with a theory of corporatism that underestimates the state factor and that has a hard time avoiding a reduction to class relationships only. Paradoxically, such a perspective leads to underestimating phenomena of power, as well as those inherent in the conflict, in order to shed light, rather ahistorically, on the mechanisms of functional adaptation.

When Offe considers the problem of corporatism, he attempts to interpret the new structures of group representation in terms of social classes, stressing the extent to which the business world occupies a position within the state that is far more advantageous than that occupied by the working class. These groups draw uneven advantages from their institutionalisation in the state, and from the diminution of their latitude of action. As Offe observes, 'whereas capital can bring its obstructive power to bear even if *it is not* organised as an interest group, the withdrawal of labor power can function as an instrument of power only if it is practiced *collectively*, that is, if it is organised in at least a rudimentary way'.[18] Offe has the merit of interpreting the corporatist system from notions of social class, class conflict, and power. However, his notion of state is purely reified. It does not correspond to any existing organisational structure; it remains totally ahistorical. This difficulty appears, for example, in the way Offe treats the German case without reflecting on the historical origins of the German state, and without taking into account the difficult formation of a German political market and democracy.

In the same vein, Bob Jessop also approaches corporatism in a relatively ahistorical manner. Even if he correctly reproaches Schmitter and Winkler for having an 'instrumentalist theory of the State' resulting in an 'inadequate theorization', he himself simply uses a theory of the 'structural selectivity' of the state to explain its 'form'. To him, the growth of monopoly capitalism is expressed through a corporatism that institutionalises the representation of capital and of the working class. Parliament would thereafter simply be the forum where the interest of the traditional petite bourgeoisie and of petit capital can be expressed. The social bases of corporatism and of parliamentarism would thus become contradictory. This would explain the birth of a 'strong State', which Schmitter calls 'State corporatism', that is to say, an authoritarian state.

According to Jessop, those European countries where a strong social democracy comes to power can avoid an authoritarian state and rather experience a 'liberal corporatism'. Here, only social democracy is capable of integrating the working class and the petite bourgeoisie. In short, the social-democratic state is understood as liberal corporatism; if favours the accumulation of capital and checks the mobilisation of the working class, which might otherwise be directed against it.[19] Jessop then attempts to describe the 'form' of the state of liberal corporatism. However, this presentation remains ahistorical; the state is the same in all capitalist countries, the only thing that changes is the weight of social democracy and, consequently, the type of corporatism. The state proper is not considered in its specificity. Only the history of political centralisation and the birth of the democratic political market are used to account for the degree and type of corporatism to be established by representational mechanisms. To Jessop the democratic system is thus the best 'shell', where capital resides as long as the bourgeoisie remains dominant, and where corporatism is no longer a 'fascism with a human face' (Winkler) but, rather, 'the highest form of social democracy'.[20]

According to Jessop, this corporatism appears in northwestern Europe, in the United States, in Australia, and in Japan.[21] Without making fully explicit the significance of this restrictive list (which includes as well countries where social democracy did not become predominant), Jessop implies that in Europe countries like France, Spain, or Italy remain quite distant from liberal corporatism. If he means to introduce here an interesting distinction, he does so without reference to the history and specificity of these states. Are they, simply because of their distinctive origin, condemned to become 'strong States' of the authoritarian type? Or do their structures and modes of function permit them to confront new crises in different ways and according to their own logic? The analysis sheds little light on the functioning of the differentiated state *à la française* and of its particular situation vis-à-vis the problem of corporatism. With reference to corporatism in Great Britain, however, his analysis is somewhat more advanced.

Here, he emphasises the fragility of such a system, since the participation of trade unions in administrative organisations is largely 'symbolic' and encounters the opposition of the business world. Above all, given an account of the absence of any real 'incorporation' of these opposing interests, he stresses that it 'requires an institutional framework within which to articulate functional representation with parliamentary representation and to coordinate intervention through corporatist channels with that through regional–legal administration. Little progress has been achieved in meeting any of the requirements despite frequent attempts and pious appeals to develop and extend corporatism.'[22] Among the present theorists of corporatism, Jessop is, then, the one who seems most concerned with that structure of politico-administrative organisation most likely to give birth to a corporatist system.

This analysis, however, appears insufficient, for it does not shed enough light on the historical particularities of political development in Great Britain. This may explain, as we shall see, the quasi-impossibility of establishing corporatism there. This absence of historical perspective appears clearly when the author suggests that we are witnessing today the creation of a 'strong State'.[23] It then becomes impossible to distinguish the British political system from those that have states, or even from those that have states that, while not really differentiated, have become so strong that they appear to be simply authoritarian.

Starting from the works of Panitch and Jessop, Christine Buci-Glucksman and Goran Therborn attempt to consider the political dimension of corporatism. Probing further into the diversity of situations affecting Western countries, they nevertheless encounter the same difficulties present in the works of the authors who inspired them. According to Buci-Glucksman and Therborn, the formation of corporatist structures was made possible by the appearance of the Keynesian state, which promoted growth, full employment, and social peace. They then stress the crisis that for fifteen years has affected this type of state, a crisis that ultimately promotes authoritarian solutions.

'Are all these forms and tendencies toward authoritarianism which are present in Germany, France and England sufficient to define a new form of State?' ask the authors. To them, 'if authoritarian statism responds to German or French developments, it does not at all cover the Scandinavian or even British cases'.[24] They thus attempt to shed some light on the particular situation in which each of these countries finds itself, without, however, considering the particular history of each type of state. Consequently, we encounter a great deal of analytic wavering. Can we, like these authors, liken the authoritarianism of France to that of Germany, yet contrast Sweden to Great Britain and to Germany? Both Great Britain and Germany would be strongly affected by authoritarian corporatism as an answer to the crisis of the Keynesian state, and in fact, the authors often find the two countries comparable as well as in contrast to each other.[25]

Even if Buci-Glucksman and Therborn insist on the 'multiple national variations' of the Keynesian state, or of its successor, their analysis still remains ambiguous.[26] In their claim that England, France, and Germany now possess identical strong states, they fail to take into account the particular modes of state construction, each of which, in turn, is a result of a particular history. Moreover, the authors do not pay sufficient attention to the diversity of democratic processes and political regimes that results from these two different forms of the division of political labour. These two forms developed into profoundly opposite political systems.

Such analytic wavering on the nature and future of capitalist states indicates how fragile these theses on corporatism are. Few authors consider the structure of the state as an essential variable that might explain the presence or absence of corporatism. One such author is Robert Salisbury, who remarks that in the United States corporatism cannot develop precisely because that country lacks a 'monist' state.[27] Guillermo O'Donnell, in his turn, contrasts 'statalising' corporatism (*corporatisme 'estatizante'*), where the state extends its influence over civil society (Brazil, Argentina and Mexico), to 'privatising' corporatism (*corporatisme 'privatista'*), where interests penetrate the heart of the state. However, this distinction is still not satisfactory. By isolating those states where bureaucracy reigns in conjunction with an army, O'Donnell unfortunately groups all the countries of Western Europe and the United States together to illustrate the second type of corporatism. Again, he remains silent on the specificity of each state and hence on what differentiates France from Great Britain.[28] The 'strong State' is now Brazil and Argentina, not Great Britain.

Even so, O'Donnell offers us a fecund path of research in distinguishing between state types and their relationships with corporatism. He compares the Brazilian or Argentinian states to Germany, Italy, and Japan before the war. Inspired by the 'development from above' analysis of Barrington Moore and A. Gershenkron (which states that accelerated growth necessitates the formation of an immense bureaucracy and a differentiated state) and by the Marxist analysis of Bonapartism (which stresses the differentiation of state structures), O'Donnell emphasises that in Latin America the state cannot be autonomous, for the bourgeoisie is linked to international capital and to persisting agrarian structures. Only similar research on the structure of the state will permit us to remove some of the ambiguity still present in corporatist theories. By re-examining contemporary works of historical sociology, such research must begin by better distinguishing among the Western capitalist countries. These countries today benefit from the advantages of democracy but nevertheless still manifest essential differences in their mode of political centralisation and, accordingly, in their relationship to corporatism. Only such research will enable us to understand the particular actions undertaken here and there by the working class in such countries as France and Great Britain.

III

Since World War Two, countries with profoundly different political systems, like Great Britain (where centralisation has led to an avoidance of differentiation and to an encouragement of representation) and France (where the hardships of centralisation led to differentiation and to the emergence of a state), are facing, as capitalist systems, relatively similar economic crises. As might be expected, they react to and resolve the problem of corporatism in accordance with their particular type of political system.

A quick survey of the history of the Labour party in Great Britain reveals the tentative character of critical proclamations the party makes when in opposition; when Labour comes to power, however, a more realistic policy is followed. Numerous historical examples bear witness to such fluctuations. The Party's 1918 programme, 'Labour and the New Order', advocated a series of progressive measures, such as the democratic control of industries, a radical transformation of the system of taxation, and a very sophisticated concept of social legislation. Within the framework of a regime that had to remain parliamentary, 'Clause 4' was adopted under Fabian influence yet remained the Labour party's central point of reference. It stipulated public control of the means of production, distribution, and exchange and nationalisation of land, and so forth. A few years later, R. H. Tawney, in *The Acquisitive Society*, offered a virtually definitive presentation of Labour ideology. The Labour party was to be a gradualist party, using the state to effect profound socio-economic transformations. This recourse to the state has remained constant in the programmes of the Labour party. Confronted with the realities of power, however, Ramsay MacDonald, as prime minister of a party that won elections for the first time, seemed to be struck with amnesia. From his first speech on, he no longer mentioned those structural reforms contemplated earlier and was satisfied with enacting social measures that benefited the old, the sick, and the unemployed. Later on, and again in opposition, the Labour party adopted a programme ('Labour and the Nation', 1928) that again was inspired by principles of social transformation. With Labour victorious in 1929 and amidst a worldwide economic crisis, these principles were once again forgotten, and MacDonald had to turn to American banks for credit. He went even so far as to ally himself with the Conservatives - the great 'treason' of August 24, 1931.[29]

Back in power in 1945, the Labour party, led by Clement Attlee, nationalised the mines, gas, electricity, and the means of transportation, and established a national health system. Except for the automobile industry, Attlee did not attack large enterprises that do not fall under public service, and he justified nationalisation less on ideological grounds than on the need to ensure full employment. Defeated in the elections of 1951, the Labour party was tempted to place in question once again the renowned 'Clause 4', but internal reactions were such that it still remained untouchable. Long after between 1964 and 1970, the Labour party increased pensions decreased citizens' share of payments for health expenses, and developed a programme of construction. However, it also reinforced private industry by letting it benefit from numerous loans aimed at increasing productivity and exports; nationalisation was no longer a question. And yet, Harold Wilson, the new prime minister, had resigned in 1951 from the Attlee government, along with Nye Bevan and John Freeman because he considered it too reformist. Once in power, Wilson showed himself a pragmatist and ruled from the centre. According to him socialism will be more the result of technological progress than of structural reforms linked to old ideologies. Henceforth, the 'technological revolution' pushed socialism into another perspective. The government strove to limit the range of industrial strife. Although it failed in the face of great trade-union reaction, this attempt nevertheless revealed the ambiguity of Labour policy.

Such ambiguity became all the more extreme in the next period. Again, while in opposition during 1973, the Labour party elaborated *Labour's Programme for Britain*. It is 'the most beautiful socialist programme I have ever seen in my life', declared Michael Foot. The party claimed that when in power it would put the squeeze on private property, nationalise a great many enterprises, increase the public appropriation of land, extend economic planning, and so forth. Victorious in 1974, Wilson named representatives of the party's left-wing, like Foot, Benn, and Heffer, to high posts. He also announced his intention to control prices and, in particular, he created the National Enterprise Board in order to further intervene in the economy. For a trade-union leader like Jack Jones, the 'New Jerusalem' was on the horizon. However, disillusionment set in for the last time. Instead of planning, incentives were used. Private industry was reassured instead of nationalised, plans to tax wealth were abandoned, and a moderate industrialist concerned with industrial democracy was appointed as head of the National Enterprise Board. In December 1976 there were 1,270,000 unemployed, compared to only 678,000 in 1975. Inflation increased dramatically and economic growth was out of reach. The government indeed agreed to ameliorate the rights of the trade unions; it abandoned the Trade Union Act by which the Conservatives had earlier attempted to legalise industrial relations. The trade-union movement accepted a severely restrictive wage policy that Mr Foot, himself, declared necessary. The rank and file, however, reacted violently, and a wildcat strike movement began. Although the government's economic policy was hardly revolutionary, it found itself fiercely accused of leading Great Britain to collectivism by state action. The distance that separated the radical programme itself from its conciliatory practices underscores, once again, all the ambiguity of the Labour party and testifies to the extreme fragility of its position.

Still today, in 1982, other 'utopians' placed at the head of the Labour party seem to threaten the traditional order. An identical process seems to be repeating itself. How can it be explained? Why, in spite of its repeated proclamations, has the Labour party failed to touch the foundations of the social system? To analyse this distortion, some authors accept the elitist perspective of Mosca and Michels, which holds that any party, whatever its ideology, will present itself as a machine functioning democratically. The 'betrayal' of the Labour party is attributed to the pursuit of personal interests, to the pursuit of the prestigious positions a political party can dispense for the profit of its leaders. While invoking utopian and universalistic ideologies to win power, the leaders of the Labour party, after winning power, pursue pragmatic policies, even to the detriment of the working class that had trusted them. This is the thesis advanced by R. T. McKenzie and, more recently, by Hugh Jenkins.[30] From a Marxism strongly mixed with elitism, Ralph Miliband, in his famous book *Parliamentary Socialism*, has similarly accused the Labour party of being, in reality, only a parliamentary party and of having constantly betrayed a working class that had fundamentally revolutionary values.[31] Its leaders are 'bourgeois politicians' who develop a 'rhetoric' that is, for the most part, 'illusory', even when it is advanced by the Labour party's left-wing. Its episodic revolts, which we have been stressing here, take on – according to Miliband – a functional character: they exploit and divert the revolutionary values of the working class.

This thesis has been often criticised because it presupposes the revolutionary character of the British working class. As Stephen Haseler has said, British workers are not drawn to socialism and thus have not been betrayed.[32] This idea is also advanced by Henry Drucker, when he affirms that the Labour party only mirrors the conservative, loyalist, respectful ethos of British workers, one that makes them sceptical of utopias.[33] Many observers stress the profound integration of the British working class, its preference for parliamentary methods that permit it to be rapidly heard, and its rejection of Marxism and anarcho-syndicalism. In this view, the pragmatism of the Labour party in power reflects that of the working class itself.

Perry Anderson and Tom Nairn, for their part, have argued that the pragmatism of the British working class echoes the empiricism of the British bourgeoisie. Insofar as the latter did not adopt a triumphant philosophy, the working class was not compelled to oppose it; hence, its defeatist ethos and its passivity.[34] The Marxism of Anderson differs from that of Miliband, although both note the parliamentary character of the Labour party. Anderson seems to feel that the Labour party does express the real values of the British working class. He thus advocates the creation of a new type of party, one that would be of Leninist inspiration and that alone could escape those constraints that inevitably lead to trade unionism (one finds here again the attacks of Lenin in *What Is to Be Done?*); Miliband proclaims the existence of a truly revolutionary working-class culture and concludes that it was betrayed by the Labour party.

These multiple interpretations are hardly satisfactory. The Labour party is not a simple political machine, and its radical programmes are not simple functional strategies. Nor can the British working-class culture be considered as purely pragmatic, even if it does not appear eminently revolutionary. All these ideas appear reductionist and simplistic, an expression of an objectivist Marxism or, on the contrary, of a depoliticised and utopian vision that conforms to the traditional 'end of ideology' thesis. The British socialist movement has, in fact, constantly remained a solid force throughout time. Marked by evangelism, it has remained utopian. Its belief in a new and fraternal world should be interpreted not as functional rhetoric but as an attachment to social justice, an attachment demonstrated by the bitter struggles led by the British working class throughout its history.

Nevertheless, these struggles do not assume any character of 'exit'.

Throughout its history and to the detriment of other social groups, the British working class has mainly attempted to increase its representation in the centre by using the political mechanisms of the parliamentary democracy already in place. Neither the Labour party nor the trade unions can appear as faithful apparatuses of the state in the service of capitalism.[35] At the turn of the century, the working class, organised in trade unions, created a party to act in the centre that called itself the Labour Representation Committee. By being present in the centre, the working class has helped limit the development of a differentiated state.

By using the processes of representative democracy (voice), the working class has similarly preferred to negotiate directly with management and has refused to give the state essential regulatory functions. British industrial relations rest, in fact, on vigorous voluntarism with social partners settling conflicts by themselves.[36] During the 1950s, when an abundant society thought it saw the end of ideologies and an end to the decomposition of social classes, these voluntarist practices, as theorised by the members of the Oxford School, looked like normal means of conflict resolution.[37]

Faced with the excesses of voluntarism, both political parties have attempted to establish a system of controls over the trade unions, so that they were not required to register with the public authority. (The Conservatives began the attempt in the framework of the Industrial Relations Act in 1971, and the Labour party continued it to a lesser degree afterward; when the Conservatives were in power, the trade unions were regulated by law and a national court of industrial relations.) This push for the extension of state power has been understood as leading to corporatism. Many authors have argued that Great Britain was now experiencing a corporatist regime, in which the interests of labour and management were integrated in, and controlled by, the politico-administrative structure. This corporatism, furthermore, was seen as the ultimate outcome of privileged 'triangular' relations first established during World War Two. At that time, when Bevin, then minister of labour, declared to the trade unions: 'I have to ask you to place yourself at the disposition of the State', he created a kind of 'new social contract' (to use Samuel Beer's expression). From this period on, according to Keith Middlemas, the trade unions and the employers associations became, like the state, 'governing institutions'; they abandoned their previous status as pressure groups in order to integrate themselves within a Keynesian-type 'extended State'.[38] Whether stable or fragile, corporatism, for most of these theorists, appears particularly advanced in Great Britain.

In reality, this integration has been greatly overestimated: public power did not succeed in controlling private enterprises opposed to any corporatism; and the trade unions, the employers associations and public power reached agreements only with great difficulty – opposition was very strong.[39] This is why planning structures have been virtually nonexistent.[40] Public power was satisfied with giving subsidies to declining economic sectors. Thus Great Britain still does not have a corporatist system.[41] Instead, there is a deliberate return to traditional voluntarism.[42]

Corporatism, as Colin Crouch suggests, requires an institutionalised bureaucracy and, I would add, a state. Thus, corporatism is incompatible with British society, in which the state remains relatively unstructured. The failure of corporatism might be attributed to the centralised character of employers' interests, the relative weakness of British trade unionism (incapable of controlling delegates from the base who react against any intervention that might deprive them of their role),[43] and the inability of the political system. More likely, however, the failure stems from the very nature of the British state – nondifferentiated, nonautonomous, noninstitutionalised, and without a particular personnel of high functionaries to serve it and to impose its will.

If the state has played, as Crouch further remarks, a noncoercive role in British industrial relations, this is because of its historical origin (neglected by Crouch), one that prevented the formation of a state capable of intervening efficiently.[44] Thus, the trade unions have succeeded in maintaining their autonomy, in avoiding integration into the political apparatus, and in forcing the return to voluntarism, which expresses the primacy of civil society. In Crouch's own expression, instead of a corporatism that requires a state, we find in Great Britain a 'private corporatism'.[45] This private corporatism, as Dominic Strinati points out, emphasises both the role of coordinating financial and industrial interests and the action of trade-union organisations.[46] Thus, the influence of the establishment is such that its very existence directly implies the absence of a differentiated state. There is, furthermore, considerable osmosis between the direction (*dirigeantes*) categories (political and economic),[47] in which numerous leaders of the working class also participate.[48]

Under these conditions, we can better explain the fluctuations of the Labour party and the distance that separates actual practice from the proclamations. Instead of interpreting such contradictions with elite theories, instead of seeing them as proof of Labour's betrayal of the working class's revolutionary values, let us stress that the doctrine of the Labour party has been, from the very beginning, *étatiste*, while the practice has almost constantly been voluntary and based on negotiation. Doctrinal recourse to the state appears disfunctional because of that society's precocious development of representative democracy and hence its non-*étatiste* centralisation. Thus, the particular formation of the British system, whose consequences have never stopped being felt, help us understand both the impossibility of corporatism and the difficulties that await the Labour party's efforts to change society.

IV

The contrast between those countries where productive relations are regulated by the state and law and those where private negotiations are victorious is often considered no more than *une image d'Epinal* that should be abandoned. However, after formulating such a judgement, Gérard Adam and Jean Daniel Reynaud analysed the situation in France and in Great Britain and concluded that in France 'there was never, as in the Anglo-Saxon mode, an institutional and almost automatic relation between the strike and negotiation, between negotiation and agreement, between agreement and social peace'.[49]

In France, the trade unions were late in being recognised. With difficulty they opposed a state that always wanted to exert strong control over them. The working class has always been excluded from the state; it had immense difficulties in having its voice heard and always had to act conflictively. As I have demonstrated, this opposition to the state accounts for the importance of Marxism and anarcho-syndicalism in France, as opposed to their near absence in Great Britain. Consequently, in France, strikes are often very political and are not directly linked to a process of negotiation.[50] As Walter Korpi and Michael Shalev observe, 'lacking an "inside track" to the state, the working class responds by activating an alternative vehicle of collective pressure, the strike'.[51] Already at the end of the nineteenth century, as Michelle Perrot has shown, both management and workers rejected negotiation; management preferred 'action on the state apparatus',[52] and workers sought state support by appealing, especially after the Republic was established, to prefects and *sous-préfets* for intervention. For Perrot, 'such an attitude [on the part of workers] reflects a belief in the high priority and the omnipotence of political factors and leads to the search for the key to happiness in a change of regime'.[53] According to the author, 'after 1800, the weight of politics lightens up. The curve of strikes becomes more liberated from politics and responds more to largely economic factors.'[54]

Clearly, as Charles Tilly states, 'the historical inheritance' of France and, more particularly, its type of state, still exerts today an essential role in the nature of industrial relations and renders impossible any corporatism. Tilly finds that, from the nineteenth century to the present, strikes stand in close correlation with political crises. And it is precisely the working class's inclusion in, or exclusion from, the state that accounts for the outcomes and the types of strikes that spring up in Great Britain and in France.[55] The strike in France is thus linked to an absence of working-class representation, as is the increasing intervention of public authorities in the resolution of industrial conflicts.[56] For example, as shown in Tilly's analysis, there is the ever-increasing action, from 1898 to 1935, of police officers, work inspectors, *sous-préfets*, prefects, and ministers.[57]

Although those involved do not always see a strike as being essentially political, it is usually the particular structure of the state, linked to the difficulties of democratic representation, that explains how social conflicts are resolved in France. In numerous historical instances, the state in France has played a vital role in searching for a solution to industrial conflict. I would like here to mention the advice that Denis Poulot gave to the people sometime after the Commune: 'Do you know what you need first in order to have the instrument of work? Well, you must be big enough to get it by yourself, and not wait for providence from the state. If you reply "impossible", look at the British.'[58] Poulot thus returns spontaneously to the contrast between France, where the role of the state is pre-eminent, and Great Britain, where there is an autonomous organisation of the working class.

Since the nineteenth century, the Jacobin tradition appears in the very conception of labour law, which Waldeck-Rousseau defined in terms of public liberty. In France, litigations take place on the terrain of law, not on that of negotiation (hence the essential role of the French courts in the resolution of industrial conflicts); in Great Britain, where

the law seldom intervenes, litigations will most often be solved in
equity. For Adam and Reynaud, 'Anglo-Saxon liberalism, contrary to
French Jacobinism, restricts intervention, even at the price of a
trade-union monopoly'.[59] Further, 'the Jacobin tradition of the state
has always had a hard time reconciling itself to negotiation between
social partners'.[60] Collective negotiations in France are still exceptional today; instead, strikes, as in the nineteenth century, reflect a
fundamental rejection of order. The 'politicisation of strikes in France
is first of all this: the absence of a domestication of demand through
negotiation'.[61] Given the distorted nature of professional relations, the
May movement of 1968 can be seen as 'primarily either the failure or
the revelation of the utopian character of this intended social pacifi-
cation'.[62] Faced with such a failure, the social actors can only have
recourse to the state and to the law; this is why the law substitutes itself
so often for negotiation between interested parties.[63]

Rejected by management and often combated by the state, the
working-class movement in France has remained unorganised, weak,
and in the minority. Its trade unions include a very small proportion of
workers (from 5 to 25 percent in the private sector). It is divided
between organisations that oppose each other politically and strategi-
cally. Its resources are few, compared to those of Anglo-Saxon trade
unions. It has relatively few executive officials (at the national level,
the Confédération Générale du Travail has about 150 officials, and the
Confédération Française et Démocratique du Travail 120).[64] And
because the state and management have never tried to reinforce it, the
French trade-union movement remains poorly structured; it is only
recently, after the events of 1968, that trade-union sections within the
enterprises have become legal. Such a contested and fragile movement
cannot exert great power on the workers as a whole, which explains the
high number of wildcat strikes outside and sometimes against the trade
unions. Each of these traits only further distances France from the
corporatist model.

After 1968 the French state appeared willing to promote a contractual policy favourable to negotiations, which might have put an end to
those conflicts around which traditional trade-union relations are
structured. Negotiation had to become the rule in order to 'unblock'
society, as J. Chaban Delmas then maintained. Towards this end,
employers had to recognise the trade unions and establish trusting
relations with them. Disillusionment came quickly; the trade unions

were immediately hostile to these forms, and management hardly appeared ready to negotiate. This is why 'the persistence of authoritarian and centralising attitudes by management and by government facilitates the ideological and strategic tasks of the trade unions; they can combine both immediate demands and global transformations of society'.[65]

After these attempts at reforms, the French working-class movement returned to its traditional position of complete opposition to management and to the state. Thus, in France, where the state has always exerted a strong influence on the whole of civil society, the introduction of a British mode of negotiation failed – just as in Great Britain, attempts at strong state intervention failed. The political logic of each system therefore still conserves each system's power of action.

In France, antagonistic social actors would rather turn toward the state and its courts, and preserve their own autonomy, than negotiate. The strength of the state thus shows itself through a threesided game in which management and the working class remain on the outside. The state, as a product of differentiation, cannot promote the integration of particular social interests in its centre without jeopardising its own institutionalisation and its own autonomy – hence, the impossibility of corporatism. The failure of voluntarism therefore does not lead to corporatism but to the state, by reinforcing the differentiation so characteristic of the French mode of political centralisation.

Under these conditions we can understand why management and trade unions have refused to integrate themselves into the state planning structures, and we can also understand why the state, in turn, has refused to give them a place in its own administrative structures.[66] The history of planning illustrates how the state in France draws its inspiration from a long interventionist tradition going back to the ancien régime. It also illustrates how trade unions have been permanently excluded from the state. Although they remain in the Commissions de Modernisation du Plan, trade unions have been there essentially as 'active spectators'.[67] In any case, at least formally, participation in these commissions is based upon personal competence and not upon the representation of specific social interests. Here again, one of the essential conditions for corporatism is not met, since workers appointed to these state structures do not officially represent the trade-union movement and cannot then be used to control it.[68] Their role was further limited by the principled hostility of the trade unions, which refused to be integrated, as well as that of the state, intent upon preserving differentiation.[69]

The only corporatism that has existed at all in France is of the authoritarian type and was installed under the Vichy regime;[70] societal corporatism in France is unthinkable as long as the trade unions refuse to be integrated into the state and as long as the state itself sees it as a threat to its specificity. Of course, this same state has established privileged relationships with the world of business; high state functionaries often act in conjunction with management or, alternatively, force management to apply a policy of economic moder-nisation through state planning.[71] By preserving its autonomy vis-à-vis the business world, the French state continues to give high function-aries an essential role; representatives of the working class thus still find themselves excluded from administrative positions. The state and the political regime reinforce each other to keep the working class at a distance and to prevent, at the same time, any corporatist leanings.

In sum, in Great Britain, the weakness of the state and the presence of representative democracy stand in the way of corporatist expansion. In France, to the contrary, the very strength of the state forestalls any corporatism, with the difficulties of democracy further alienating the working class.

7 ❦ The Nazi collective movement against the Prussian state

Totalitarian régimes, such as that of National Socialist Germany, undergo an intense mobilisation of their many social groups. This would even seem to be their defining feature. Juan Linz, in advancing a clearcut distinction between totalitarian and authoritarian régimes, reckons that the former are essentially characterised by multiple processes of mobilisation, conducted by a mass party, in the name of an ideology and to the advantage of an omnipotent leader. He therefore deems a totalitarian system to be one which eliminates all pluralism, and which endows itself with an exclusive ideology and with a closed and constraining conception of the world, so as to integrate individuals more fully by provoking an intense collective mobilisation within the framework of a single party and various other secondary associations.[1]

Conversely, authoritarian systems are in Juan Linz's view characterised by a limited pluralism, as also by the absence of a highly structured ideology to which everyone is subjected; there is, instead, a wide range of different beliefs. Political mobilisation is not very intense in a régime of this kind; the leader, or the small group holding power, wields it by means of frameworks which are ill-defined but which rule out what is purely and simply arbitrary.[2] Because no ideology is forced upon the social actors, and because they do not identify emotionally with their leaders but prefer to concentrate upon problems arising in their private lives, mobilisation is significantly weaker under such régimes. In an authoritarian régime, one would therefore find oneself in a situation of extreme depoliticisation rather than one of intense mobilisation. Furthermore, for Juan Linz, the lack of mobilisation and the depoliticisation have immediate consequences for political power in an authoritarian régime, with the traditional élites in the civil and military bureaucracies conserving their power, whereas in a totalitarian régime they are replaced by élites which are more marginal as regards both their social and professional origin and their values.[3] There is thus a clear correlation between a high level of institutionalisation and an authoritarian form of political power and, on the other hand, a low level of institutionalisation and a totalitarian form of power.[4] This also returns us to the relationship already analysed above between types of mobilisation and types of state. I would further stress that political power may itself undergo far-reaching developments: a totalitarian system may be transformed to some extent into an authoritarian one; the 'routinisation of charisma' turns the power of a leader into an authority role; mobilisation is thereby itself attentuated, the role played by ideology becomes less crucial, and recourse to violence – which some authors, Hannah Arendt among them, regard as a feature consubstantial with the wielding of totalitarian power[5] – no longer seems so crucial a variable as once it did. Such transformations are not, however, linear and, just as the emergence of a democratic régime depends upon numerous different factors,[6] so, too, the formation of an authoritarian régime is not the necessary consequence of the institutionalisation of a totalitarian system.

This discussion of the opposition between totalitarianism and authoritarianism, conducted mainly in terms of analyses concerned with types of power and degrees of mobilisation, is clearly at odds with Carl Friedrich's classic definition of totalitarianism. For Friedrich, a totalitarian régime has six characteristics:

1. A totalist ideology; 2. a single party committed to this ideology and usually led by one man, the dictator; 3. a fully developed secret police, and three kinds of monopoly or, more precisely, monopolistic control: namely, that of: (a) mass communications, (b) operational weapons, (c) all organisations including economic ones. Such monopoly control is not necessarily exercised by a party: it is however in the hands of whatever 'élite' rules the particular society.[7]

This now classic definition of totalitarianism has numerous shortcomings. I would simply note here that it pays no heed to the phenomenon of mobilisation and that it only tackles the problem of power in terms of élites or of leaders.[8] If we only take account of the role played by the leaders, we will construct a model of totalitarianism which covers quite diverse power structures: this, however, is what Carl Friedrich and Zbigniew Brzezinski are doing in maintaining that Stalin, Hitler and Mussolini all held 'absolute' power.[9] In reality, the rise to power of each of these leaders was realised in the context of very different state structures. Thus, in some cases, as for example in

Germany, these state structures were highly institutionalised and served at first to place limits on a leader's power, whereas in others such structures were barely institutionalised at all and would never have been able to assume such a function of control.[10] An analysis of totalitarianism thus demands that one should also undertake an analysis of the types of state which have been constructed in each of the societies in which one or other of the 'isms' was successfully established.

Hannah Arendt has shown, in a remarkable analysis, how the Pan-Germanic and Pan-Slavist movements undermined the structure of the then existing states, for in both cases they refused to surrender to them the right to grant citizenship solely on the basis of their own criteria. Thus the Pan-Germanic movement had already argued that the German people could be said to comprise all those who shared German culture or who belonged to the German race. As a consequence, 'hostility towards the State as an institution runs through the theories of all pan-movements'.[11] As far as Arendt was concerned, the fascists in Italy 'wanted a fascist State and a fascist army, but it was still a State, it was still an army';[12] by contrast, in Germany and in Russia, with the undermining of the state's sovereignty, 'the "totalitarian State" [was] a State in appearance only, and the movement no longer truly identified itself with the needs of the people. The Movement by now [was] above State and people.'[13] Whilst it is true that Hannah Arendt does not examine the specific qualities of each of the states which was undermined by totalitarianism and is also in no position to analyse their capacity for resistance, which varies in accord with their greater or lesser institutionalisation, her analysis does nevertheless have the merit of throwing light upon the irremediable opposition between totalitarianism and the state.

The state is in fact the outcome of a process of differentiation separating it off from the rest of the social system; its existence presupposes strong barriers which protect, by means of, for example, administrative law, the highly institutionalised politico-administrative apparatus.[14] Totalitarianism undermines the state's independence; it 'annihilates all boundaries between the State and the groupings of society'.[15] This is why 'totalitarian systems are characterised by the elimination of the carefully cultivated distinction made in Western democracies between the state and society'.[16] This 'totalist'[17] conception of the social system, applied in the name of a systematic ideology aimed at mobilising all actors and at eliminating the slightest trace of independence which might serve as a space for resistance, makes the end of the state inevitable. In this respect, those who choose to speak, as many do, of a totalitarian state, are clinging to 'contradictory terms'.[18] To confuse totalitarianism with the absolute state is to betray a misunderstanding of the nature of totalitarianism, which challenges all particularism and, *a fortiori*, that of an absolute state with a particularly high degree of power of its own.[19] An absolutist state is meant to rule over society and hold sway over each of its parts, in accord with its own interests; a totalitarian movement, on the other hand, aims to eliminate all institutions which result from the operation of the principle of differentiation; the state is a victim of the 'cancer of totalitarianism'.[20] As Hans Buchheim has shown, 'after its "seizure of power" the totalitarian movement converts the state, which until then had been its energy, into its slave'.[21] One can conclude with this crucial point, namely that totalitarianism seeks 'to throw the state overboard',[22] to destroy its power and consequently to challenge the results of a long process of differentiation. One is plainly concerned here with a movement of dedifferentiation.[23]

Each totalitarian movement has to confront a different type of state, which, depending upon its level of institutionalisation, will show varying degrees of resistance. The present chapter will be dedicated to an analysis of Nazi totalitarianism, which I shall rapidly compare with Italian fascism, through taking into account the type of state constructed in each of the two countries. I shall not consider the case of the USSR, which differs in many respects from that of Germany and Italy. National Socialist ideology had adopted a completely hostile attitude towards the state from the start. From the very first pages of *Mein Kampf*, Hitler forcefully and repeatedly asserts: 'I did not want to become a civil servant.'[24] In the course of three long chapters, he violently attacks the authority of the state conceived as an end in itself, as an organisation assumed to be suited to the shaping of civilisation: for him, 'the state is a means to an end . . . it must first of all preserve the original racial elements'.[25] In contrast to the Hegelian conception of the state, regarded as an instrument of universalist reason or, indeed, to the Weberian theory of rational–legal power, which are both particularly applicable to the highly bureaucratised Prussian state, Hitler assumed an anti-state perspective and sought to entrust an élite with the task of realising the union of the race.[26] The absolute power of the élite was thus supposed to break the power of the state.

As early as February 1920, the programme of the National Socialist Party expressed the desire to constitute a Germany in which 'in order to be a citizen, one must be German in origin'; article 5 also excluded non-citizens from holding public office.[27] If one bears in mind the close relation binding every universalist state to those that it acknowledges, without applying any particularist criterion, to have a right of citizenship – such that everyone has an equal right to participate in a neutral public office, in the service of the general interest – one can grasp the extent to which Nazi totalitarianism presented itself as above all else a necessarily anti-state movement. As Hitler quite clearly put it, in the autumn of 1934, at Nuremberg: 'The state does not command us, we command the state.' Similarly, Heydrich declared: '[our] enemies have spread their tentacles through every branch of our public life and state structure'.[28] Conversely, Italian fascism seems to have been a movement that favoured the strengthening of the state. Thus, in a speech at La Scala in Milan, Mussolini declared that everything was in the state, that nothing was against the state, and that nothing was outside the state. By contrast with Nazism, fascism aimed to strengthen the state, not to demolish it, to further the extension of the public sphere rather than to abolish it. According to Mussolini, 'The fascist conception of the state is all-embracing; outside of it no human or spiritual values can exist, much less have value. Thus understood, fascism is totalitarian.'[29] This is why 'the fascist conception of authority has nothing in common with that of a police state'.[30] Mussolinian totalitarianism was therefore the polar opposite of Nazi totalitarianism: this is because in reality it was not totalitarianism but an authoritarian régime which aimed to strengthen the power of the state.

The debate on the nature of totalitarianism, and on its relation to the state, does not therefore date from the Cold War; it had already begun in the inter-war period. If Nazism sought to abolish the state and to destroy differentiation, it was because it claimed to be returning a total power to the *Volk* itself. As George Mosse has quite brilliantly demonstrated, the critique of civilisation and the return to 'culture', the rejection of towns and of modernity and the nostalgia for the organic, informed a large part of German ideology and, in particular, permeated nineteenth-century irrationalist romanticism before coming to dominate all of reactionary thought at the beginning of the twentieth century. The 'new romanticism' defended by the review *Die Tat*, edited by Eugen Diederichs, sought to re-establish the guilds and organic relations between groups, so that all might be considered members of one and the same *Volk* and be led by an aristocratic élite. This is why 'at best, the state was a servant of the *Geist*, of the *Volk* and its interest'.[31] For many authors, writing from many different points of view, the *Volk* was structured as a *Bund* and the state was thereby reduced to being nothing more than a number of purely instrumental functions which no longer enjoyed any sovereignty.[32] From Pan-Germanism to National Socialism, it was therefore considered necessary to yield power to an élite expressing the unity of the *Volk* which the state had destroyed. It was after Hitler had transformed *bündisch*-type organisations into a mass movement capable of promoting a totalitarian mobilisation on the basis of multiple forms of social organisations either collective or associative that he assumed the role of Führer. The 'nationalisation of classes',[33] when seen in this light, expresses the organic unity of the *Volk* reconstructed at another level than that of *bündisch* structure.

As Otto Koellreutter, a professor of constitutional law well versed in this line of argument, put it:

from this *völkische* totality it follows that, as far as National Socialism is concerned, the continuity of the political event is assured by the people, as the incarnation of political greatness, rather than by the state. This being the case, the Hegelian conception of the state as 'the reality of the moral Idea' constitutes a non-*völkische* position which is alien to National Socialism.[34]

Thus the theoreticians of the Third Reich emphasised the total opposition between fascist and National Socialist conceptions of the state; in the former case, the *stato totalitario* is invariably deified, whereas in the latter it is stressed that 'the designation of our Reich as an "authoritarian" or "totalitarian" state is inexact'.[35]

As far as the leaders of National Socialism were concerned, the state ought not to be totalitarian, for that would be to give it an absolute power. It was, on the contrary, the Aryan movement – an expression of the unity of the *Volk* and its leader – which was supposed to enjoy a total power of that kind. Carl Schmidt formulated this in juridical terms: 'society which is itself organised as a state . . . is now in the course of being transformed from the neutral state of the nineteenth century into a potentially total state'.[36] But 'total mobilisation', a category which Ernst Jünger had used before Carl Schmidt, was

realised this time through 'society having itself become a party state'.[37]
In Carl Schmidt's writings, as in those of his disciple Ernst Forsthoff,
the author of *Der totale Staat*, the formula of the total state undoubtedly
implied a rejection of the neutral and constitutionalist state, but did
not therefore imply a commitment to fascist 'statism'. These writers
thus tend towards the doctrine of the *völkische* total state, according to
which state and *Volk* are confused one with the other. But inasmuch as
the original, Italian version of the formula of the total state expressed a
desire to increase the actual power of the state, it contained ambigui-
ties which the theorists of National Socialism found unacceptable. It
was therefore quickly abandoned.

It was, by contrast, the advocates of a German National Bolshevism
who were to celebrate the might of the total state, thereby aligning
themselves with the Prussian tradition which fought against National
Socialism. From 1919 on, the theorists of this current – men such as
Eltzbacher – therefore regarded Bolshevism as a dictatorship wielded
by a strong state;[38] Eltzbacher himself believed that Bolshevik Russia
had taken up the torch of the Prussian state. It was because they
believed that the Bolshevik régime was about to restore the Russian
state to its former greatness that the German National Bolsheviks
turned their attention towards it, as if Prussia, too, might regain its
might of days gone by. Ernst Niekisch, the most important theorist in
this current, held that the military state constructed by the Bolsheviks
was none other than the 'Potsdam state'. This was the real meaning
of the Bolshevik Revolution: 'Russia, being at death's door, resorted to
the Potsdam idea; indeed, it stretched it to the limit, so as in the end to
distort it and create an absolute warrior state'. Germany may well
have allowed Russia 'to pre-empt it in creating such a state', but it now
had to 'recover lost ground'.[39] Another advocate of 'revolutionary
nationalism' advanced a similar argument in *State and Marxism*, which
was published in 1921: 'In Lenin we see a head of state who, though he
admittedly denies the idea of the state in theory, displays an
unprecedented coolness and decisiveness, as all observers will allow, in
his practical realisation of it.' This writer, intent upon drawing the
Soviet experience ever closer to the Prussian model, observes that 'the
dictatorship implicit in the Prussian Idea of the State was itself an
anti-democratic and anti-capitalist one'.[40] This perspective was
directly opposed to that of the National Socialists, who therefore
showed no hesitation in eliminating its key figures. In this sense, the

Nazi leaders professed a lasting hostility for the old structures of the highly differentiated Prussian state and devoted all their energies to combating it.

However, since Prussia played a central part in the construction of the German Reich, it was difficult to declare open war upon it. This is why the National Socialists sometimes made themselves out to be its heirs. Thus, in April 1933, Joseph Goebbels declared: 'National Socialism must declare itself to be, with good reason, Prussian. Wherever we National Socialists are to be found, throughout Germany, there too we are Prussians.'[41] References to Prussia and, during the war, to Frederick the Great, were a constant feature of German propaganda. While it may have seemed more effective to maintain a degree of ambiguity, which could have served to bolster the legitimacy of National Socialism, it should nevertheless be emphasised that, under Nazism, as William Ebenstein observes: 'it was the Reich which administered Prussia and not *vice-versa*. As a geographical and administrative unit, Prussia has never been so emasculated and overshadowed as under Nazism.'[42] Nazi totalitarianism in fact tried to impose its ideology and methods upon Prussian authoritarianism, and I will analyse the latter's drawn-out and structured resistance to it below. So passionately opposed to the state were the National Socialists that they even sought to return to a period prior to the state. This explains their enthusiasm for a return to the political structures of the Middle Ages, a period which preceded the process of differentiation whereby a separate space for the state was established. Through its admiration for the Teutonic order, its romantic conception of law (*Treue*) and honour, binding leader and vassal to each other, its vision of justice modelled on the example of Saint Louis, National Socialism literally 'cannibalised'[43] the German political system by undermining state unification.

In order to complement this analysis of the ideological dimension of National Socialism, I propose now to consider how this ideology was translated into fact and how the Nazi movement managed to break up the state and install its own totalitarian order. A large number of interpretative models have been advanced, and it is right and proper that I should begin by examining these. The majority of them were developed either in the inter-war period or during the Second World War. This being the case, the models in question are often blatantly biased or else concerned more with moral philosophy than with empirical research of the kind I shall consider below.

When Hitler's party seized power, the Communist Parties advanced an orthodox Marxist interpretation of Nazism, so that, for the Third International, in 1932, 'fascism grows organically out of bourgeois democracy'.[44] Regarded as an expression of imperialism, fascism was thought to unmask the true nature of political systems formed in the framework of a capitalist economy. The state was thus seen as having an interventionist function which had grown in response to worsening social contradictions, which is why Dimitrov, in August 1935, at the Seventh Congress of the Comintern, defined fascism as 'dictatorship of the most reactionary, chauvinist and imperialist elements of finance capital'.[45] This was to interpret Nazi power as a dictatorship of a particular fraction of the bourgeoisie. It hardly matters here if one decides that this fraction did or did not benefit from the help of the Social Democratic Parties, and I will therefore not go into the Third International's waverings on this point. It is worth bearing in mind, however, that for Marxist theorists of the inter-war period, such as Otto Bauer, 'the dictatorship of capital . . . narrows down so as to become a dictatorship of the most bellicose fraction of the capitalist class'.[46] The purely economistic and instrumentalist interpretation of Nazi state power has been entertained, with a few variations here and there, throughout the course of the twentieth century, so that even in recent years it is possible to find an author declaring that it is 'a perfect monopoly capitalist state'.[47] Since the theory of state monopoly capitalism is applied indiscriminately to the Weimar Republic, to Nazism, to the American political system or to Gaullism, it necessarily has nothing to say about the specificity of the state itself.

However, since the inter-war period, there have been many theories attempting to account for the autonomy of the Nazis' political power. Thus August Thalheimer formulated an original interpretation of Italian fascism in 1930, applying to it the Bonapartist model developed by Marx in relation to Louis Napoleon. Thalheimer himself attempted to analyse the authoritarian phenomenon by regarding it as the result of an equilibrium between antagonistic social classes, thanks to which the executive power managed to establish its own independence. Whereas Marx, however, had placed the emphasis upon the institutional conditions governing this independence, which was connected with the fact that the state had its own resources (the development of a civil and military public function), Thalheimer began by emphasising that the fascist régime corresponds to the organisational form of

Bonapartism, a political framework enabling the bourgeoisie to invent a form of power which would rescue it in social terms while doing violence to itself politically,[48] but he did therefore recognise that the institutional independence won by the state was a genuine one. To apply the Bonapartist model to fascism is in fact to distort it: since fascism, in the last analysis, enables the bourgeoisie to put up a better defence of its economic power, it is, for some interpreters, a functional translation of that power. Though attacked by the advocates of a more economistic Marxism, this impoverished version of the Bonapartist model rests in its turn both upon a rejection of the political specificity of Nazism and its relation to a state which it sought to undermine. Finally, even those Marxist theorists who, being conscious of the specifically political character of fascism, take their distance from the monopoly capitalist state model, conclude by subordinating it, directly or indirectly, to the holders of economic power.[49] Nicos Poulantzas, for example, has consistently opposed the reductionism of the monopoly capitalist state model; nevertheless, he reckons that the advent of an exceptional state such as fascism finds expression in an ' "institutional crisis" which, although it has its own effects on the class struggle, is itself simply the result of it. Institutions do not determine social antagonisms: it is the class struggle which governs the modifications in the state apparatuses.'[50] This is why, in Germany, according to Poulantzas, fascism established 'the overwhelming domination of big capital by a process of regulation (a process having nothing to do with the myth of a "planned" or "organised" capitalism)',[51] this argument culminating in a very summary description by Poulantzas of the exceptional state itself.[52] The Bonapartist model, as is the case with all models designed to reflect the specificity of the political, should encourage one, as I shall try to show below, to pursue a scrupulous investigation into the development of the state, with the help of materials furnished by, for example, the science of administration.

The theory of state monopoly capitalism, even where qualified by the Bonapartist model, has been still more flatly rejected by all those theorists who, from this period on, predicted the emergence of a simple state capitalism which would effectively dominate the monopolies and steer their actions to suit its own interests. Such theories were developed in the main by the Frankfurt School. Thus Frederick Pollack, mindful of the consequences of technological advances, conceived of National Socialism as the emergence of a new social order within which a divorce between power and the ownership of the means of production is effected. Advanced during the same period, but independently of Burnham's thesis on the rise of a managerial class, Pollack's thesis stresses the novel features of the state capitalism which National Socialism establishes. According to Pollack, it abolishes 'the last vestiges of such free economic subjects; property and income are no longer the foremost determinants of the individual's social position'.[53] Invoking Harold Lasswell's analyses on the 'garrison state', Pollack also draws attention to the situation of dependence industrialists from now on find themselves in with respect to those who possess the means of exercising violence.[54] For Pollack, 'Under a totalitarian form of state capitalism the state is the power instrument of a new ruling group, which has resulted from the mergers of the most powerful vested interests, the top ranking personnel in industrial and business management, the higher strata of the state bureaucracy (including the military) and the leading figures of the victorious party's bureaucracy.'[55] Pollack does, it is true, use the notion of totalitarianism in his analysis of Nazism, while the Marxist thinkers of the period tend to refer instead to the notion of the dictatorship of capital. He does not therefore talk of a totalitarian state for, to his mind, it is actually the ruling class which wields such power through the mediation of a capitalist state, a class consisting of those who hold the highest posts in a number of different institutions. For Pollack, as for Max Horkheimer, Nazism tends to eliminate the market and to favour 'integral statism',[56] so that 'state capitalism is the authoritarian state of the present period'.[57] Even if, as the reader will no doubt have noticed, these Frankfurt School theorists employ the notions of authoritarianism and totalitarianism as if they were interchangeable, even if they undertake no study of this state itself, preferring rather to focus their researches upon the consequences of the Enlightenment, upon the relations between reason and technique or, again, upon the authoritarian personality itself, they do nevertheless distance themselves from a purely economistic vision of the phenomenon of Nazism (though other members of this same school do in fact entertain such a vision).[58] Franz Neumann was, however, the member of this school who produced the most searching analysis of the nature of the power enjoyed by the Nazis. Although his analysis seems compatible in some respects with Marxism, in other respects it veers towards – without ever being identical to – that proposed by Pollack. For Neumann, in contrast to Pollack, 'the very term "state capitalism" is a *contradictio in adiectio* . . . Such a state is therefore no longer capitalistic. It may be called a slave state or a managerial dictatorship or a system of bureaucratic collectivism – that is, it must be described in political and not in economic categories.'[59] Franz Neumann therefore rejects both the notion that the régime is a capitalist state and the idea that it constitutes a state monopoly capitalism. For him, Nazi society would seem rather to be 'a private capitalistic economy, regimented by the totalitarian state. We suggest as a name best to describe it "Totalitarian Monopoly Capitalism".'[60] By contrast with most of the other members of the Frankfurt School, Franz Neumann holds to his belief in Marxism and, refusing to accord a special significance to technology and to the power it can sometimes confer on those who own it, maintains that the National Socialist régime still depends upon a capitalist economy. But the power of the state is not therefore, it would seem, any the less increased:

The political structure of national-socialism exhibits a number of divergent elements. The concept of the strong, all-embracing totalitarian state, though now rejected in ideology, is by far the most characteristic. The rule of the bureaucracy and of the armed forces . . . is complete. The state is restricted only in the police and youth administrations, in which the party is sovereign.[61]

Emphasising that 'to the extent that the political power of the state has increased, the idea of the totalitarian state has been rejected',[62] Neumann is able to conclude that the state, not society, is totalitarian in nature.

This claim is open to question since, as I have already observed, the Nazi leaders actually hoped to destroy the state by imposing upon it a totalitarian power which would not tolerate the existence of a state at all. I shall therefore consider below the measures taken by the Nazis when in power to undermine state organisation where it resisted their totalitarian aspirations. Franz Neumann's analysis is nevertheless of interest insofar as it confronts the problem of totalitarianism within a Marxist framework, and thereby prevents us from regarding the Nazi state as being simply the expression of the dictatorship of capital, whose might it recognises.

Furthermore, having several times asserted that the state was growing ever stronger within Nazi society, Neumann went on to emphasise that this state could not be compared with Hobbes' Leviathan, whose power was limited by the law. It would be more appropriate, Neumann suggested, to compare the Nazi state with Behemoth, which is a 'non-state', a total power which, by contrast with Leviathan, 'swallows all [of society]'.[63] If Nazi power 'swallowed' all of society, it was because it undermined the differentiation of the political which Leviathan, by contrast, respected. In the last analysis, the Nazi state was not so much a state which was totalitarian but in fact a 'non-state', a power which wielded total control over society through the process of dedifferentiation analysed at the beginning of this chapter. This negation of the state by totalitarian power implies, according to Neumann, the destruction of the public function.[64] Once he had, a little like Pollack, distinguished between four rival groups within the ruling class (refusing, again like Pollack, a too strictly economistic conception of power), namely the Nazi leaders (in charge of the police and of propaganda), the army, economic power, and public high office, Neumann concluded that public bureaucracy was gradually declining and would in the end be eliminated.[65] Neumann is thus ready to conclude that Nazi power was not a 'capitalist state' nor a monopoly state capitalism but in fact a non-state.[66] In spite of its ambiguous and at times contradictory nature, the analysis of National Socialist power advanced by Franz Neumann seems to me to be still a fundamental one today; in the last analysis it is compatible with the theoretical analysis advanced above of totalitarianism, which implied that the state was disappearing, and enables one to grasp the extent to which Hitler's anti-statist discourse was successfully translated into fact.

Very few writers nowadays would subscribe to a reductionist and economistic analysis of Nazism.[67] Where the political dimension of Nazism is emphasised,[68] one is logically led to highlight the profound transformations which it imposed upon the former Prussian state in the name of a political, anti-statist conception of totalitarianism. The Prussian state was in fact constructed upon the French model, so that it was a highly institutionalised state. The 'Sparta of the North' appeared to be like a 'garrison state' relying upon substantial civil and military bureaucracies. This 'civil servants' state', or *Beamtenstaat*, delimits a political space which, though admittedly penetrated by the Junkers, nevertheless wielded a massive degree of power over the whole of the society. The state bureaucracy glorified by Hegel and admired by Weber subscribed to, and imposed, a system of values which Hitler, as I have already noted, challenged. High civil and military public office presented itself as a meritocratic ensemble, recruiting from the upper classes, and turned in on itself to such a degree that numerous civil servants were themselves sons of civil servants. Since a large proportion of the politicians were recruited from their ranks, these civil servants would seem to have been the indispensable and effective instrument of authoritarian power.[69] It was this state which pushed its differentiation sufficiently far for the Pan-Germanist movements, first of all, to seek to destroy it; the National Socialist Party then took up the attack, arguing that the Prussian state shattered both the unity of the *Volk* and that of ethnic groups, and proceeded to impose its own conception of a more limited citizenship. As National Socialism undermined the pre-eminence of this state, which is connected even now to the Junkers, some have actually considered it to be a modernising element insofar as, after the totalitarianism which succeeded authoritarianism, it is democracy and a parliamentary régime which have finally taken root in Germany.[70]

It is feasible to regard the National Socialist movement as an attempt to demolish the Prussian state for, after having had to coexist with it for a long time, given the strong defences that it was able to muster (a 'prerogative' state thus being constructed in parallel to a 'normative' state, which successfully defended its own structures, its mode of functioning and its particular values), National Socialism gradually managed to eliminate this 'double state'[71] through the setting-up of a society which tended towards totalitarianism.

The dedifferentiation of the state was marked by the abandonment of the title of Reichskanzler and its replacement by that of Führer. As William Ebenstein observes: 'Hitler rejected the title of *Reichskanzler* on the grounds that this was too functional a term. If one was addressed as "the Führer" one would seem to be the head of the German people, and not head of an institution, no matter how eminent a one.'[72] Soldiers swore an oath to Hitler as Führer and not as head of state; from the time of the law regarding public office of 26 January 1933, the same was true for all civil servants. In order to break up the old administrative order and its particularisms, the estates were scrapped and the whole national territory unified by the law of 10 January 1934 on the Reorganisation of the Reich, thus putting an end to the independence of the *Länder*[73] and thereby replacing state structures with political centralisation. The administrative law which testified to the state's differentiation was gradually whittled away and, in November 1939, every trace of an independent administrative jurisdiction was eliminated. The Statute for the Defence of the People and the State of 28 February 1933 established the state of emergency as a permanent feature in Germany and thus dealt a mortal blow to the state of law, with the SA being exempt from state jurisdiction; on 2 May 1935 it was decided that the Gestapo's warrants were no longer within the competence of the administrative courts.

The dedifferentiation of the state worked to the advantage of the party. The law of 1 December 1933, Guarantees of the Unity of Party and State,[74] was in reality intended to mark the supremacy of the party over the state, with the former even acquiring a public status. It was the party which from then on represented the state, and there was a gradual fusion of their respective personnel, which invariably worked to the advantage of the party leaders. The Führer's councillor, who was appointed by Hitler himself, became a member of the government of the Reich, signed decrees and laws and was involved in the procedure for the appointment of civil servants. Likewise, the head of party propaganda became Minister of Propaganda, the head of the SS became Chief of Police, and the 45 Gauleiters, the local party bosses, were appointed provincial governors.[75] As Hans Buchheim emphasises, this crucial law was meant to 'affirm the dominance of the party over the state; the Führer's power depended upon it, and it was through it and not through the state that the new Reich was built'.[76] As Hitler declared, from 6 July 1933, 'the party became the state'.

The reality was somewhat different, however. Jewish civil servants, communists and socialists were, it is true, immediately barred from holding office, but the civil and military bureaucracies managed to preserve a degree of independence for several more years. The National Socialist movement was forced for a period to arrive at an accommodation with the élites of the authoritarian state and, so great was the prestige enjoyed by these bureaucratic institutions, that a number of Nazi militants who were appointed to serve in them actually adopted their values and became integrated into them.[77] Ludwig Gravert, who had been appointed Secretary of State in the Prussian Ministry of the Interior under Göring, spoke out against the law of 7 April 1933, which threatened the independence of civil servants, and called to mind the need for a homogeneous, competent and effective civil service. As far as Gravert was concerned, the corps of civil servants ought to be preserved as an institution, with its expertise being placed at the disposal of the National Socialist movement. In much the same spirit, Frick, a minister of the Reich and a member of the Nazi Party, spoke in defence of the corps of civil servants and attempted to limit its politicisation. Frick wished the administration of the state to take precedence over ideological forces. Bormann, Hitler's adviser, proposed on the other hand that the administration be restricted to management and the decision-making process, with the National Socialist Party enjoying a monopoly over the development of global perspectives and guaranteeing the allegiance of civil servants by means of appointments which were basically political in nature. Frick wanted to limit the number of purely ideological appointments and reckoned, as did Schulenburg, who in 1935 drafted a report entitled *Krise des Beamtentums*, that it was in the Nazi authorities' best interests to maintain the bureaucracy as functionally independent. This position, which was shared by a number of other Nazi leaders, was defended by Frick up until November 1941, at which date his last report on the subject was definitively rejected by Hitler.[78] Frick resigned and wrote Hitler a letter, in which he declared:

I have, my Führer, always seen it as my duty as your civil service Minister since 1933, to make available to you for the great tasks of state policy a highly qualified professional civil service and to develop it in the old Prussian conception of duty as well as the National Socialist character, as is the case with the German armed forces. The course of the last years makes me doubt, however, whether my efforts can in any way be regarded as successful . . . There can no longer be any talk whatever of the professional civil service being preferred as a body enjoying the special trust of the state leadership . . . The civil service is also suffering badly from the fact that new tasks are not being entrusted to it, but to the Party organisations.[79]

As the war spread further and further, totalitarianism managed gradually to eliminate the brake that the Prussian authoritarian and bureaucratic state represented. This attempt on the part of the civil and military bureaucracies to defend their own identity and functions, even at the cost of serving the Nazi authorities, did therefore last for several years and *esprit de corps* prevailed for some considerable time. It was only in 1939 that a decree stipulated that, in order to hold public office, every applicant would have to belong, or to have belonged to the party or to one of its affiliated organisations.[80] However, even before they had curtailed the attempts of the bureaucratic structures to maintain their own specific identities, the Nazi authorities had also tried to skirt around them by creating their own institutions, which would perform the functions usually devolving upon the Prussian administration. The most telling instance of this strategy was the formation of a kind of surrogate Ministry of Foreign Affairs, the official one being too deeply attached to its prerogatives and traditions. A new ministry was therefore created, with Ribbentrop in charge, and its members were no longer professional civil servants, but, rather, Nazi militants.

Likewise, the economic administration concerned with the completion of the Fourth Plan (run by Göring), the Todt organisation for the development of the motorways, the SS, the labour service and the youth organisations (together with the schools, whose task it was to train the youth of the country) were all organised outside the traditional structures of the civil and military administration.[81] This gave rise to a plurality of conflicting sources of power. Insofar as the state organisations did in the end lose their old functions, there was something of a return to face-to-face contact, to lord and vassal relationships and to attempts to build up personal fiefdoms. These changes were reminiscent to some degree of the period prior to the formation of the state, namely the Middle Ages.[82] In the wake of Ernst Fraenkel, who saw Nazism as a double state, and of Franz Neumann, who analysed the struggle between the four pillars of power in Nazi Germany, authors such as Martin Broszat and Hans Mommsen nowadays place the emphasis upon the large number of centres of power, which often performed identical functions in competition with each other. Far from regarding Hitlerian totalitarianism as a system allowing Hitler to wield absolute power, these scholars stress the dysfunctional character of the decision-making structures, and the often irrational aspect of the decisions taken in the many centres of power. In a 'polycracy'[83] of this kind, the great diversity of the instruments of power and their fragmentation could not help but lessen the totalitarian aspects of the system and thereby make the decisions which were taken less 'intentional'.[84] I do not want to go more deeply into the polemic between those who hold to the polycratic thesis and those who oppose to it the intentionalist thesis.[85] Whether one lays most emphasis upon the power of opposed groups or upon that of a dictator acting intentionally, one would in both cases be recognising that the power of the Prussian state was at an end. In the relentless struggle which it waged against the strong Prussian state, which was so intent upon preserving its specificity, the totalitarian movement radicalised itself all the more, overturned institutions, to a great extent destroyed the state, and gave rise instead to a multiplicity of rival powers threatening its own coherence and efficacy. In this sense, the relative failure of totalitarianism may also be accounted for in terms of the solidity of the Prussian state institutions which, through their very strength, gave rise to so many parallel and competing structures.

The Prussian state was not replaced by a totalitarian state. Indeed, the latter term would be best discarded. Faced with a highly institutionalised state, the Nazi totalitarian mobilisation, notwithstanding its radicalism, with all its tragic consequences, ended up by disintegrating into a large number of rival powers dominated by a modern tyrant.

When faced with a 'strong' state, an extreme mobilisation therefore arises through social structures which alone permit it to blossom and to grow. The correlation between a 'strong' state and high mobilisation ought, *a contrario*, to be matched by a similar correlation between a 'weak' or relatively undifferentiated state and a mobilisation which is weak, or at any rate which assumes less radical forms and less extreme political objectives. One could likewise imagine that, in a system in which associative or communal relations had been all but obliterated, no strong mobilisation would ensue through confrontation with a state which was a particularly powerful one; or, again, that in a society in which such relations were still a crucial element in collective existence, a strong mobilisation would nevertheless occur, thus endangering a state which was weakly constituted and which would thereby find it still harder to put up a serious resistance. Collective actions of this nature might, furthermore, arise one after the other within the same society, with the state either growing stronger or weaker, with social relations also undergoing profound changes, with networks of acquaintanceship being obliterated or, conversely, being reestablished. In this sense, the above pages are meant as an introduction to a genuine, and still unrealised, typology of the many forms of political mobilisation.

8 ❧ Territorial and ethnic mobilisation in Scotland, Brittany and Catalonia

History sometimes produces some surprising coincidences. Thus, in 1707, Scotland voluntarily negotiated its union with England while Catalonia, at the same date, had the laws of Castile imposed upon it, 'in the name of the just rights of conquest'; during this same period, Brittany endured harsh repression at the hands of Louis XIV's armies. Just as each state conducts a specific foreign policy, so too does it pursue a particular line of conduct domestically, in relation to national minorities. If one considers the policies followed by England, a weak state, in relation to Scotland, those of France, a strong state, with respect to Brittany, and finally those which Spain, a weak state that wished to be a strong one, pursued in relation to Catalonia, could one perhaps identify a political logic at work within the political system, and thereby explain the extreme diversity of the strategies adopted by nationality movements when confronted with different types of state?

Some writers, adopting a developmentalist perspective, have felt able to maintain that industrialisation ought to bring about a decline in ethnic tensions and further the homogenisation of society through the spread of modernising and universalist values.[1] According to others, nationality movements fade into the background during the capitalist period when faced with the main conflict, which is that of social classes in perpetual struggle.[2] Thus Rosa Luxemburg condemned the claims advanced by nationalities, on the grounds that they distracted from class conflict. Most Marxist theoreticians have accepted this point of view, though there have been some, such as Lenin, who for strategic reasons have sought not to scorn this type of conflict, thinking it capable of dealing an initial blow to the social order. Through modernisation in the one case, class struggle in the other, ethnic particularisms are thrown into the background and the movements which reflect them thus lose their *raison d'être*.

In Western industrialised societies, however, we find what is in fact a powerful revival of nationality movements, and these sometimes give rise to a significant political mobilisation. Far from ethnic and cultural particularisms seeming dysfunctional and ill-adjusted to a modern world, a growing awareness of them seems entirely compatible with political development. In societies of abundance, socio-economic divisions turn out to be rivalled by divisions along ethnic lines which have remained latent, and which are a historical expression of the resistance of peripheries dominated by centres which are becoming increasingly distant in cultural terms and which even today still incarnate different political values.[3] Within the capitalist system, between the dominant, capitalist centre and the exploited and dominated periphery inhabited by the nationalities, links of dependence are established which are analogous to those which are formed, on the international scene, between the imperialist countries and the societies of the Third World. In this respect, far from tending to weaken, the opposition between the centre and the periphery is hardening, reflecting very precisely the more and more severe struggles which are appearing in the international domain.

With modifications of this kind, the Marxist approach to ethnic and cultural particularisms turns out to be compatible with the idea of class struggle. From the twelfth century on, even before the advent of capitalism, 'regional modes of production' in Western Europe provoked various different types of reaction on the part of the nationalities, reactions which were founded upon dissimilar relations between social classes which, moreover, entered into a range of different alliances with those who held a central position. The feudal mode of production, which later turned out to be so propitious for the creation of modern states 'in spite of the important variations that exist within each zone', presented 'an appearance of homogeneity at a macroscopic level'.[4] Consequently, Scotland may be compared with Brittany, and both of them on the other hand differ from the final region in my sample, Catalonia, which more closely resembles northern Italy and Flanders, where an arable agriculture and early form of capitalism emerged.

This sophisticated version of Marxism therefore provides a new way of analysing regionalist phenomena. It suffers, however, from the same shortcomings as the dependence or world-economy theses, for it, too, underestimates the specificity of the type of state in relation to which this or that kind of mobilisation of a nationality arises. Consequently, it

interprets the English state as a 'strong' state,[5] similar to the kind
which emerged in France or in Flanders, also both feudal regions. This
thus brings us back to the thesis advanced by Wallerstein, according to
which strong states are constructed at the centre of capitalism, with
peripheral regions experiencing a different political development as a
consequence of their subordinate position within the international
division of labour. Studies of this kind do not take into account specific
processes of state construction and disregard the features which, from
this period onwards, divide England from France or from Spain. This
is why authors who take their cue from this kind of position, when they
focus their attention on nationalities, tend to group Scotland and
Brittany, for instance, within the same category. I, by contrast, would
prefer to emphasise what differentiates these regions one from the
other, with Brittany in this respect presenting characteristics analogous with those of Catalonia, so that the nationality movements
which arise there therefore differ from those which emerge in Scotland,
for they confront quite opposite types of state.[6]

In 1707, Scotland opted to unite with England; this agreement
followed on from the Union of Crowns, decided upon in 1603, through
which James VI of Scotland acceded to the throne of England.
Scotland then became one of several peripheral provinces, persecuted
on grounds of religious belief and impoverished through the English
taxes which weighed upon it and the trade restrictions which were
imposed upon it. In spite of the hostility aroused in one part of the
population, the new Act of Union was signed by the ruling classes of
both the centre and the periphery. Much that was specific to Scotland
was nevertheless preserved in this agreement, since the legal system
was not altered, the Presbyterian religion was maintained, the language was not abolished and the educational system was kept.[7]
Parliament was dissolved, but Union allowed 45 Scots to sit in the
House of Commons. Since representation during this period was a
function of wealth rather than of population, Scotland enjoyed higher
levels of representation than England did.

This process of integration of a peripheral nationality into a political
system is unique in Western Europe. Although it may have arisen from
an agreement entered into by two ruling classes, it did nevertheless
enable Scotland to survive both institutionally and culturally, so that
in this case cooption was preferred to destruction by the state. No
representative of the central power was appointed to rule over Scot-

land, and administration and justice were in the hands of the local nobility, who kept their independence. As James Kellas observes, 'while possessing neither a government nor a parliament of its own, [Scotland] has a strong constitutional identity and a large number of political and social institutions'.[8]

If we apply here the theory developed by Albert Hirschman, one can advance the proposition that, in accordance with the nature of the British political system, which has a weak state, a representative mechanism was installed in such a way that the periphery could make itself heard (through its 'voice') by the centre, as has been borne out from then on by the uninterrupted loyalty, throughout the history of Great Britain, shown by numerous Scots in their service with the British armed forces. The temptation to 'exit' has been restricted to a number of revolts emanating above all from the Highlands, in 1715 and in 1745, which perhaps expresses a religious refusal, Catholic in motivation, rather than an assertion of nationalism.[9]

In this sense, the process of representation peculiar to Great Britain, which has been under consideration upon numerous occasions in the course of the present book, whether it is applied to a social class, such as the working class, or to an ethnic and cultural reality, such as Scotland, has proved its efficacy in each and every context. Centralisation here depends upon representation whereas, in other countries, that representation runs up against an uncompromising commitment to the construction of the state.

Michael Hechter is nevertheless right in emphasising the extent to which, even today, Scotland is dependent on London; it has undergone only a limited degree of industrialisation, it has not been able to maintain its own market, it has become harder for it to export, its income remains lower than that of England, its territory is depopulated and its population has been anglicised. Hechter reckons that his account of the enduring nature of such inequalities stands as proof of the validity of the 'internal colonialism' hypothesis, although he acknowledges how original the process of integration of Scotland, thanks to which it has maintained its own personality, has been.[10] Indeed, Scotland suffers from no legal discrimination against either its language or its religion, and its law has remained independent; the Scots enjoy the same rights as the English do, and they have even managed to play a crucial role in British cultural and political life. The sole argument in favour of the 'internal colonialism' hypothesis which remains convincing is that concerning the external control of regional wealth and industries.[11] Domination of a thoroughgoing kind does, however, exist in other societies, where the peripheries inhabited by minority nationalities have not managed to ward off the attempts of strong states to break down their specificity and to destroy all forms of independence.

We must therefore turn our attention once more to the peculiar nature of the British political system. I would emphasise that a Marxist writer such as Tom Nairn admits the unique character of Scottish destiny. Nairn holds that, insofar as union with England allowed Scotland to keep its privileges, it did not undergo, even in the nineteenth century, a genuine nationalism; since the *petite bourgeoisie*, the class which traditionally provides a country with intellectuals ready to contest the prevailing order, had no real cause for discontent, the working class remained deprived of any nationalist culture. Given these conditions, intellectuals of Scottish origin preferred rather to play a role, indeed one of great importance, in English letters (from Carlyle to Ruskin), with Scotland also furnishing the English labour movement with illustrious leaders (from Keir Hardie to Ramsay MacDonald).[12] This integration into Great Britain accounts for the success enjoyed by the Labour Party in Scotland, which is today one of its most faithful bastions, and for the fragility of any nationalist party which has been launched there.[13] The British system has therefore served to encourage a representation at the centre of the nationalist peripheries, such that their internal social diversity is taken into account. It is my view, in fact, that only the logic of the state will shed light upon the specific nature of the processes involved in the integration of the peripheries.

In order to lend further weight to this argument, I shall now take Brittany as an extreme example of an integration effected by a genuine incorporation into the state of a peripheral nationality. Whereas Scotland voluntarily entered into several agreements with England, Brittany had to confront the might of an absolutist state. I shall not linger here over the two occasions upon which Anne, Duchess of Brittany, was forced to marry Capetian sovereigns. François I preferred an 'Act of Union' to this somewhat unstable method of achieving integration. The edict of Plessis-Macé, which was signed in September 1532, therefore entitled Brittany to preserve the same kind of privileges as were granted in perpetuity to Scotland and, in addition, the Parliament of Brittany was not eliminated: it supervised the new taxes, together with all institutional reforms or changes brought forward by France; furthermore, customary law, including 'the Very ancient Custom of Brittany', was preserved.

However, the vicissitudes of the Wars of Religion and, above all, the formation of a genuine absolutism in the seventeenth century put an end to this relative independence. Cardinal Richelieu acceded to the office of Governor of Brittany and considerably reinforced the powers of the central government. Louis XIV and Colbert sought to increase it still further, in accordance with the strategy appropriate to every strong state proposing to subdue its various peripheral appurtenances, each of which is then liable to become a focal point for collective resistance. New taxes were imposed on Brittany, this time without the agreement of the Estates; the insurrections which then broke out were met by a violent and large-scale repression which resulted, in spite of the unceasing resistance of the Breton Parliament, supported by the majority of the population, in the final loss of the region's independence.

The Revolution was to pursue the same objective as the *ancien régime*, but with a still greater emphasis upon state construction, so that from then on Brittany ceased to exist as an administrative entity. The establishment of the *départements* dealt a mortal blow to its specificity, as did the suppression, proposed by the Abbé Grégoire, of all the regional languages.[14] As the Attorney General of the Estates of Brittany, Monsieur de Botherel, put it in his protest of February 1791, 'from being allies, as we now are, the new arrangements will turn us into the subjects of France'.[15] Even if during this period Brittany no longer existed as an entity that was genuinely conscious of itself,[16] its political and administrative specificity could not be denied; the state brought it to a brutal close. The uprising of the Chouans, which may be interpreted above all as a struggle against the central government, was then violently put down and, little by little, the state made Brittany French.

Resistance movements do nevertheless arise, with varying degrees of success, throughout the nineteenth century and up until the modern period, aiming in each case to assert the special value of Breton nationalism and to win recognition for it.[17] Yet Brittany has become an integral part of the French state and the laws of the Republic are applied there in a universalist manner. Its fate could therefore not have been in greater contrast to that of Scotland.

There are a number of writers who, disregarding the particular features of this history and paying no heed to the brutal process of integration undergone by Brittany, show no hesitation in invoking an impoverished version of the 'internal colonialism' thesis to account for its development. It is true that Brittany has industrialised less rapidly than the rest of France, that its economic structures remain predominantly pre-capitalist, that its inhabitants have often had to emigrate abroad or leave their own region in order to come to Paris and, finally, that it has suffered, under the Third Republic in particular, a genuine linguistic repression. The confrontation between region and centre is further complicated by social struggles, with the dominant categories of the centre provoking a strong response on the periphery. Nationalist claims cannot, however, be solely conceived as 'a way of gaining an entrance into the class struggle',[18] for an argument of this sort disregards the peculiar characteristics of the history of French society. In this context, too, the reductionist thesis of a monopoly state capitalism, when applied to regionalism, tells us nothing about the state itself and about its particular logic, which is clearly expressed in the fact that nationalities on the periphery of societies with an identical mode of production may nevertheless undergo a quite dissimilar integration.

Whereas the insertion of Scotland into the United Kingdom was realised through negotiations and representation at the centre, and the integration of Brittany into France was effected through the might of a state which tolerated no peculiarities on its periphery, since it claimed to operate in a universalist manner, the way in which union between Catalonia and Spain was achieved bears witness, by contrast, to the hybrid character of the Spanish state, which had sought in vain to be strong and absolutist.

In 1707, as I reminded the reader at the beginning of this chapter, Castile attempted to impose its rule upon Catalonia, which had long remained independent, by forcing it to accept a form of state control analogous to that in operation in absolutist France. In Spain, as in France, the origins of the construction of the state date back to the tenth century, but subsequent development occurred within the framework of the *Reconquista*, during which regions like Aragon and Catalonia succeeded in safeguarding their own role. While it is true that Castile played a crucial part in this process, it was never sufficiently strong on its own to effect a unification of the country.[19]

Numerous territories therefore maintained their own independence, their rights (*fueros*) and their cultural particularisms.[20]

Castile, being weaker than France and proving incapable of building a significant military and civil bureaucracy, was not able to have systematic recourse to force in order to extend state centralisation in the way that the French monarchy had done. Furthermore, the Spanish state did not manage to win the support of an active bourgeoisie and thus to differentiate itself from the nobility. The essential principles of state construction, namely differentiation and institutionalisation, could therefore not be put into practice.

Finally, I would emphasise that, at the beginning of the sixteenth century, the very success of Charles V's Empire, which grew ever larger, uniting numerous, heterogeneous and distant territories, would seem to have been one more factor standing in the way of the construction of a Spanish state. Empire and state obey two different kinds of logic,[21] European imperialism being ultimately very harmful to Spain. As Perry Anderson emphasises, 'the very sprawl of the Habsburg Empire thus overextended its capacity for integration, and helped to arrest the process of administrative centralisation within Spain itself'.[22]

One could further add that Castile's expansion was mainly realised abroad, in its conquest of the wealth of the Americas, which it took every care to keep for itself. This attitude shows still more plainly how much it disdained peripheries such as Catalonia and how incapable it was of constructing a genuine state.[23] Castile was therefore not affected by the monetary consequences of the massive importations of gold and by the inflation to which they gave rise; but it would clearly have done much better to have built up its own economic strength, to have conquered its own markets, to have developed its exports, and thus quite rapidly to have endowed itself with an active bourgeoisie which from then on would have reinforced its economic potential.[24]

In conditions such as these, the peripheral nations succeeded in preserving their particular features and, in the seventeenth century, in the period of absolutism, the Spanish political system remained by and large a decentralised one. While the French monarchy continued with a remorseless extension of the power of the state, the Count of Olivares still had to recommend to Philip IV, in a memorandum drafted in 1625, that he 'become King of Spain; I mean that your Majesty should not settle for being King of Portugal, of Aragon, of Valencia, and

Count of Barcelona; he must make preparations for the destruction of all these kingdoms of which Spain consists, so that the style and the laws of Castile are imposed upon them, with no other difference remaining'.[25] In the eighteenth century, Philip V attempted to carry out such a strategy and to subject the whole of the peninsula, with the exception of Portugal, to a unitary state constructed on the French model. It was during this period, according to Jaume i Vives, that there was 'close cooperation with Castilian Spain', to which Catalonia was subordinated. This was brought about by the decree of 29 June 1707, mentioned above, which 'in the name of the lawful right of conquest', imposed the laws, manners, customs and internal organisation of Castile. After its defeat, Catalonia was reduced, in 1716, to the rank of a 'Spanish province', and its public law, together with its political institutions, was abolished; from this time on it was governed from Madrid. It was the express wish of the Council of Castile that 'one abandon, obliterate and entirely remove the *fueros*, usages and customs of this principality . . . imposing upon it the laws of Castile . . . conducting affairs in the Castilian language . . . that one not allow books in the Catalan language, nor any speaking or writing in Catalan in the schools'.[26] Only Catalan civil law would survive.

Curtailed as a state, Catalonia turned its energies towards economic expansion, so that the imbalance between the political and administrative centre and the real economic centre, which was the Catalan periphery, was accentuated still further.[27] The attempt to impose complete unity was, however, to fail. One can gain a better idea of the true extent of this failure by contrasting the almost complete lack of Catalans within the Spanish national élite[28] with the important part played by the Scots, as I have noted above, in British politics.

From the nineteenth century up until modern times, Catalan nationalism has been constantly asserted, regardless of the attempts by the various régimes in Spain, whether authoritarian or democratic, to check its vigorous growth.[29] Always present in one form or another, the demand for an *Estat Català* resulted in the statute of Nuria, then in the independence statute of 1932 and finally, after many clashes, in the Constitution of 1978, which 'recognises and guarantees the right to autonomy of the nationalities and regions of Spain and the solidarity of all of them'. Catalonia then entered once more into possession of the majority of its rights and privileges.

If one compares the construction of the French state with the formation of the Spanish one, one must conclude that the latter process has not yet ended.[30] Whereas Brittany is a region which, like so many others, has been turned, in the context of a unitary state, into a *département*, Catalonia enjoys a vague constitution which confers a limited autonomy upon it, under the control of a Spanish state which has been forced to acknowledge its specificity but which still strives, in spite of everything, to function as a state.[31] Conversely, Scotland, thanks to a devolution, which will probably occur in the future[32] and which is compatible with the British system with its weak state, should finally improve its own representation without being reduced to the level of a province plain and simple, but without having any pretensions either to constituting itself as a genuine counter-state.

9 ꧁ Nation, state and culture: the example of Zionism

Do the Jews constitute a people or a nation, and can they therefore have a state? This question, which remains, even after the creation of the state of Israel, a highly complex one, was still more so at the turn of the century, during the period when Zionism emerged and slowly took shape as a collective movement. It was in eastern Europe that Zionism made genuine advances, that is to say on the east of the conceptual map imagined by recent political sociologists,[1] a zone where the state, because it was unable to differentiate itself from the landed aristocracy, could not be properly constituted. Power in these areas remained autocratic and no space for a state with universalist juridical boundaries could be cleared. A fortiori, no genuine 'public space' was created, such as would allow actors to have a voice and achieve a legitimate expression of their interests, which is as much as to say that, after the Bolshevik Revolution had taken place, the many social and nationalist mobilisations that then occurred did not have to confront an already established state, nor was there a genuine political market where they might express themselves. As a consequence, conflicting claims became confused and found expression, in a quite contradictory manner, at one and the same time, whereas in the West, where the state–citizenship dyad had long been established, the national framework existed in an embryonic form also, so that social conflicts unfolded within it.[2]

In France the state attained a high level of institutionalisation, destroyed all peripheral allegiances in order to further, above all else, its own legitimacy, and therefore made the Jews, for example, into citizens enjoying equal rights and at the same time allowed only a strictly private expression to their Judaism.[3] In Germany, by contrast, where the state's institutionalisation was less advanced, as was its universalisation, the emancipation of the Jews was delayed and, indeed, never completed.[4] On the conceptual map of Europe devised by Stein Rokkan,[5] Germany in fact features on the north of the band running across the centre, and the construction of state and nation was both difficult and delayed there. Since it came into existence only in the nineteenth century, Germany produced a very different formulation of the Jewish question, in contrast both with the East – that is, with the territory of Poland, Galicia (partly subsumed within the Austro-Hungarian Empire) or with Russia[6] – and with the West, and with France in particular. This gives us a different perspective on the comparative sociology of the state for, if the idea of a return to a Jewish nation was imaginable in the East, where communal structures remained strong with respect to an autocratic power, it was less so in France, where emancipation depended upon individual citizenship. In Germany, which may be regarded as an intermediate case, love of the *Vaterland* and the call of the Promised Land found expression at one and the same time.[7]

When the Bolshevik leaders had to confront the nationalist movements which arose after the collapse of the Russian Empire, they gave the class struggle precedence since, according to Marx and Engels, 'the working men have no country. We cannot take from them what they have not got. Since the proletariat must first of all acquire political supremacy, must rise to be the leading class of the nation, must constitute itself as the nation, it is . . . itself national, though not in the bourgeois sense of the word.'[8] Even though they made an exception of Poland and Ireland, the only two nations whose creation, for strategic reasons, Marx and Engels accepted, their hostility towards nationalism – which had always, in their view, to remain subordinated to the class struggle – was to leave its mark on the whole of the workers' movement and, more particularly, on the Russian Social Democratic Party, when it had to consider the claims of the various national minorities. Given these circumstances, one can more readily understand the part played by the Jewish question in the communist movement at the turn of the century, even if the extent to which it preoccupies the main theoreticians is still surprising. For Lenin, the Jewish question was a matter of either assimilation or isolation. The idea of 'Jewish nationality' as such seemed to him intrinsically reactionary, not only when held by the real partisans of this notion (the Zionists) but also when proposed by those who sought to link it to the social democratic idea (the Bundists). Lenin believed that the idea of a

Jewish nation was contrary to the interests of the Jewish proletariat, and that, directly or indirectly, it would foster a hostility to assimilation and therefore would create ghettos.[9]

A considerable number of Lenin's and Stalin's writings are devoted to refuting the idea of the Jewish nation. In his key text on this subject, *Critical Remarks on the National Question* (1913), Lenin tirelessly contests the claims of those calling for the recognition of the Jewish nation. As far as Lenin was concerned, 'Jewish national culture' was a slogan of the Rabbis and of the bourgeoisie. Whoever voiced such a slogan, whether directly or indirectly, was, Lenin maintained, an enemy of the proletariat, and, in advocating whatever was old and represented the Jews as a caste, was acting as an accomplice of the Rabbis and of the bourgeoisie. Lenin argued that the Jewish proletarians should assimilate and dissolve into the Russian proletariat, so as to constitute 'a great centralised state', for Marxists are 'opposed to federalism and decentralisation' and reject any form of 'medieval particularism'.[10] The alliance of the proletarians of all nations should result in the creation of a single, powerful, centralised state: the nations cannot therefore be constituted as specific states and, *a fortiori*, neither can the Jews, who do not make up a nation. Nevertheless, the Bundists[11] – 'philistine nationalists' as far as Lenin was concerned – in no way toned down their claims to *cultural* independence. Being both Marxists and opponents of Zionism,[12] the Bundists defended Jewish culture and refused assimilation pure and simple, though they did not lay claim to national independence, still less to the construction of their own state. Stalin, in his texts on the national question, published in the years from 1904 on, also took issue with the Bund and with Zionism. Since language and territory were for him the crucial criteria governing the spread of a national identity, 'the Russian, Galician, American, Georgian and Caucasian Highland Jews . . . do not constitute a single nation'.[13] Stalin was the first author within the Marxist tradition to have conceived of territory as a crucial factor in the definition of a nation, and in this sense he was realigning himself with various currents within conservative nationalism. Criticising the perspective of Otto Bauer (the leader of the Austrian Social Democrats and himself a Jew), which involved 'divorcing the nation from its soil', Stalin added:

what sort of nation, for instance, is a Jewish nation which consists of Georgian, Daghestanian, Russian, American and other Jews, the members of which do not understand each other . . . inhabit different parts of the globe . . . No, it is not for such paper 'nations' that Social-Democracy draws up its national programme. It can reckon only with real nations . . . Bauer is obviously confusing *nation*, which is a historical category with *tribe*, which is an ethnographical category.[14]

Stalin was later to give this territory to the Jews, so that, on 29 August 1936, a decree promulgated in Moscow proclaimed: 'for the first time in its history, the Jewish people has seen its deep desire realised to found a party, to build a national state'. For the President of the USSR, Mikhail Kalinine, 'the Jewish proletarians have their country, the USSR, and a national Jewish state. They have become a nation.' This was Birobidjan, an independent region established in the years after 28 March 1928, bordering on China. Instead of doing as the Jewish Bolsheviks had wished, and building 'a Palestine in Moscow', so as to be better placed to combat Zionism and supervise the Jewish problem, the Jews were given a territory where they might constitute themselves as a nation.[15]

The question of territory would therefore appear to be a crucial aspect of the constitution of a Jewish nation. While the Zionists located this territory in Palestine, and while a number of other options were considered in the course of the first half of the twentieth century – an outlandish and eclectic selection for the most part (Uganda, Argentina or Madagascar) – the offer of Birobidjan was to be a total failure, which in no sense represented a proper response to the single demand formulated by the Bund, that of national cultural autonomy, nor to those of the Zionist movement itself.

The case of Borochov provides perhaps the best illustration of the different aspects of the question of the Jewish nation. He belonged at first to the Marxist social democratic movement; later, he was to break free of it, in order to take into consideration, still from a Marxist perspective, the specificity of Jewish culture. As far as Borochov was concerned, socialism ought not to cause the Jewish nation to disappear; he rejected the perspectives of both orthodox Marxism and of the Bund, placing his emphasis rather on cultural independence alone. Borochov rejected both outright assimilation and the spiritualist theory of a thinker such as Dubnov, who held to an individualist vision of what a nation was, maintaining that the Jews would belong to it deep within themselves while at the same time living in the midst of other nations. In their stead, he proposed another solution, namely, Marxist Zionism. Borochov believed that, given a Marxist perspective,

territory was a crucial precondition – for the formation of a Jewish
nation, where a class struggle within the Jewish people might unfold.
To his way of seeing things, 'The conditions of production are
abnormal when . . . a nation is deprived of its territory.'[16] In the
Diaspora, the Jews had been placed in just such an abnormal situation.
In a now classic text, *Our Programme*, first published in 1904, Borochov
declared that 'long before a state is established the territory must
actually belong, in an economic and political sense, to that people
which desires to form a centre in it'.[17] As a right-thinking Marxist, he
was bound to affirm that it was the 'conscious Jewish proletariat' that
would have to lead this migration into Palestine, where the Jews would
be able to create normal conditions of production, and become a nation
within which the class struggle would find expression. Borochov held
that '*The most vital of the material conditions of production is the territory.*'[18]
There were thus strictly strategic reasons why this territory could not
be chosen at random; later, *a fortiori*, those who adopted Borochov's
perspective could not help but reject the offer of Birobidjan.

The Jewish question therefore overturns the traditional framework
of Marxism. One can gauge the extent to which this is the case by
considering the various currents within Austro-Marxism. It is well
known that Otto Bauer, in 1906, proposed a definition of the nation
which was to be violently rejected both by Lenin and by Stalin, for the
reason (among others) that it would allow a degree of legitimacy to the
Bund, even though Bauer himself maintained that the Jews were a
'nation without history' and that, even if they did not in the end
disappear, they could not help but join up with the proletariat and
become assimilated into it. According to Bauer, 'the nation is the
totality of men bound together through a common destiny into a
community of character'.[19] For Bauer, class, for example, constitutes a
community of character which is able to unite the workers. But only a
nation is able to constitute a community of character which is at the
same time a community of destiny. Hence the crucial importance of
language, which alone makes possible an intense communication
between the individual members of a common nation.[20] It was on the
basis of an interpretation of this kind – which takes neither state nor
territory into account – that Bauer was able to acknowledge that a
Jewish nation existed. However, reviving Engels' notion of a 'people
without history', Bauer applied it to the Jews: 'their culture is stunted,
their language decayed, and they have no national literature'.[21]

Although Jewish himself, Bauer made fun of Jews coming from the East – from Galicia perhaps, or from Bukovina: 'Imagine Jewish children being taught Yiddish in their independent schools! There the children will be taught the culture of a nation without a history.'[22] Paradoxically enough, while Bauer refuses to apply his own definition of nation to the Jewish people, who nevertheless have all the appropriate characteristics, the members of Poale Zion were to employ this same definition to claim cultural independence for the Jews. The Jewish leaders of the Austrian Social Democratic Party, on the other hand, preferred to welcome the support of anti-Semitic movements, which were often Catholic, in their struggle against 'Jewish' capital, an extremist mobilisation which would, they hoped, provoke a general revolution.'[23] In this sense, not only did the Austrian Marxist leaders reject the idea of a Jewish nation and consistently oppose the growth of the Zionist movement but, in addition, they even refused to acknowledge a specific Jewish identity in the ranks of the proletariat.

In the West, the Jews had to be assimilated as citizens; in the East, as far as the Austrian socialists were concerned, they had to be assimilated into the proletariat, thus losing their specific identity there also. For the *Volkstribune*, the weekly paper of the Austrian Socialist Party, 'Zionism means to bring about an active and positive national consciousness identical to that of the Germans, the Czechs or the French . . . Zionist national agitation cannot, however, turn the Jews into a nation.'[24] In Germany, too, the Marxist leaders rejected all Jewish separatism. Kautsky adopted the notion of a 'people without history' in order to assert that the Jews 'constitute a caste rather than a nation', whose destiny it was to disappear with capitalism itself. In two important texts, *Das Judentum* and *Rasse und Judentum*, Kautsky maintains that the Jews form a hereditary caste of merchants, financiers and professional men and that it would be vain to seek, as the Zionists did, to turn it into a nation by creating a 'global ghetto' in Palestine. As far as Kautsky was concerned, Herzl's actions could be equated with those of the anti-Semites, who likewise affirmed that the Jews would remain for ever foreigners in the Diaspora.[25] Herzl was therefore accused, because of his negotiations with the Tsarist authorities, of shattering the unity of the revolutionary movement.[26] Each of the various kinds of Marxism, be it Bolshevik, social democratic or Austro-Marxist, therefore rejected both the idea of Jewish nation and that of a more specifically Jewish working class. Given these refusals, men such as Borochov, on the one hand, and the Bundists, on the other, though they still owed allegiance to Marxism, were attempting to bring about an almost impossible reconciliation.

The re-creation of a Jewish nation was, however, undertaken in terms of perspectives of a more strictly cultural or political nature. Political Zionism was set up by Herzl, who maintained that it had been created in the West, where emancipation was the general rule. As early as 1894, in one of his plays, *The New Ghetto*, Herzl expressed the frustration of the emancipated Jewish middle classes, who ran up against 'walls and barriers which had now become invisible'. Faced with the violent anti-Semitism unleashed at the time of the Dreyfus Affair, Herzl argued that, since the most large-scale emancipation, as effected by the strong state established in France, had not managed to eliminate anti-Semitism, the latter must itself now be being provoked by emancipation itself.[27] From then on, Herzl held that the only feasible solution was the construction of a Jewish state, or rather, to give a more precise translation, of the state of the Jews. 'I no longer regard the Jewish question', declared Herzl, 'so much as a social question but rather as a national question, and to solve it we must formulate it above all as a political question.'[28] This was because, for Herzl, if 'we are a people, a united people', in order to constitute it and guarantee its survival in history, it was indispensable to create a state whose defining features he then describes with some care, specifying, for example, that it would be 'neutral' and, above all, that the religious heads would stay 'in their temples' and the military leaders 'in their barracks'. The state would therefore be neither theocratic nor military, even if Herzl anticipated that its form would be that of an 'aristocratic republic' and not a pure democracy. Consequently, 'the new Jewish state should be explored and settled using all the modern techniques'.[29] Herzl's project was essentially a 'practical' rather than a Utopian one. He believed that one should act fast, assemble the necessary sums of money and win over the great personages of the world, such as the Kaiser, the Sultan, the Marquis of Salisbury and the Grand Duke of Baden.[30] Herzl believed that it was the state which constructed the nation on a given territory. Where, then, would it be located – in Palestine or in Argentina? Herzl answered that the movement 'would accept what was granted to it'.[31] The state thus reinvents the nation, a state which transcends private interests and is of a universalist type, structured as a 'highly centralised administration'.[32] Adhering to a Prussian model of the state, of the kind that Hegel, and after him Weber, employed as the basis for their paradigm of rationality and bureaucracy, Herzl imagined a Jewish nation, structured by a strong state and therefore drawing its inspiration from the kind of strong state existing in certain countries in the West. But this state, although it has been described by sociologists concerned with a comparative history of the state, in fact derived from quite distant and original historical processes.[33] As far as Herzl was concerned, the Jewish nation should depend, like the French and German nations (which in fact, as we have already observed, follow wholly distinct trajectories), upon the might of the state. But can one readily transpose this kind of highly differentiated state, which emerged in particular societies in the aftermath of feudalism, and export it to a given territory, since it was the outcome, in the West, of a specific cultural framework and, more particularly, since it was constituted in relation to the Catholic religion and in the image of its Church? Contemporary sociologists concerned with the state have judged that such a generalisation of the state, its superimposition from the outside on to a wholly different social and cultural reality, cannot help but fail or, at any rate, give rise to a great number of difficulties.

Ahad Ha-'Am would seem to have intuited as much for, from the time of the 1877 Congress, he violently rejected a purely political approach of this kind and judged that Herzl, in proposing that a state be constructed 'organised exactly on the lines of other states', had aligned himself with Western tradition. There would, he maintained, be nothing specifically Jewish about such a state. Ahad Ha-'Am's Zionism, although it was not essentially religious, was from then on presented as being predominantly 'cultural'. Thus, whereas Herzl was influenced by the statist model of certain Western countries, Ahad Ha-'Am steered closer to those aspects of the populist vision which appealed to him. This vision, at any rate in the East, and in Russia in particular, implies a development of the community and not of the state, with the Jewish ethic supposedly emerging organically from a social body moulded by culture rather than appearing as the product of a state operating from above. The state, Ahad Ha-'Am maintained, should be cut down to a minimum and should only be established, in fact, when the nation has already been welded together on the basis of its own culture. Only such a reversal of priorities between nation and state would enable one to impose a limit upon the authoritarian claims of the state, while guaranteeing at the same time its genuinely Jewish character, to the extent that it would be the product of a nation constructed on the basis of Jewish ethics.[34] Because of these views, Ahad Ha-'Am campaigned tirelessly against Herzl's political Zionism, opposing him at the various congresses and attempting to influence the many movements scattered across Europe. He sought to further a cultural Zionism of a kind that a state based upon Western models, 'assimilated by', and superimposed in an arbitrary manner upon, Palestine, could never have promoted, given its neutral, universalist dimension and its detachment from the values peculiar to Judaism, which were, of course, of paramount importance to him. There was thus, in addition to the debate on the nation, a controversy respecting the nature of the state. One may gain a deeper understanding of this controversy by considering present-day discussions concerning the differentiation between state and religion, which is regarded either as the necessary foundation of every state or, conversely, as the distinctive feature of a number of states in the Western world but not therefore something that would serve as a general model applicable to all cultures. This discussion, which has played so central a part in the demolition of those Western evolutionist perspectives which link the advent of the state to a political modernisation conceived of in a purely linear manner, could also be applied to the present situation of the Israeli state, to its strictly Jewish character, and to the transformation of Jewish religious ideas once the religious dimension has been integrated with the political.[35] In a crucial text, 'The Jewish state and the Jewish problem',[36] Ahad Ha-'Am thus asserts that political Zionism simply constitutes the logical culmination of assimilation, of the normalisation of the Jews once they are deprived of their own culture. The state that the Jews would later construct ought consequently to emanate from the *Volksgeist* of the Jewish nation. It would only become possible, Ahad Ha-'Am believed, to build 'not merely a State of Jews, but truly a Jewish State', once the Jews had begun 'to return to its *historic centre* . . . to develop and complete its natural heritage'.[37] As far as Ahad Ha-'Am was concerned, 'this ancient people' could not rest content, after thousands of years of suffering, with a small state, which would be nothing more than 'a plaything of the Great Powers'.[38]

By opposing the 'centre' to the state, by emphasising the cultural dimension of the first model *vis-à-vis* the neutral and therefore assimilationist orientation of the second, Ahad Ha-'Am tackles, in terms which still seem innovatory, a distinction which has become crucial in recent years for the comparative sociology of the state.[39]

However, if one adopts a position of this kind, one risks delaying the passage from nation to state until the millennium. As Lilienblum declared, in no uncertain terms, in 1897, even if the Jewish state could not be as large as the German or the English one, the Jews would do better to avail themselves of a 'small' state, which might even become neutral like Belgium or Switzerland, rather than remain dispersed for any longer[40] since, from 1881 onwards, the uninterrupted succession of pogroms in Russia had begun to threaten their actual existence.[41] Lilienblum, being an advocate of the territorial solution, thus defended the strategy which Herzl had elaborated. He maintained that, in order to avoid disputes between orthodox and lay Jews, it was crucial to go to Palestine, for on that territory and *within our autonomous political life everything will find its place*.[42] Through this reversal of priorities it was the territory which came first, since the state could be constructed upon it and it would thus be possible, through the development of a national liberation movement, for a nation to emerge. It is thus clear how great a divide there was between Herzl's and Ahad Ha-'Am's conceptions of Zionism. Arthur Herzberg saw one as the Mirabeau, the other as the Edmund Burke of Zionism, with the former being quite indifferent to Hebrew and the latter searching for a spiritual dimension, and a basis for action, in language.[43] For someone advocating Herzl's approach, such as Jacob Klatzkin, 'what is really new in Zionism is the territorial–political definition of Jewish nationalism . . . Getting our land is an end in itself, that of arriving at a free national life . . . Essentially, [Zionism], consciously or unconsciously, denies every conception of Jewish identity based upon a spiritual criterion.'[44] The question then arises: which territory?[45] Both the cultural Zionists and the Marxist Zionists insisted that it had to be Palestine; the former felt that only Palestine would provide a suitable context for the renewal of the *Volksgeist* of the Jewish nation, whereas the latter also saw it as providing a framework for the development of the class struggle. Herzl agreed that no effort should be spared to establish the Jewish nation in Palestine and he devoted all his energies to this end; yet he was also tempted by the Argentinian solution. The adoption of this latter scheme would involve pursuing the proposal advanced earlier by Pinsker, in his famous essay *Autoemancipation*, published in 1882:

'Perhaps the Holy Land will again become ours. If so, all the better, but *first of all*, we must determine – and this is the crucial point – what country is accessible to us.'[46] It was, above all else, a question of obtaining a territory, irrespective of its symbolic connotations. Pinsker did not even employ the notion of state, which was to prove so central to Herzl's arguments; as far as he was concerned, the territory was in itself the crucial factor and one could as well create it in the United States as elsewhere.[47] Was it to be in Palestine, the United States or in the Argentine? The stage was thus set for the great quarrel which was to split the Zionist movement; after the failure of the Congo projects, Herzl went on to defend the choice of Uganda and, after 1903, that of El Arish.

Since he encountered such difficulty in persuading the Great Powers to allow the Jews to go to Palestine, Herzl accepted the offer of Joseph Chamberlain, who was then British Secretary of State to the Colonies, to create a Jewish state in East Africa. Herzl's initiative was violently contested at the Sixth Congress of the Zionist movement and was finally defeated in 1904. It was, of course, Ahad Ha-'Am who led the fight against political Zionism, on the grounds that it showed itself too willing to abandon the Jews' own culture and values, together with the role that a possible return to Zion had always played in creating a spiritual 'centre' liable, through its influence, to revive Judaism. As far as Ahad Ha-'Am was concerned, the territorialist position did, admittedly, present itself as a form of nationalism, but it could no longer be regarded as intrinsically Zionist. The debate over these conflicting strategies was a crucial one and, once Herzl was defeated, he declared: 'No one could rightly reproach me with disloyalty to Zionism were I to say: I am going to Uganda. It was as a Jewish-state man (*Judenstaatler*) that I had originally presented myself to you. I gave you my card: Herzl, *Judenstaatler* . . . But, gentlemen, I also learned that the solution for us lies only in Palestine.'[48]

Zangwill was virtually the only one to hold to this territorialist strategy and attempt to see it through. For him, 'Zion without Zionism is a hollow mockery'; it is 'better [to have] Zionism without Zion', that is 'a Provisional Palestine', for 'any territory which was Jewish, [and] under a Jewish flag, would save the Jew's body and the Jew's soul'.[49]

Zangwill, together with a number of other delegates, therefore seceded from the Congress and formed the International Jewish Organisation (IJO); it was their intention to create a Jewish colony

within the framework of the British Empire. Once he had failed in
Uganda, Zangwill opted in turn for Canada, Australia, Angola and so
on, until he came to a complete dead end and the territorialist position
was abandoned forever.

By the beginning of the twentieth century, the territorialist strategy,
which Pinsker, Herzl, Lilienblum, Nordau and Zangwill had all to
various degrees defended, had lost all credibility. Conversely, both
those who thought to preserve the specificity of Jewish culture in
Europe, either in its exclusively spiritual dimension, that is to say in
the conscience of each and every Jew, in the depths of their private
being, as Dubnov believed, and those, at the other end of the spectrum,
who appealed to the class struggle and hoped for the spread of a
specifically Jewish proletariat, as the members of the Bund did, met
with failure.[50] When the new generation of Zionists emerged, their
commitment was wholly to Zion, a territory imbued with a genuine
symbolic and cultural dimension and which, against all the odds, was
chosen by them as the site for the renewal of a Jewish nation.

If, as Ernest Gellner maintains, 'modern man is not loyal to a
monarch, or a land or a faith . . . but to a culture',[51] we are the better
able to understand the immense influence enjoyed by figures such as
Ahad Ha-'Am, with their advocacy of a cultural Zionism, within the
modern Zionist movement. This is apparent in, for example, the attitude of someone like Chaim Weizmann, who, together with Martin
Buber, attacked Herzl in 1903 for being a *Juden von gestern*, a Jew born
yesterday, and lacking in a culture specific to the Jewish people, and
who, much later, while in Palestine, set in motion, in 1912, in collaboration with Ahad Ha-'Am, a project for founding a Hebrew university.
It would constitute 'an intellectual centre where Jews could learn,
teach, and do research in a sympathetic atmosphere free of hind-
rances, in the fellowship of Jews, free from the oppression of an alien
culture',[52] furthering the renaissance of the Jewish national spirit in
the whole people. Cultural Zionism consequently results in concrete
effects likely to guarantee both a return to a form of ethical commitment and, for example, the renaissance of Hebrew as a national language. The 'synthetic Zionism' advocated by Weizmann, influenced
in this by Martin Buber, sought to transcend the longstanding dispute
over the relative merits of cultural and political Zionism, and to reject
an outright deification of the state as state, with regard to which Buber
declared: 'I do not know anything about a "Jewish state with cannons,

flags and military decorations", not even as a dream'.[53] But Buber did not therefore renounce immediate political action, holding talks, for example, with Lord Balfour, whose famous declaration in November 1917 was the first occasion when the national rights of the Jews were recognised as legitimate, or requesting, as Herzl had previously done, the help of Churchill, together with that of various of the other great statesmen.

If it is indeed 'nationalism which engenders nations, and not the other way round', if it is up to nationalism to construct 'potential nations', language must serve as a crucial instrument in the affirmation of a culture.[54] This is why Ahad Ha-'Am's disciples spared no efforts in spreading and teaching Hebrew. Other Zionist leaders participated in this cultural campaign, even though it had its origin in intellectual and political milieux quite different from their own. Thus, Berl Katznelson, who was responsible, with Ben Gurion, for the building of a Labour Party, Ahdut ha-Avoda, in Palestine, and played a crucial political role up until 1944, almost up to the actual creation of the state of Israel, was also concerned with the teaching of Hebrew. *Rapprochements* between the different political currents did therefore become possible, though priorities invariably differed. Thus, when the Peel Commission visited Palestine for the first time in 1936, and proposed that it be divided, Weizmann gave its secretary an English translation of Ahad Ha-'Am's work, in the belief that it was still relevant and topical. Berl Katznelson, however, responded as follows: 'Ahad Ha-'Am is an important author but his English translation is dangerous. Between the moment at which this book was written, it was not thirty but three hundred years that passed.'[55] As the situation grew more perilous, Zionism of the minimal, cultural kind began to seem inadequate, in part because it required a very long time scale; what Katznelson basically believed in was the slow construction of the nation, through the Kibbutz, unions and parties, that is through civil society, and this too seemed inadequate now. Even though the nation was not yet genuinely constituted, a state had nevertheless to be rapidly constructed. This task fell to Ben Gurion, who decided to favour Zionism over the socialism of Borochov, even though he saw himself as belonging to the latter tradition. Katznelson had aligned himself with the anti-Marxist Narodnik movement, which, in according precedence to communal and spiritual activities, was exclusively concerned with the self-organisation of civil society. This approach, though relevant in pre-revolutionary Russia, with its authoritarian, non-statist traditions and its slow rate of historical change, was no longer feasible. From now on, emphasis upon the political and upon the state was obligatory. The communal idea had, for the time being, to take second place to the task of constructing a state, for this alone could guarantee that the nation survived. The order of priorities was therefore once again reversed. From now on, on a given territory, Palestine, where a large number of Arabs (whose rights were much emphasised by Buber and Ahad Ha-'Am) also lived, it was the state which had to assume responsibility for the nation and ensure its cultural and linguistic permanence. What kind of state was it to be? The polemical debates conducted in Herzl's day were not yet fully resolved. To what degree and in what way would the state be in itself Jewish? Admittedly, it is clear that the majority of the leaders refused to link the Jewish character of the state to the idea of race, as Jabotinsky and the revisionist current had explicitly proposed: 'a nation's substance, the alpha and omega of the uniqueness of its character – this is embodied in its specific physical quality, in the component of its racial composition'.[56] In a pamphlet published in Warsaw in 1933, Jabotinsky maintained that 'Every race has a different spiritual mechanism . . . For this reason, every race seeks to become a state.'[57] Darwinist ideas current at the end of the nineteenth century, which was so nationalist in temper, therefore left their mark on the Zionist movement as well, just as, at the turn of the century and in the inter-war period, they gave rise to extremist mobilisations throughout Europe; likewise, on the old Continent, such ideas were sometimes the occasion for violent confrontations between the protagonists of opposed ideologies. However, in an increasingly ominous political climate, those who favoured a rapid construction of the state managed to set aside their differences and, for a period at any rate, prevailed over those who wished to place the emphasis, as far as the process of building a nation for the Jewish people was concerned, upon culture. Once the state of Israel had been created, in 1948, the task remained for political theory, employing the paradigms of a present-day comparative sociology of the state,[58] to assess the degree of differentiation this state might undergo while still being a Jewish state, that is a state in which one could still recognise a society which continued in large measure to subscribe to the values of cultural Judaism and rejected, for instance, the kind of thoroughgoing secularisation which a differentiated state would usually undergo.[59]

10 🦋 The state, the police and the West Indians: collective movements in Great Britain

In 1811, at a time when political crisis and social disorder was resulting in an upsurge of criminal activity, the British Parliament rejected Bentham's proposals regarding the construction of the panopticon and of industrial houses. The panopticon, as readers of Michel Foucault's *Discipline and Punish* will know, was a prison whose structure was designed to allow each and every prisoner to be surveyed. No one within this imposing 'machine' could escape surveillance. Foucault observes that Bentham nowhere states whether his project drew its inspiration from the menagerie which Le Vaux had built in Versailles.[1] He also emphasises the extent to which these plans for a system of total surveillance, which Bentham wanted to extend to the 150 industrial houses (containing some 2,000 persons each), were influenced by the French example.

From the time of Louis XIV, policing in France grew and grew, until constant surveillance of the whole population was achieved. Thus, the Lieutenant-General of Police in Paris was in charge of 48 commissioners of police, allocated to 20 different districts, 20 inspectors, the officers of the watch, the constables, the mounted watch, the foot-watch, in addition to which there was a whole army of spies. This immense police force also received help from the Marshalsea. The French police continued to grow in strength and, in the aftermath of the Revolution, Fouché had made it yet stronger and more centralised.[2] As the *Encyclopaedia Britannica* then observed, France already had 'the most developed policing machinery'.

In Great Britain, on the other hand, policing was still organised on a local basis and was therefore fragmented and weak. This being so, France gave the impression of being a police state. Nevertheless, those who wanted to reform the English police tended to look to France, and they therefore challenged the traditional system, which was Norman in origin, and which relied upon volunteers accepting responsibility for surveillance for a period of a year. English policing therefore remained local, unspecialised, voluntary, and was almost always the citizens' own responsibility. The word 'police' was still virtually unknown in England at the beginning of the eighteenth century. It was only after the Gordon Riots, which took place in 1780, that Pitt, in 1785, proposed that a police force be established that was wholly independent of the municipal authorities and that was therefore centralised. This proposal was rejected, as was Bentham's project in later years.

As early as 1775, in his *Rationale of Punishment* (published first in French as *Traité de législation civile et pénale*), Bentham had questioned Adam Smith's claim that the French system led directly to a police state. Bentham supported the creation of a preventative, developed, centralised and specialised police force. For him, 'government action is necessary to guarantee defence and policing'; consequently, 'Government cannot be exercised without coercion'.[3] Bentham was later to produce a very careful analysis of the French manner of effecting an arbitrary division of a territory into *départements* and *arrondissements*, which, if it were applied to Great Britain, would render the old system of control through local collectivities null and void. The panopticon and the industrial houses, rejected in 1811, therefore belonged to a wider project for police control through the establishment of a range of new institutions. I would further add that Bentham's proposed reforms constituted a coherent plan for the global transformation of a society regulated by the market alone. Indeed, he favoured the emergence of an absolutist and centralised political system and, in his *Constitutional Code*, he even argued that a professionalised and hierarchised bureaucracy, such as Weber was later to conceptualise, be established.[4] Bentham thus played a key part in early nineteenth-century projects for the reforms of the police, and his influence was especially evident in the writings of Chadwick, who was his secretary and who also, in 1829, advanced a project aimed at creating an efficient, centralised police system. The French example was genuinely seen as a radically different model for social regulation and some, such as James Mill, were inspired by it to attempt to introduce something similar into a society where socio-political regulation had always obeyed a wholly different set of rules.

If Bentham's proposals were rejected, it was because they rested upon an excessive belief in the capacity of institutions to effect social

control. Some modern historians and sociologists actually maintain
that social control in nineteenth-century England did not depend
either upon prisons or upon factories. In direct contrast to the
interpretation advanced by Michel Foucault, it has been claimed that
it was the market or the law itself which made total surveillance
possible, independently of any institution or machinery.[5] This would
account for Bentham's failure. Conversely, France naturally seemed
more sympathetic to his projects, for they fitted better with its mode of
control.[6] This said, one would still have to explain, in terms of the
sociology of knowledge, how it was that the Benthamite Utopia
appeared in a country whose repressive institutions were infinitely less
developed and where the police force was still integrated into the local
communities.

As Charles Reith, a historian of the English police, observes, the
creation of a centralised police force would be in no sense 'the product
of the character and genius of the English people'.[7] For Raymond
Fosdick, the author of one of the few comparative histories of police
forces, Great Britain is so much the polar opposite of France that it
belongs in this respect to the nineteenth century. This author therefore
advances an opposition between the kind of police which is a centralised force eluding the control of citizens and serving as the instrument
of an all-powerful administration (France, Germany, Austria) and the
kind which continues to be a local force in the service of the community
and is closely controlled by it, the latter being a natural consequence of
a democracy where liberties are safeguarded by the Magna Carta and
the Bill of Rights.[8]

The organisation of the various police forces is thus connected to the
type of state which has arisen in France and in Great Britain. Where
there is a differentiated state that claims to oversee the whole of society,
there is a huge police apparatus (France); conversely, a political
system in which representative centralisation avoids state encroach-
ment gives rise to a weak police force, an expression of society's
capacity for self-regulation. In the eighteenth century, and at the
beginning of the nineteenth century, as Douglas Hay has demonstrated, a police force still did not exist in Great Britain. The
aristocracy was opposed to the very idea of one because it reminded
them of Stuart claims, of French absolutism and of Jacobin methods.
The law ruled in its stead, and it threatened offenders and criminals –
those who made off with private property, in particular – with the

death penalty. The law in its majesty was able to arrange the death of those who challenged it: 'the criminal law, more than any other social institution, made it possible to govern eighteenth-century England without a police force and without a large army'.[9] At a time when, in France, huge repressive apparatuses existed, in Great Britain it was not so much through panoptica and the police forces that the regulation of the social system was achieved as through the market, which was able to organise, and the law, which was able to control. The law in England, which used to punish all offenders with a public death organised in a terrifying manner, was only rarely applied.[10] The threat counted for much more, and thus testified to the power invested in social norms.

Studies by Eric Hobsbawm and E. P. Thompson have, however, taught us that, between 1820 and 1830, Great Britain passed through a period of social and political crisis in which protest movements were so powerful that 'revolution was possible'.[11] The crisis occasioned by the refusal to extend the suffrage was further exacerbated by religious crises and confrontation between classes. This was also the period chosen by Charles Tilly in his study of the way in which movements of collective action may develop as much through friendly societies, clubs, artisans' societies and communities as through the support of the early trade unions.[12]

I shall not attempt an analysis here of the diverse forms of social protest which were a feature of this period in Great Britain. What I wish to emphasise, rather, is the fact that this rising tide of collective action was in fact accompanied by a decline in the recourse to violence. The protest and reform movements thus found expression not so much in the occasional insurrection as in the employment of more traditional political methods, through participation both at the local and at the national level. This line of argument accords with what John Stevenson has shown us, namely that the decline in violence is not attributable to police action, as was often believed; it was, on the contrary, cultural changes affecting British society which accounted for and permitted the incorporation of those previously excluded.[13] Even if one sometimes finds, between 1820 and 1830, the role of the local police diminishing and that of the troops increasing,[14] even if, as I observed above, the question of a radical transformation of the structure of the police apparatus was on the agenda, with some wishing to adopt the French model, changes affecting the organisation of policing were, all in all, minimal. Even so, it was during this period that the first reforms of the police force were put into effect. The Metropolitan Police Act of 1829, which was set in motion by Peel, anticipated the organisation in London of a 'new police', which would be unified and which would thereby end the independence of the parishes with regard to the activities of their constables. In London, policing became a full-time, uniformed profession; judges had no control over it and it therefore depended wholly upon the executive, which naturally remained under the control of Parliament. Other measures were decided upon in 1839 (County Police Act), which made policing more uniform at the national level.

Notwithstanding these various reforms, which were greeted with hostility almost everywhere, policing in Britain cannot be said to have undergone any real upheavals even if, in 1856, the County and Borough Police Act required that a professional police force be established everywhere and the parish system be dismantled. In practice, the policemen continued to depend upon the local authorities and the 'bobby' was still unarmed and integrated into the community which he protected while on the beat.[15] The police force remained decentralised and its numbers did not really increase.[16] Of course, there were occasions throughout the nineteenth century when its actions were brutal, as when it confronted the working class during strikes in the mining areas, in Scotland at the end of the century, or again in Wales in 1910. Likewise, in the inter-war period, the police had to confront the working class, in 1932 in particular, in Liverpool, Leeds, Glasgow and, above all, in Birkenhead.[17] Yet, violent though they may have been, the police charges almost always involved the use of truncheons only,[18] with the notable exception of those which took place in Belfast, in which arms were used more often and deaths occurred. During this period, just as in 1820–30, it was above all the Irish question which raised the level of violence and brought about changes in policing methods.

I shall argue here that, since 1970, Great Britain has witnessed the installation, in the space of a few years, of a wholly different police force and one which seems, both qualitatively and quantitatively, wholly different from the traditional one. In a matter of ten years or so, the police may well have undergone more transformations than in the course of its whole history. This mutation would seem to have been provoked by factors wholly external to the British political system. As I have already observed, the English working class lost no time in entrusting its party and its unions with the responsibility of representing it to the centre;[19] it turned away from systematic violence, just as it almost always showed great reservations as regards Marxism or anarchism. The transformation of the British police has therefore been brought about through the Irish question and, nowadays, in response to the problems posed by the integration of immigrants from Jamaica, Pakistan, Uganda or Bangladesh, whether they are or are not British citizens.

In April 1981, a violent riot broke out in Brixton, in south London, which was to last for several days. Many streets were burnt out and there were violent confrontations between police and young people, who belonged in the main to the black community. Although the police were not armed, several hundred people were wounded and there were about the same number of arrests. This violence appeared to be the final episode in a long series of confrontations which, since 1965, in Brixton in particular, had seen police and immigrants ranged on opposite sides. In July, almost all the big cities had similar riots and houses burnt down in the inner-city areas.[20]

The whole of Great Britain followed, hour by hour, the course of events as they unfolded, analogous, it seemed, to those of Bristol or of Notting Hill (1958). The riots in fact reflected the rising tide of racism and the rapid change in the role of the police. In a matter of ten years, British society had moved with brutal suddenness from the permissiveness of 'swinging London' during the affluent 1960s, to repression and strict control.[21] In line with these developments, unemployment rose (in April 1981, there were over 2.5 million people unemployed or, in other words, over 10% of the working population). This was the highest figure since the war and poverty was spreading in a society which has been all the more badly hit by economic recession inasmuch as the rate of reinvestment of capital has been traditionally low.

A spate of recent opinion polls suggests that anti-immigrant racism, directed at British subjects from Caribbean islands such as Jamaica, or from Pakistan or Bangladesh, is now operative in all social classes. This racism even affects the least skilled members of the working class, thereby helping to disrupt class solidarity in the face of unemployment.[22] There is thus a general atmosphere of racism, which is reflected in the aloofness, tinged with varying degrees of hostility, of all the major political parties. This explosive situation has also swelled the ranks of the National Front, a deeply racist organisation of the far right, which devotes all its time to harassing and attacking immigrants, sometimes with the complicity of the police. Furthermore, in both the general elections of 1974 and the local elections of 1977, the National Front won up to 20% of the vote in a number of London boroughs.[23] The response of the immigrant communities to police violence, to the increasing number of arrests under the Vagrancy Act of 1824, which allows one to arrest 'any suspect . . . assumed to be a thief . . . intending to commit a crime' (in 1975, 30,000 people were arrested in this manner, half of whom were black), to the attacks of the National Front, and to the pervasive atmosphere of racism, has been to develop self-defence organisations, independently of the unions and the political parties, which have done nothing to defend them. The emergence of Black Power in Great Britain has been responsible for a wide-ranging cultural renewal. This has found expression in a number of different ways: in an often highly politicised and radical reggae (such as that of Linton Kwezi Johnson, whose refrain 'Shout it loud, I'm black and proud' is well known), in the apocalyptic half-political and half-religious movement known as Rastafarianism, and in the use of distinctive clothing to reinforce identification within a group and to emphasise differences between it and the outside world still further. The journal *Race Today*, which has become extremely influential, thus proclaims the need for a caste-based rather than a class-based organisation, with the blacks uniting together and turning down work of their own free will in order to weaken the economic power of the employers.

For the first time, therefore, Great Britain has been confronted with a significant minority which it does not wish to assimilate and which, in response, is itself less and less prepared to abandon its own particularisms. For the first time, a way of life which has been unanimously accepted, and interiorised through an effective political socialisation, has been challenged. Consensus has given way to repression and to racism. There has been political repression of radical black movements, which are often Marxist in inspiration, and there has been day-to-day repression, on the street, of blacks, who are all presumed to be thieves. Since 1972, a new myth has arisen, that of mugging.[24] The existence of a term of this kind, brought in from the United States, testifies to the fear that the black population inspires. It covers all common law offences (theft of cars, of commodities, assault, and so on) and as a myth it serves to justify an astonishing development of police power. No statistics suggest, however, that the crime rate worsened during the 1970s.[25] It is simply that a moral panic seems to have spread, and an anxiety, connected to the economic crisis, has led, as it invariably does, to the search for a scapegoat. The myth of mugging suggests to the British that the American ghettos are already upon them, with their high rates of poverty and violence, drug addiction and sexual freedom. It is also an expression of the decline of the inner cities and the deterioration of the fabric of the city, which is often as evident in Great Britain as it is in the United States. For many, the foreigners are a threat and a living testimony to the decadence of a once powerful Britain which has lost its Empire. Mugging creates a collective panic of a symbolic kind and thus legitimises reaction and an urgent return to the healthy but lost traditions of the past. So it is that a number of Western countries, sometimes invoking slightly different dangers, have one after the other adopted a harsh 'law and order' politics.

This explains why a whole string of repressive laws have been hurriedly passed, beginning in 1962 with the Commonwealth Immigration Act and culminating with the Immigration Act of 1971, which came into force in 1973. The latter enabled the authorities to impose very strict controls upon immigration and to send immigrants back to their countries of origin for no other reason than that their presence was judged to be not 'compatible with the common good'. These legislative measures thus dealt a heavy blow to the rights of British subjects who had come from, for example, the West Indies and who wished to set up home in Great Britain. They were drafted by members of both the Labour and the Conservative Parties; other, still more repressive laws are at present being considered, and these are a cause of great anxiety in the black community. Along with this social violence, there has been the threat posed by the bombing campaigns conducted by members of the IRA. Civil liberties have been seriously undermined. The Prevention of Terrorism Act (1974) has enabled the authorities to arrest anyone suspected of planning terrorist activities. They can be arrested without a warrant and held for 48 hours, and subsequently for five days, at the Home Secretary's behest. These measures have effectively destroyed the traditional right of *habeas corpus*, for so long a crucial feature of the British democratic tradition, and the judiciary has thereby relinquished much of its power to control a repressive administration. In this respect, the troubles in Ireland have also played a part in the radical transformation of British society. Because of the new judicial measures and the threat posed by the IRA, thousands of people have been arrested, put on file and questioned at length, only 1.5% to 2.0% of them in fact for supposed terrorist activities. They are wholly isolated during their period of detention and are not entitled to any legal aid throughout this period.[26] It was also Irish terrorism which led to the establishment, inside Scotland Yard, of the Bomb Squad (1971), which was later turned into the Anti-Terrorist Squad (1976). This team of specialist policemen works hand in hand with the Special Branch, which itself emerged out of the Special Irish Branch, founded as early as 1883 with the express purpose of combating the Irish movement. The qualification 'Irish' was then dropped, and the Special Branch was given the job of checking up on potential enemies of the state, placing a watch upon foreigners, trade unionists, militants of far left and far right parties, civil servants, and even the leaders of the Labour Party. It has also grown rapidly in size.[27]

Special Patrol Groups, noted for the part they have played in suppressing immigrant movements, have also been set up. These groups of policemen are of especial importance because they would seem to be a third force, halfway between the police and the army, with some resemblance to the French CRS, even though they are not so numerous and do not always have access to such sophisticated equipment. It is the SPG who have been involved in the often violent suppression of various forms of self-organisation within the black community and in the protection of the activities of the National Front. Their repressive activities have, moreover, often been coordinated with those of the army. 1974 saw the first joint operation at Heathrow; subsequently it was revealed that there had been no real danger. This operation was repeated in 1977 at Manchester, where there was a massive show of strength of both the police and the army, with the latter deploying tanks.[28]

A new kind of police force has thus emerged, as a direct response to Black Power and to the IRA. The peacable bobby, accessible to all and sundry, calmly patrolling his allotted area, to which he in some deeper sense belongs, is a thing of the past. The police have lost their local character. Nowadays, the police force is completely centralised, deeply specialised, uses police cars more and more when answering calls, is authorised to carry guns (there were 14,574 armed expeditions

between 1975 and 1978), and has in almost all cases lost all contact
with the communities which it has under its continual surveillance.
Policemen tend now to live outside the towns, in middle-class areas,
abandoning the crisis-torn and decrepit inner cities to the immigrants.

The police patrol this now alien territory in the American manner,
with a direct line to headquarters, which is able to make a vast amount
of computerised information available to them at a moment's notice.
Great Britain is quite possibly the country where computerisation has
been developed the most in police work. We know that in Ulster more
than one out of every two persons is at present on file, indisputably the
highest percentage in the world. The police have access to highly
detailed information and the Lisburn computer has played a crucial
role in counter-insurrection strategy since 1974. Few people are aware
that the Metropolitan Police has to hand, for Greater London alone,
computerised information on some 4 to 5 million files. In this way data
is collected regarding the civil status of suspects, the individuals with
whom they have been in contact, and their own personal details
('race', colour of hair and hairstyle, accent, type of car and so on). The
Special Branch, which gathers information on all those who are liable
to 'pose problems to state security', has nearly 1½ million computerised
files at its disposal. The Police National Computer (PNC), located in
Hendon in North London, is connected up to 800 terminals across the
country, which are always available to all policemen on patrol. This
system is being constantly updated by a team of officers who are
trained in computer science and who cover the whole of the country. In
addition, specialised computers centralise information on drug
addicts, offenders or political activists; all of these storage systems
appear to be closely interconnected and seem by and large to elude the
surveillance of Parliament and of its commissions of enquiry.[29] Finally,
a communications system which is more advanced perhaps than any
other is at present operative in London and allows computer print-outs
to be installed in certain police vehicles. This modernisation of the
British police force, in a context of moral panic and a rejection of
permissiveness, has been quite deliberately embarked upon by its chief
officers, in particular by Sir Robert Mark, who was appointed head of
the Metropolitan Police. Mark succeeded in waging an effective
struggle against corruption in Scotland Yard, a by no means negligible
number of whose officers had set up very profitable relations with the
underworld.[30] Given this perspective of moral revival, Mark wanted to

Table 10.1 *The police force in Great Britain*

	England and Wales		Scotland		Ireland (N. Ireland from 1930)	
	No. of forces	No. of police	No. of forces	No. of police	No. of forces	No. of police
1900	179	41,900	61	4,900	1	12,300
1910	190	49,600	63	5,600	1	11,900
1920	191	56,500	59	6,500	1	11,600
1930	183	58,000	49	6,600	1	2,800
1940	129	57,300	48	6,800	1	2,900
1950	125	62,600	33	7,200	1	2,800
1960	125	72,300	33	8,700	1	2,900
1965	120	83,300	31	10,200	1	3,000
1970	47	92,700	20	11,200	1	3,800
1977	43	106,700	8	11,800	1	5,700

Source: David Butler and Dan Sloman (eds.), *British Political Facts, 1900–1979* (London, 1980), p. 292.

proceed much further and reconstruct the whole social order: 'The British Police must provide a stabilising and reassuring influence in a changing and often perplexed society.'[31] For James Anderton, who has been in charge of Manchester police since 1976, 'each defeat suffered by the police, since it is a crucial force in the struggle for law and order, is a blow to democracy and will ensure the triumph of anarchy'.[32] One could give any number of quotations bearing witness to the politicisation of the heads of a rapidly expanding police force, which is also flanked by the militias – the groupings of carefully selected civilian volunteers (the Special Constables and the Territorial Army), several hundreds of thousands strong – and finally the counter-espionage organisations (MI5, MI6).[33] An indication of the growing numbers and increasing centralisation of the police in Britain is given in Table 10.1.

It is worth noting that the mechanisms of representation continue to function effectively enough at the centre, and thereby serve to check the intensity of social conflicts, which have not provoked any violence so extreme as to render further reinforcement of the police acceptable. Just as in the nineteenth century, when 'the problem of controlling civil conflict in nineteenth-century London was not a serious one' – except in exceptional cases, such as Bloody Sunday (31 November 1887) – so, too, in the twentieth century, workers' protest and the policing of it has almost never resulted in deaths.[34] It has mainly been the resistance of the peripheries which has forced the centre into adopting authoritarian traits, a resistance which has been evident as much on the territorial peripheries (Ireland, Scotland) as on the social ones (the question of immigrants). This is where both communism (in industrial towns in Scotland and among Scottish migrants in London) and nationalism develop, flanked by a wide range of different forms of rebellion which reflect the continued existence of communal structures. These communal structures confront a centre whose constant use of the army or the police gives it, as far as the peripheries are concerned, a more or less authoritarian identity.[35]

Although it is not as well equipped as the French, the English police force thus has a powerful armoury of weapons to employ in its control of the population. It may use different means but it carries out its surveillance in what is perhaps an even more effective manner. The surveillance techniques of Bentham's panopticon, which were rejected at the time, now seem to have been extended to the entire social system and to have won a legitimacy of their own; they are applied, however, in more than just a purely organisational context, with the computer replacing the institution of 'prison'. The French model of policing, so slandered in earlier historical periods because it smacked of authoritarianism, seems now to have been adopted, and if the instruments that are used differ somewhat, insofar as they are less institutional in form, they may well be just as effective.

⚜ Conclusion: the end of the state? From differentiation to dedifferentiation

In the 1950s, when industrialisation seemed to be triumphing and the welfare state was spreading, numerous theorists were prepared to announce that, in a world where rationalisation was extending ever further, the end of ideologies was at hand. Political sociology also ceased to be concerned with the concept of power and the idea of conflict. In a period in which politics was declared to be at an end, it remained *a fortiori* anachronistic to enquire into the role of the state. Apolitical, developmentalist perspectives, which saw modernisation in evolutionist terms, with the state being nothing more than a function within a system, were only abandoned much later, when a return to the political – to its history, to its diversity within a range of different cultural spaces, to its structuring in terms of types of specific power – was effected. This accounts for the return, in our own period, to the question of the state, which may be regarded as just one of the many forms of constituted political power. If one rejects both the purely philosophical and the purely institutional conceptions of the state, if one also refuses to regard it as simply a subject of international law endowed with attributes of legitimacy, and if, finally, one wishes deliberately to adopt an ideal-typical approach, one can choose, in one's attempts to account for the extreme diversity of existing institutions, to regard as a state every differentiated political power which is differentiated from social, territorial or partisan peripheries, and which is set going by actors associated with functions whose efficacy increases the more this power, with all its claims to universality, is realised.

A number of authors have been especially concerned to shed light on the particular conditions surrounding the emergence of a state of this kind.[1] I would simply note here that, if one treats differentiation as the defining feature of a state, one significantly reduces the scope of the concept. Not only does the state cease to be regarded as either the potential instrument of man's liberation, or indeed of his enslavement, but, more generally, its ideal-typical status is curtailed. One would no longer be entitled to define as a state, at least as far as political sociology was concerned, all non-differentiated political powers, for instance that of a social class of one kind or another, that of a party, whether single or dominant, or again that of a particular ethnic ensemble. This would be to deliberately restrict one's field of enquiry as regards the state. In order to extend our framework somewhat, and to make for a better overall understanding, fragments of state, as it were, which are emerging in non-state societies, can be treated in the same sort of way.[2] In the light of what has been discussed in previous chapters, I would like to show here how the state is these days under threat from a number of processes of dedifferentiation which are liable to interfere with its complete or merely partial institutionalisation. At the very time when the state appears to be making sure of its own ascendancy, we seem, paradoxically enough, to be witnessing its decline and fall also.

Democracy against the state?

All forms of participatory democracy quite clearly undermine the differentiation of the state, for they propose, indeed, that the distance between what is private and what is public should be eliminated. From Rousseau to Hannah Arendt, there is the constant desire to increase political commitment, the *vita activa*, and to extend public space (Habermas), which in this context is taken to be that belonging to citizens rather than to the state. Politics is then neither given over to élites[3] nor, *a fortiori*, to the state: citizenship is conceived as linked in its essence to participation in a political community, which therefore manifests itself as a 'strong democracy',[4] rather than as being the main aspect of membership of a state. Relations between the actors themselves become public, hence the privatisation of citizenship. We then find, for example, an extension of associative forms,[5] the development of local democracy or, again, the rise of a variety of self-management movements whose declared aim, even in a country such as France, where the state is especially differentiated and institutionalised, is the abolition of the state's autonomy.[6] It is also perhaps worth adding here that Eurocommunism, which made a brief appearance in countries which did in the main have strong states, was itself a movement for dedifferentiation also.[7]

Although wholly distinct from the above perspectives, the theories of representative democracy also undermine the differentiation of the state. De Tocqueville has thus stressed how, in the United States, 'political associations are, if one may put it so, the only powerful people who aspire to rule the state'.[8] In a context like this, 'society acts by and for itself', for 'there are no authorities except within itself'.[9] This accounts for the importance of decentralisation in all its various manifestations, for this shatters the state's hankering after despotism.[10] According to de Tocqueville, in France, by contrast, 'the central power kept all Frenchmen in quasi-parental tutelage'.[11] He therefore seems to regard the strength of the state as a measure of the weakness of democracy. For him, as for nineteenth-century liberals, the spread of democracy would of its own accord prevent state differentiation. Adopting a similar line of argument, a number of authors have posited an opposition between societies which undergo a modernisation 'from below', by virtue of their representative institutions, and societies which effect a change 'from above', that is through the state, with democracy invariably being more fragile in the latter case, as in France or Prussia,[12] and with the state claiming the right to represent society all by itself. Even in the latter situation, however, representative democracy and the parties which operate within it, and which claim to be the sole holders of sovereignty, may attempt to undermine state differentiation. Thus, in France, the Third and Fourth Republics rested upon an opposition between the legitimacy of the parliamentary Republic and that of the state; in this sense, it was the Republic itself which was the state.[13] This accounts for the predominance of the party system, and for the decline in the role of the state and of its senior civil service. Representative democracy thus manages to undermine state differentiation, to contain it (and to eliminate it on the periphery), by doing its utmost to smash the state whenever it lays claim to a greater autonomy[14] – by placing ever greater emphasis upon 'the sacred rights of notables'[15] when, in socialist France, for instance, the state, of its own accord, shows itself willing to sacrifice a part of the state differentiation habitual within Jacobin tradition.

The market against the state

When Robert Nozick wonders 'how much room . ... individual rights leave for the state',[16] he tends to answer that, when all is said and done, they leave no room for it at all. Nozick thus opts for an atomistic conception of society that rests upon a realism which makes the quest for individual self-interest the sole acceptable criterion. This is why he pleads the case for anarchy, for a minimal state which ceases to enjoy any function of sovereignty whatsoever and presents itself as no more than an agency to which its clients can have recourse for their own protection. Nozick's work would seem to be the most systematic refutation, in recent years, of the notion that the state's legitimacy consists in its being a differentiated institution serving the general interest. It does, however, undoubtedly represent an extension of Hayek's position which, within the framework of classical liberalism, entails a defence of the pre-eminence of the market as a means of invisible regulation. For Hayek, as for Nozick or for those who in the present day advocate, in the majority of Western European countries, a return to the market as against any further growth of the welfare state, it is the 'invisible hand' which alone is capable of realising individual adjustments by respecting efficiency, which the state, when it claims the right to intervene in the name of the general interest, tends to endanger.[17] A libertarian perspective of this kind seeks to establish a democracy without the state.[18] It tends to be advanced in societies which a sociologist would regard, in terms of his ideal type, as lacking a differentiated state. It is therefore opposed to the emergence, in the United States and Great Britain (societies in which the market has spread as a regulatory mechanism), of components of the state arising out of the New Deal[19] or, more generally, to the appearance in both of these societies of a welfare state. In the United States, as in Great Britain,[20] a state intervention of this kind, giving rise to a far more limited differentiation than has occurred in, say, France, throughout its history, has been rejected because it clashes with an individualist conception of democracy, which is effectively identified with the simple logic of the market. In countries with a strong state, such as France,[21] where more and more are setting out to wage war on the state,[22] this return to the law of the market has also found many advocates. I would simply note here the degree to which this desire to return to the market is deliberately presented as a strategy for the dedifferentiation of the state, but I would further emphasise that it assumes a different meaning depending upon whether it is a society with a weak or a strong state that is involved. In the case of the latter, where the logic of state differentiation is the outcome of a long history, it is not certain that it will so readily be breached by the revival of liberalism. By way of conclusion, I would also emphasise how, on the basis of an equally individualist point of view, some authors are concerned to justify not so much the predominance of the market as the formation of small communities which, since there is sufficient time for information to be exchanged and trust to be built up, deprive purely individual free-rider strategies of all meaning. The community may well seem to be a framework for anarchy, yet it is nevertheless the case that the social order is constructed without the state.[23] Thus, in spite of their internal disagreements, these more recent theories link up with earlier anti-statist ones advanced by the advocates of a participatory 'strong democracy' endowed with a communal or self-management structure. This return to self-government in all its various forms is in the last analysis fairly consistent with the logic implicit in the working of societies with a weak state, such as those in Great Britain and the United States. Although some have wished to effect a similar return in France, it may well be that it could not be so easily realised where there is a state which would seem intent upon maintaining its own logic.

Interest groups ranged against the state

The model of the strong state implies that it assumes the form, paradoxically enough, of an institutionalised 'invisible hand' which would manage, precisely because of its distance from all peripheries, to impose the general interest on the basis of a universalist politics implemented by civil servants with little inclination to sacrifice anything in order to satisfy particularist interests. If, on the other hand, we consider the opposite model, in any one of its variants, the undifferentiated state is treated as a locus for the representation of a range of different interests which, wholly legitimately, do all they can to make themselves 'heard'. This accounts for the crucial role played by pressure groups and associations of all kinds, and by the represen-tation also of social categories and of, for example, ethnic or cultural groupings. Thus, in Great Britain and the United States, to the extent that the state is still weak, interest groups are not against the state; no matter how diverse such groups are, they legitimately occupy the space of the political by restricting all the more effectively any attempts at further differentiation of the state. This accounts for the crucial role played by the élites which are emerging from the many peripheries; it also explains the part played by mechanisms for the representation of socio-economic interests, which contemporary theories of corporatism are designed to illuminate. In societies with weak states, societal corporatism may well spread, for it does not clash with a state concerned to protect the degree of differentiation which it already enjoys; it must obviously limit pluralism to some degree, by legitimising some interests at the expense of others, and it will also undermine the theory of representative democracy by favouring particular socio-economic groups, over whose members it will, in return, exercise a strict control, and whose union action will be to some extent hampered.[24] This perspective suggests that interest groups with access to this corporative sphere gain a sense of being 'ruling institutions'.[25] Private and public then tend to become confused and the government itself assumes a quasi-private status. I would further add that organisations on the margins of the state are becoming more and more widespread in countries like Great Britain, West Germany and the United States, and tend to have administrative functions.[26] There is thus constituted a kind of complex network mixing private with public institutions, and civil servants with representatives of private interests, who enter into decision-making negotiations with each other.[27] Whether corporatism is then regarded as 'macro' or as 'meso', appearing in this latter case as the locus of negotiation with respect to a number of particular economic policies,[28] it is manifestly incompatible with a highly institutionalised state.[29]

Such corporatist practices would seem to strike a blow at the universalist claims of the state. This makes it all the easier to grasp why it is that pressure groups in a country such as France, where the general interest is supposed not to be the result of the aggregation of individual and partial interests, but rather the outcome of the sovereign deliberations of a differentiated state, are virtually illegitimate. This explains why in France the representatives of private interests are refused access to the state apparatus, why its internal 'frontiers' are absolutely closed, why the top civil servants recruited by the major state Ecoles play such a decisive role, and why these same civil servants openly admit to feeling complete contempt for pressure groups and for deputies who are supposed to be acting in the name of particular groups.[30] The French state is nevertheless threatened with the loss of certain aspects of its differentiation, for a number of private interests are already an integral part of its structures. This is the case, for example, with French peasants,[31] small tradesmen in charge of administrative boards, notaries, private persons vested with public functions, members of the business world in control of planning committees and, to a great extent, with bodies responsible for the management of economic policies.[32] Since 1981, there have been other signs in France of the dedifferentiation of the state. Thus representatives of the world of trade unionism have been appointed to state jobs:[33] the 'third way' of the Ecole Nationale d'Administration guarantees, on a particularist basis, the integration within the state of union members, with the civil service having therefore to become, as the communist Minister of Public Offices, Le Pors, has declared, 'the social reflection of the nation.'[34] From this comes the idea of setting up a kind of *proportz-democratie*, which would hardly be compatible with a highly differentiated state. I would further add that the randomness which would result from the application of an approach involving 'spoils', as in the American system – in which the circulation of élites is compatible with the relative weakness of the state – would seem to be found also to damage the institutionalisation of the state. Generally speaking, at any rate where political discourse is concerned, 'changing ways of life' had to involve 'changing the state', challenging Jacobin statism, developing self-management and all the forms of self-government, in a word giving civil society pre-eminence over the state. This explains why books by French intellectuals which were supposed to provide a theoretical account of this sort of view of society against the state,[35] justifying in advance all attempts to dedifferentiate the state,[36] have been greeted with such enthusiasm. This political perspective has thus been expressed both by the integration within the state of actors and of sectional interests deriving from society as a whole, and by the devolution to representatives of local interests of functions formerly performed by public officials. This shift is seen in the important law of 1982, which overturned relations between centre and periphery, transformed the prefect system, which had for so long epitomised the state's power and its degree of institutionalisation, and actually transferred to local worthies a power that, inasmuch as it could call upon a constant plurality of numerous electoral mandates, was all the more significant. From then on, 'the peripheral was central' and each of the state's provincial administrations had no choice, if it wished to be effective, but to establish privileged links with a number of local worthies.[37] There was also set up a sort of step-by-step, incrementalist politics, which ought strictly speaking to be classified as a practice of the clientelist type, that is, as involving ways of going about things which are incompatible with a universalist and differentiated state. Since such 'deals' would occur as easily in central government as in provincial administrations, and since they would be accompanied by the penetration of specific interests into the space of the state, by a greater permeability in the upper echelons and by a change in the values of civil servants (who thus became less committed to the notions of public authority and the general interest), one would be witnessing a real tendency to dedifferentiation, a tendency which should also be regarded as one aspect of a socialist perspective on self-government and the return to society. These tendencies would seem, however, to clash with the inherent logic of a strong state, which appears to ensure its own continued existence by curbing corporatist or neo-clientelist practices, so that calls for a return to a logic of the market, such as dominates in countries like Great Britain and the United States, which lack a differentiated state, are probably purely ideological. On the other hand, in these latter countries, institutions enjoying a degree of differentiation from the state appear to be more threatened by this tendency towards privatisation, in a weaker and less coherent public sector. This perhaps accounts for the recent attempts, as far as the economy is concerned, to establish regulation through the market, for the attacks levelled against the partial structures of the welfare state, and for denationalisation.[38]

Mobilisation against the state

How extreme the character of mobilisation is seems to be linked both to the solidarity of the internal networks upon which the structuring of collective action depends, and to the power of the state against which it is unleashed. For a long time now, the theory of collective action has been solely concerned with the conditions for the aggregation of individual choices that would allow the formation of a social movement or of social structures which would facilitate such collective action. One can, however, demonstrate how the mobilisation of the working class, of ethnic minorities, or, again, of political groupings also depends upon the type of state in relation to which they are constituted. It is not merely that social revolutions tend to occur, as Theda Skocpol has shown,[39] in opposition to particular kinds of bureaucratic state (in societies with weak states, the many peripheries manage to a greater or lesser degree to make themselves 'heard' and therefore remain 'loyal' (Hirschman)), but mobilisations themselves seem to be more frequent, more widespread and more violent in such bureaucratic societies. In France, for example, strikes differ markedly in function and nature from those taking place in Great Britain, which only rarely assume a political character and are not meant to overthrow the state.[40] From the French Revolution up until the present day, movements proposing to impede or, subsequently, to eliminate state differentiation, have been quite commonplace. From the collective counter-revolutionary actions in the Vendée[41] to the various revolutions in the course of the nineteenth century, culminating in the Paris Commune, which challenged the state structure precisely in order to bring about a form of participatory democracy featuring, among other things, the election and rotation of the holders of public office, from the anarcho-syndicalist movement, which has always seen it as its basic mission to challenge the power of the state, and which has for so long exerted a powerful influence over the French working class, to May 1968, which defied the state's claims to be all-powerful, collective action in France has always been characterised by an anti-state dimension which grows in intensity as the state confronting it increases its powers. Nevertheless, the French state has gained such solidity and legitimacy in the course of its history that no mobilisation has ever managed to breach its institutionalisation. As we have known since de Tocqueville, the French state has grown ever stronger, not only through the French Revolution but also in the process of being confronted by all the other forms of collective action which have disputed its legitimacy.

In the last analysis, it is feasible to suppose that it is because the differentiation of the state has been so strong and so legitimate that it managed, between the wars, for example, to restrict the role of the far right and to contain extremist agitation. In a somewhat paradoxical manner, the power of the state gives rise to a significant mobilisation against it, which in turn provokes a further strengthening of the state and not, so far, its disappearance. A logic of this kind is at work in countries with strong states and with solid political democracies, such as Great Britain, where extremist mobilisations are still limited to the far left and the far right and where ideologies, as I have already observed, have little impact. On the contrary, when a state wishes to be strong but in reality is not sufficiently so, when it produces an even more extreme mobilisation, when democracy itself is still fragile, mobilisation will destroy the state rather than strengthen it. The end of the state, according to this last hypothesis (that of a recoil effect), will be inevitable; the example of Nazi mobilisation against the Prussian state seems a perfect example of such a pattern. Hitler's mobilisation was in fact wholly directed against the state. As Hans Buchheim shows, 'after its "seizure of power", the totalitarian movement converted the state, which up until then had been its enemy, into its slave'.[42] The expression 'totalitarian state' would seem to be wholly contradictory inasmuch as totalitarianism presents itself as a movement which rejects state differentiation: since it aims to establish a new and total order over the whole of a society, it necessarily clashes with the state, attacks its boundaries and destroys those of its structures which enjoy an independent space. Totalitarianism seeks to bring about the end of the state; it develops enough to be able to destroy it, and finally succeeds in doing so. In a word, German totalitarianism sought 'to throw the state overboard'[43] by breaking the administration's resistance to it, by setting up 'double' organisations and replacing the machinery of state,[44] and by boosting the interests of the party, which was granted public status. In Hitler's own words, from 6 July 1933, 'the party [had] become the state'. The state, whose existence had never been wholly guaranteed, then proceeded to disintegrate, to be replaced by relations of vassalage resembling those of the Middle Ages,[45] and by a 'polycracy',[46] that is by the struggle of a large number of rival powers, opposed to each other at both local and national levels, within the framework of decision-making processes. In place of state power, Nazi mobilisation therefore carried one man to power and produced a confrontation between groups; at all events, it spelled the end of state differentiation.[47]

At the present time, other extreme mobilisations have arisen in response to states constructed on the model of the strong state. The refusal of state differentiation, the desire to destroy the state are here based upon a revival of religious fundamentalism in Arab countries, some of which have imported the model of the strong state, which rests upon a wholly lay identity, that is a differentiation between religious and political power. The desire for dedifferentiation is just as evident in Turkey as it is, for example, in Tunisia. Turkey appears to be an exemplary instance of a society which, from the time of the Ottoman

Empire to the reforms of Atatürk, had set out to build a strong and differentiated state. There is thus a sense in which 'one can describe the Kemalist state as Jacobin'.[48] During this period, there occurred, in imitation of the French and Prussian models, an institutionalisation of the state, the constitution of a concept of citizenship which served to negate peripheral allegiances, and the emergence of a notion of lay culture, influenced by ideas from France of a differentiation between religion and the state. Secularisation and the construction of a powerful bureaucracy went hand in hand, in a manner which reflected the universalist ideas of Durkheim, who had proved so deep an influence in the France of the Third Republic. This notion of a lay culture appeared to involve the imposition of the state upon a Muslim civil society.[49] The differentiated bureaucracy, once it was established, seems to have been a crucial element in the modernisation of Turkey, standing outside, and in opposition to, Islam, the religion which was dominant in civil society.[50] This attempt at differentiation, which could never have been successfully completed, was based upon an underestimation of the weight of a religion which regarded the Umma, the community of believers, as a political community also, and therefore refused all notions of a separation between the political and the religious.[51] This explains the reaction which has occurred in recent years, which can in fact be understood as the expression of a desire for the dedifferentiation of a state whose establishment of a separate space is seen as being in breach of the prevailing religious code. The revival of fundamentalism in modern Turkey and the challenge to the notion of a lay culture and of a universalist state may thus likewise be regarded as processes in the dedifferentiation of a strong state of the French type.[52]

One could well make a similar analysis of, for example, Tunisia, which in the modern period has quite clearly introduced a state on the French model, that is highly differentiated, bureaucratic and lay;[53] there, too, the modern period has seen the development of a back-to-Islam movement which, in the long run, is bound to endanger the state.[54] By way of conclusion, I would emphasise that the formation within France of a large Algerian immigrant community (because of the Algerian War of Independence, because of the importation of manpower, and so on) also has consequences which pose a challenge, for example, to the idea of citizenship conceived as exclusive allegiance to a differentiated state. Thus, for the very first time, the idea is now being mooted that, in order to take account of the presence in France of this community, which is being called upon to take up permanent residence, one should separate citizenship from nationality in order to give, for instance, voting rights to such citizens, even though they would remain foreign nationals. This proposal, which has won real support in France, undermines the symbol of exclusive allegiance to the state and then goes on to formulate in novel terms the problem of lay culture, another crucial factor in a differentiation which might be challenged.[55]

Wars against the state

Wars would seem to be a crucial aspect of the threat to differentiated states. Whilst it is true that, throughout recorded history, wars have often played a part in making strong states tremble and yet in the end have served to strengthen their structures, the world wars of the modern period have genuinely brought about, to varying degrees, the end of particular states. The German and French examples are again pertinent here. The First World War radically altered the nature of German politics by undermining the position of the previously all-powerful and dominant Prussian bureaucratic state. The German defeat gave rise to the Weimar Republic, in which political parties representing particular clienteles dominated a political game that rested upon a division between a large number of opposed interests, a division which reflected a marked contradiction between the institutionalised state and the parliamentary republic, in which the parties had the upper hand.[56] As I have demonstrated above, Hitler's mobilisation against parliamentary democracy and the state forced the latter to abandon its prerogatives one by one. Defeat in the Second World War undermined the German state even further, so that, while the federal form of the Reich in 1871 had allowed Prussia to wield hegemonic power, and while, at the time of the Weimar Republic, the different states tended to hold still less power, the federalism estab-lished in 1949 made each *Land* virtually pre-eminent in its own domain. Created in a wholly artificial manner, so as to shatter all sense of historical continuity, the *Länder* were vested with substantial powers: each *Land* has a highly developed bureaucratic apparatus and extreme decentralisation, which suggests that federal services are very weak indeed.[57] The fragility of the unitary state is still further emphasised by the important role performed by the Bundesrat. To sum up, it might be said that authority has to be shared out at all the different levels.[58] In a sense, it is perhaps fair to observe that the prototype of a federal system with a weak state, namely the American state, was imposed by the victors upon the vanquished because it was their own political and economic order. However, the Germans in fact received the American system in a more exaggerated form, with numerous federal decisions depending upon the agreement of the *Länder*, as did many services also. Since each federal state tends to look after its own interests, it has even proved feasible to investigate the degree to which an interpretation in terms of methodological individualism might be advanced. Seen in this way, each agent, whether individual or collective, may be tempted to opt for a free-rider politics, even if in time such a purely utilitarian strategy is bound to collapse, insofar as, as Elster has shown, a common consciousness emerges. Even if such a collective consciousness does serve in the end to place a limit upon purely individual strategies,[59] one can see the extent to which the state is under threat. Finally, I would add that, just as in the inter-war years, political parties now wield so much influence that some commentators talk of them as 'party-states' – a label that shows just how far the state's differentiation has been undermined – with the parties being henceforth more properly regarded, according to the ruling of the Constitutional Court, as 'organs of the state'; they wield, moreover, an influence which is so great and so legitimate that the state bureaucracy is itself highly politicised at every level. There is thus a sense in which the legitimacy of the political parties supplants that of the state.[60]

The consequences of the Second World War also made themselves felt in the case of France, where the defeat of 1940 dealt a heavy blow to the legality of the state. Access to public office lost its universalist character, the notion of citizenship underwent a serious shift in meaning, civil servants, as in Nazi Germany, had to swear a personal oath of allegiance, and partisan interests penetrated the state, which itself gained an explicitly authoritarian character. While the differences between totalitarianism and authoritarianism may be clearly grasped,[61] it is somewhat harder to distinguish between a state and an authoritarian state, insofar as the overturning of structures and of élites is on an infinitely smaller scale. The Vichy régime destroyed the Republic in much the same way as Hitler had eliminated Weimar Germany; but Vichy did not shatter the state so totally and, to this

degree, it differs from the Nazi order. Being more highly institutionalised than the German state, the state in France was under attack, as
far as its differentiation was concerned, from the policies pursued by
the Vichy régime, but it managed to preserve, by virtue of the actual
strength of its structures, some aspects of its institutionalisation. The
French state was perverted by the policies which it pursued and, if it
did not wholly disappear, it was because the mobilisation aroused in
opposition to it was infinitely less strong.[62] The war also deprived the
state of a part of its legitimacy, so that, when the Liberation took place,
a proportion of the administrative élite was 'purified' too.[63]

Just as the Allies had envisaged founding a number of independent
states in place of the German state, so that its end might be more
clearly marked, so too an Allied administration was set up in order to
reorganise French society. The particular destinies of the various
armies, the strategy pursued by the actors involved, and the high level
of institutionalisation of a state whose identity was so closely bound up
with the whole history of France – all of these factors were to decide
otherwise. Once again, the fortunes of war did not actually put an end
to the state. If, in a general sense, war sometimes brings about the end
of a state,[64] when it is particularly institutionalised, it manages, even
through defeats, to preserve some of its structures.

The many types of state thus find different ways of confronting the
various processes which, in each case, threaten them. The most
differentiated states are also threatened, in the present period, by the
penetration of private interests, by the various corporatisms, by
extremist mobilisations, by war or, again, by a desire to return to
society in order the better to guarantee a form of self-government
which the state, because it claims to enjoy a monopoly over sovereignty, prefers to limit. These days, even a thoroughly differentiated
state is hemmed in by communal mechanisms, such as those of the
European Common Market, which hamper its operations; it also has
to address itself to a revival, at the local level, of nationalist
movements, which regard peripheral allegiances as legitimate and,
finally, it has to face up to the activities of multinationals,[65] over whom
it has virtually no control. One can perhaps draw the conclusion,
simple though it may seem, that a differentiated and institutionalised
state is better placed to resist these numerous challenges and thereby
guarantee its own survival.

Notes

Introduction

1 See P. Birnbaum, *La Fin du politique* (Paris, 1975).
2 See C. Pateman, *Participation and Democratic Theory* (New Haven, 1970); and B. Barry, *Sociologists, Economists and Democracy* (London, 1970).
3 See R. Dahl, *Who Governs?* (New Haven, 1961).
4 See D. Apter, *The Politics of Modernization* (Chicago, 1965).
5 See B. Badie, *Le Développement politique* (Paris, 1978).
6 C. Wright Mills, *The Power Elite* (New York, 1956); T. Lowi, *The End of Liberalism* (New York, 1969).
7 P. Bachrach and M. Baratz, *Power and Poverty* (New York, 1970).
8 S. Lukes, *Power, a Radical View* (London, 1974).
9 L. Althusser, 'Ideology and ideological state apparatuses', in *Lenin and Philosophy and Other Essays* (London, 1971).
10 See N. Poulantzas, *Political Power and Social Classes* (London, 1973); G. Therborn, *What Does the Ruling Class Do When it Rules?* (London, 1978); C. Offe, 'Structural problems of the capitalist state', in *German Political Studies* (London, 1974); C. Offe, *Contradictions of the Welfare State* (London, 1984); J. O'Connor, *The Fiscal Crisis of the State* (New York, 1973); J. Habermas, *Legitimation Crisis* (Boston, 1975); J. Hirsch, 'The state apparatus and social reproduction: elements of a theory of the bourgeois state', in J. Holloway and S. Picciotto (eds.), *State and Capital* (London, 1978); B. Jessop, *The Capitalist State* (London, 1982); and M. Carnoy, *The State and Political Theory* (Princeton, 1984).
11 See P. Veyne, *Comment on écrit l'histoire* (Paris, 1971); and R. Aron, 'Comment l'historien écrit l'épistémologie?', *Annales* (November–December 1971).
12 See W. Cahnman and A. Boskoff, *Sociology and History* (New York, 1964); C. Tilly, *As Sociology Meets History* (New York, 1981); and P. Abrams, *Historical Sociology* (Ithaca, 1982).
13 See C. Ragin and D. Zaret, 'Theory and method in comparative research: two strategies', *Social Forces*, 61, 3 (1983).
14 R. Bendix, *Kings or People* (Berkeley, 1978), p. 15.
15 See T. Skocpol, *Vision and Method in Historical Sociology* (Cambridge, 1984), pp. 75–6.
16 See M. Dogan and D. Pelassy, *Sociologie politique comparative* (Paris, 1982).
17 P. Nettl, 'The state as a conceptual variable', *World Politics* (July 1968).
18 See K. Dyson, *The State Tradition in Western Europe* (Oxford, 1980); and B. Badie and P. Birnbaum, *Sociology of the State* (Chicago, 1983).
19 See R. Alford and R. Friedland, *Powers of Theory: Capitalism, the State and Democracy* (Cambridge, 1985).
20 See E. Nordlinger, *On the Autonomy of the Democratic State* (Cambridge, Mass., 1981).
21 See C. Geertz, *Interpretations of Cultures* (New York, 1973).
22 See Badie and Birnbaum, *Sociology of the State*.
23 See P. Birnbaum, *La Logique de l'Etat* (Paris, 1982).
24 See C. Tilly, *Big Structures, Large Processes, Huge Comparisons* (New York, 1984).
25 See P. Evans, T. Skocpol and D. Rueschmeyer, *Bringing the State back in* (Cambridge, 1985).

26 T. Skocpol, *States and Social Revolutions* (Cambridge, 1979).
27 See T. Skocpol, *Vision and Method in Historical Sociology* (Cambridge, 1984).
28 See P. Birnbaum and J. Leca, *Sur l'individualisme* (Paris, 1986).

1 Mobilisation theory and the state

1 A. de Tocqueville, *Democracy in America*, edited by J. P. Mayer, translated by G. Lawrence (New York, 1969), p. 692.
2 J. S. Mill, *Utilitarianism, Liberty and Representative Government* (New York, 1951), p. 165.
3 See S. Giner, *Mass Society* (London, 1976), chapters 3 and 4, together with an older study by L. Bramson, *The Political Context of Sociology* (Princeton, 1961), chapter 2.
4 H. Taine, *Les Origines de la France contemporaine* (Paris, 1881), vol. 2. Taine's position may in this respect be compared with that of J. Talmon in *The Origins of Totalitarian Democracy* (London, 1951).
5 Taine, *Les Origines de la France contemporaine*, vol. 2, p. 9.
6 G. Le Bon, *The Psychology of Crowds* (London, 1909), p. 26.
7 See R. Nye, *The Origins of Crowd Psychology: Gustave Le Bon and the Crisis of Mass Democracy in the Third Republic* (London, 1976); and Y. Thiec, 'Gustave Le Bon prophète de l'irrationalisme de masse', *Revue française de sociologie*, 3 (1981).
8 G. Le Bon, *La Psychologie politique et la défense sociale* (Paris, 1910), p. 141.
9 See T. Clark (ed.), *Gabriel Tarde* (Chicago, 1969); J. Millet, *Gabriel Tarde et la philosophie de l'histoire* (Paris, 1970); and I. Lubek, 'Histoire des psychologies sociales perdues: le cas de Gabriel Tarde', *Revue française de sociologie*, 3 (1981).
10 G. Tarde, *The Laws of Imitation* (Gloucester, Mass., 1962), p. 68.
11 *Ibid.*, p. xiv (translation modified).
12 *Ibid.*, p. 35 (translation modified). Serge Moscovici emphasises what differentiates the work of Le Bon from that of Tarde, noting that the latter includes, in his study of crowds, organisations like parties, unions or indeed the state itself (see *L'Age des foules* (Paris, 1982), p. 210).
13 Tarde, *The Laws of Imitation*, p. 87 (translation modified). As regards Tarde, Le Bon and crowds, see Yvon Thiec and Jean-René Tréanton, 'La foule comme objet de "science"', *Revue française de sociologie* (January–March 1983).
14 K. Wolf (ed.), *The Sociology of George Simmel* (New York, 1964), p. 98. For Simmel, there arises in a crowd a 'collective irritability, there is a sensibility, a passion, an eccentricity peculiar to great masses of people' (*Sociologie et épistémologie* (Paris, 1981), p. 115).
15 See L. Wirth, 'Urbanism as a way of life', *American Journal of Sociology*, 4 (1939).
16 See R. Sommer, *Personal Space* (New Jersey, 1969).
17 S. Milgram and H. Toch, 'Collective behaviour: crowds and social movements', in G. Lindzey and E. Aronson (eds.), *Handbook of Social Psychology*, vol. 4 (Reading, 1969), p. 510.
18 D. Stokols, 'The experience of crowding in primary and secondary environments', *Environment and Behavior* (March 1976).
19 D. Schmidt, R. Goldman and N. Feimer, 'Perception of crowding', *Environment and Behavior* (March 1979), p. 123.
20 See Stokols, 'The experience of crowding', p. 73; and, in the same spirit, Schmidt, Goldman and Feimer, 'Perception of crowding', p. 123. See also D. Schmidt and J. Keating, 'Human crowding and personal control', *Psychological Bulletin* (July 1979), p. 692.
21 See the studies in D. Katz, D. Cartwright, S. Eldersveld and A. McClung Lee, *Public Opinion and Propaganda* (New York, 1964).
22 See E. Laumann and F. Pappi, *Networks of Collective Action* (New York, 1964). See also, C. Fischer, *The Urban Experience* (New York, 1976).
23 R. Turner, 'New theoretical framework', in R. Evans (ed.), *Readings in Collective Behavior* (Chicago, 1969).
24 E. Durkheim, *The Rules of Sociological Method*, edited and with an introduction by S. Lukes, translated by W. D. Halls (London, 1982), p. 59, n. 3. Pierre Favre refuses to accept that there is such a sharp opposition between the perspective of Durkheim and that of Tarde, noting that, while Durkheim may be right to challenge Tarde's methodology, Tarde himself, in

placing the emphasis upon the role played by the actors themselves, avoids the reificatory perspective which is sometimes evident in Durkheim (see P. Favre, 'Gabriel Tarde et la mauvaise fortune d'un "baptême sociologique" de la science politique', *Revue française de sociologie* (January–March 1983), pp. 10–11). I would note, however, that Durkheim is careful to stress that 'there are in societies only individual consciousnesses; in these, then, is found the source of all individual evolution' (*The Rules of Sociological Method*, p. 98).

25 Durkheim, *The Rules of Sociological Method*, p. 40.
26 E. Allardt, 'Division du travail, types d'intégration et modes de conflit', in P. Birnbaum and F. Chazel (eds.), *Sociologie politique* (Paris, 1971).
27 See R. Nisbet, *The Sociological Tradition* (London, 1966).
28 C. Tilly, *From Mobilization to Revolution* (Reading, 1978), pp. 16–23. See also C. Tilly, L. Tilly and R. Tilly, *The Rebellious Century, 1830–1930* (Cambridge, Mass., 1975). In his most recent work, *As Sociology Meets History* (New York, 1981), C. Tilly persists in identifying a strict relation between anomie and social conflict in Durkheim's work (p. 102). Likewise, he reckons (p. 106) that, for Durkheim, conflict increases with industrialisation and urbanisation. I have sought to show, in the present chapter, that there is no such strict correlation in Durkheim's writings.
29 See M. Cherkaoui, 'Changement social et anomie: essai de formalisation de la théorie durkheimienne', *Archives européennes de sociologie*, 1 (1981), pp. 37–9.
30 E. Durkheim, *The Division of Labour in Society*, translated by W. D. Halls (London, 1984), pp. 314–15.
31 With regard to the relation between the social question and socialism in Durkheim's work, see chapters 1 and 2 of P. Birnbaum, *Dimensions du pouvoir* (Paris, 1984).
32 See Cherkaoui, 'Changement social et anomie', pp. 26–7.
33 See T. Gurr, *Why Men Rebel* (Princeton, 1970).
34 See A. Hirschman, *The Passions and the Interests* (Princeton, 1977).
35 A. Smith, *An Inquiry into the Nature and Causes of the Wealth of Nations* (Oxford, 1976), vol. 1, book 4, chapter 2, p. 454.
36 See L. Dumont, *Homo aequalis* (Paris, 1977).
37 See P. Rosanvallon, *Le Capitalisme utopique* (Paris, 1979), pp. 57–62.
38 See H. M. Robertson, *Aspects of the Rise of Economic Individualism* (Cambridge, 1933); and S. Lukes, *Individualism* (New York, 1973), chapter 13.
39 M. Olson, *The Logic of Collective Action* (Cambridge, Mass., 1965), p. 50.
40 *Ibid.*, pp. 106–7.
41 Karl Polanyi, however, has already shown that human behaviour cannot simply be understood in terms of individual economic rationality; he regards this type of action as characteristic in fact of nineteenth-century market societies only, inasmuch as they managed to eliminate the social dimension (see K. Polanyi, *Trade and Market in the Early Empires* (Glencoe, 1957), pp. 264–70).
42 I would note, however, that, even from this perspective, some can breathe a purer air or benefit from the right to vote, along with all and sundry, once such things have been won, but, in addition, insofar as they did more to encourage the movement which produced such goods, they would sometimes receive a minimum of their own symbolic rewards or again would professionalise themselves through the management of such actions (consider, for example, the case of consumers' groups in the United States). This returns us again to Olson's perspective.
43 H. Tillock and D. Morrison, 'Group size and contributions to collective action', in L. Kriesberg (ed.), *Research in Social Movements, Conflicts and Change* (Greenwich, Connecticut, 1979), vol. 2, p. 146.
44 B. Fireman and W. Gamson, 'Utilitarian logic in the resource mobilization perspective', in M. Zald and J. McCarthy (eds.), *The Dynamics of Social Movements* (Cambridge, 1979), p. 17.
45 Jon Elster rejects the opposition advanced by Mancur Olson between someone who prefers to get a 'free rider' only and someone who acts solely out of altruism, and holds that 'the conditional altruism of the Assurance Game is also a possible motivational structure, which may lead to collective action by tacit coordination, given information provided by the leaders' ('Marxism, functionalism and game theory', *Theory and Society*, 11, 4 (1982), p. 470).

46 M. Olson, *The Rise and Decline of Nations* (New Haven, 1982), p. 24.

47 A. Hirschman, *Exit, Voice and Loyalty* (Princeton, 1970), p. 53.

48 *Ibid.*, p. 97.

49 *Ibid.*, p. 108. Hirschman, however, emphasises the fact that black power refuses to adopt such a strategy, for individual defection serves to damage the interests of the group; for him, 'the black power doctrine represents a totally new approach to upward mobility because of its open advocacy of the group process' (p. 112). But he regards this as a 'recent discrepancy' which, furthermore, in recent times seems to have gradually disappeared, black Americans appearing themselves to prefer individual defection.

50 W. Sombart, *Why is there no Socialism in the United States?*, translated by P. M. Hacking and C. T. Husbands (New York, 1976). I would emphasise that Sombart himself observes that 'Among American workers one therefore finds none of the opposition to the state that is to be found in continental-European Socialism' (p. 19). Again, we find here a correlation between a weak state, an 'open' society and a weak socialism (see P. Birnbaum, *La Logique de l'Etat* (Paris, 1982), chapter 1). On Sombart's theory, see S. M. Lipset, 'Why no socialism in the United States?', in S. Bialer and S. Sluzar (eds.), *Sources of Contemporary Radicalism* (Boulder, Colorado, 1977). See also R. Boudon, *The Logic of Social Action* (London, 1981), translated by D. Silverman.

51 Conversely, Karl Polanyi believed that the state played a crucial role in the creation of a market. But the market, once created, 'was more allergic to rioting than any other economic system we know' (*The Great Transformation* (Boston, 1944), p. 186). In Germany, by contrast with Great Britain, the unions and the parties might 'disregard the rules of the market' (p. 190). Hence the social confrontations which occur.

52 See B. Badie and P. Birnbaum, *Sociology of the State* (Chicago, 1983).

53 D. Wrong, 'The over-socialised conception of man in modern society', *American Sociological Review*, 26 (1961), pp. 183–93. It is nevertheless true that, in a society in which individualism is triumphant, principles of socialisation and of role determination are operative while, conversely, in societies where multiple collective solidarities are organised in opposition to the state, the actors can always attempt an individual strategy.

54 B. Barry, 'Exit, voice and loyalty', *British Journal of Science*, 4 (1974), pp. 93–6.

55 At this stage, Hirschman's approach still almost always derives from a methodological individualism.

56 A. Hirschman, *Shifting Involvements* (Princeton, 1982), chapter 5. Raymond Boudon, however, quite properly notes that an event such as May 1968 may also be explained in terms of structural blockages in the political system, which is why 'an interest in political action cannot be considered as resulting from the addition of a number of individual disappointments' ('Intérêts privés et actions publiques', *Bulletin de la SEDEIS* (September 1982), p. 3).

57 A. Hirschman, *Essays in Trespassing* (Cambridge, 1981), p. 215.

58 *Ibid.*, p. 241.

59 *Ibid.*, p. 226.

60 In *The Logic of Collective Action*, Mancur Olson writes: 'This is not to deny that a theory of *irrational* behaviour leading to class action might in certain cases be of some interest. Class differences resulting from sociological factors might lead individuals irrationally and emotionally to act in a class-oriented way' (p. 108).

61 Olson, *The Logic of Collective Action*, p. 51.

62 Olson, *The Rise and Decline of Nations*, pp. 44 ff and chapter 4.

63 C. Offe and H. Wiesenthal, 'Two logics of collective action: theoretical notes on social class and organisational form', in M. Zeitlin (ed.), *Political Power and Social Theory*, vol. 1 (Greenwich, Connecticut, 1980).

64 Offe and Wiesenthal, 'Two logics of collective action', pp. 95–6. For a similar position, see C. Offe, 'The attribution of political status to interest groups', in S. Berger (ed.), *Interest Groups in Western Europe* (Cambridge, 1979). I am not entirely sure that this 'second level' is really immune from Mancur Olson's utilitarian critique.

65 K. Marx and F. Engels, *Manifesto of the Communist Party*, in *The Revolutions of 1848*, edited and introduced by D. Fernbach (London, 1973), p. 76.

66 Marx and Engels, *Manifesto of the Communist Party*, p. 76.

67 K. Deutsch, *Nationalism and Social Communication* (New York, 1953), p. 100.

68 K. Marx, *The Poverty of Philosophy* (London, 1935), pp. 194–5.

69 I would note that Mancur Olson, in accord with his own line of argument, emphasises that the peasants of the Ganges, who are isolated from each other, do not constitute a social network and cannot therefore be mobilised (see *The Rise and Decline of Nations*, p. 39).

70 Marx, *The Eighteenth Brumaire of Louis Bonaparte*, p. 238.

71 See V. I. Lenin, *What Is To Be Done?* (London, 1933), pp. 32 ff.

72 W. Kornhauser, *The Politics of Mass Society* (London, 1960).

73 M. Pinard, *The Rise of a Third Party: A Study in Crisis* (New Jersey, 1971), p. 185.

74 See J. Gusfield, 'Mass society and extremist politics', *American Sociological Review* (February 1962).

75 A. Oberschall, 'Une théorie sociologique de la mobilisation', in Birnbaum and Chazel (eds.), *Sociologie politique*, p. 234.

76 Insofar as this model rests upon such an opposition, it is liable to lead into an evolutionist perspective, with one type of social movement then being linked to a particular stage in development. To avoid difficulties of this kind, Oberschall stresses that 'A still thriving network of community relations can serve as a basis for a rapid growth in networks of modern associations' (*ibid.*, p. 240).

77 When the collectivities are 'integrated', one could argue, using the terms employed by Albert Hirschman, that 'voice' is possible, 'loyalty' normal and mobilisation unlikely. Where 'segmentation' occurred, the temptation to 'exit' might well be strong, although this hypothesis is not one envisaged by Oberschall.

78 In case C, there is no risk of violence or of mobilisation. Conversely, in A, riots involving religious or ethnic groups do, according to Oberschall, sometimes occur; in B, individual acts of banditry may also take place.

79 Oberschall, 'Une théorie sociologique', p. 241.

80 I would note, however, that when he describes the actual mobilisations or the revolts, rebellions or riots which may, in terms of the other hypotheses, occur, the notion of class is almost always discarded.

81 A. Oberschall, *Social Conflict and Social Movements* (New Jersey, 1973), p. 129.

82 *Ibid.*, p. 125.

83 *Ibid.*, p. 133. Edward Walsh undertakes an analysis of an empirical example in order to show that Oberschall's approach is a fruitful one (see E. Walsh, 'Mobilization theory vis-à-vis mobilization process: the case of the United Farm Workers' Movement', in Kriesberg (ed.), *Research in Social Movements*, p. 173). He notes, however, that Oberschall pays too little attention to the charismatic role of the leader in the development of the process of mobilisation (p. 174). As far as peasant societies are concerned, John McCarthy and Mayer Zald argue that the organisations involved in social movements may be less numerous but that the resources for mobilisation dependent upon the social infrastructure are, conversely, very powerful (see J. McCarthy and M. Zald, 'Resource mobilization and social movements: a partial theory', *American Journal of Sociology* (May 1977), p. 1237).

84 Oberschall, *Social Conflict*, p. 123.

85 See F. Chazel, 'La mobilisation politique: problèmes et dimensions', *Revue française de science politique*, 25 (1975). Chazel is justifiably astonished by Oberschall's determination to found an analysis upon Olson's problematic. By placing such emphasis upon collective organisation, Oberschall is in reality quite removed from Olson, according to Chazel (p. 514). It should be acknowledged, however, that Oberschall has more recently come to question his own position himself, to question how useful the utilitarian approach is in accounting for collective mobilisation (see A. Oberschall, 'Theories of social conflict', *Annual Review of Sociology*, 4 (1978), p. 307).

86 S. Halebsky, *Mass Society and Political Conflict* (Cambridge, 1976), p. 91.

87 See chapter 7.

88 In *From Mobilization to Revolution*, p. 63, Tilly puts it that *Catness* (unity of category) × *Netness* (intensity of the internal networks) = *Organisation*.

89 Tilly, *From Mobilization to Revolution*, p. 69.

90 François Chazel notes that Tilly places most emphasis upon resources while failing to count as

resources the values which give rise to mobilisation, such as ideologies and world views (see F. Chazel, review of *From Mobilization to Revolution, Revue française de sociologie,* 4 (October– December 1980), p. 654). Likewise, Anthony Oberschall also demonstrates that one cannot directly infer the nature of mobilisation from the type of resource held, although at the same time he acknowledges that Tilly's model does indeed give one a better chance of overcoming this difficulty (see Oberschall, 'Theories of social conflict', p. 307). For a similar line of argument, see W. Gamson, *The Strategy of Social Protest* (Homewood, Ill., 1975).

91 Tilly, *From Mobilization to Revolution,* p. 85.
92 Let me remind the reader of the definition which François Chazel gives of mobilisation: 'mobilisation consists essentially of the creation of new commitments and new identifications – or sometimes a reactivation of "forgotten" loyalties and identifications – along with a gathering-together, on this basis, of actors – or of groups of actors – in the framework of a social movement entrusted, where necessary through a direct and on occasions violent confrontation with the authorities concerned, with promoting and sometimes "restoring" collective ends' (Chazel, 'La mobilisation politique', p. 156).
93 Tilly, *From Mobilization to Revolution,* p. 77.
94 C. Tilly, *The Vendée* (New York, 1967).
95 C. Tilly, 'Does modernization breed revolution?', *Comparative Politics* (April 1973), p. 436.
96 See T. Skocpol, *States and Social Revolutions* (Cambridge, 1979). This writer would seem, however, to underestimate the importance which Tilly accords to the state and so compares him, somewhat erroneously, with Ted Gurr. Tilly certainly holds that mobilisation is intentional but he does not see it as depending in any way upon the mechanisms of relative frustration but, on the contrary, as we have already observed, upon the nature of the social ties, and upon their organisational aspect (see *States and Social Revolutions,* pp. 16, 26–7).
97 *Ibid.,* p. 29.
98 *Ibid.,* chapters 2 and 3. Likewise, James Scott shows how, in South-East Asia, revolutions have arisen in opposition to highly bureaucratised states which have tended to disregard local realities (see J. Scott, *The Moral Economy of the Peasant* (New Haven, 1976), pp. 96–8).
99 Skocpol, *States and Social Revolutions,* p. 117. Jeffrey Paige differentiates between systems with decentralised economies (such as rice-growing areas in Vietnam), where landowners cannot impose their control on a local basis and where revolutions arise against a centralised power which imposes entry into the market, and systems where a centralised economy (such as the cotton-growing areas of Peru) reinforces both the links of dependence and social control, and thereby forestalls revolution (see J. Paige, *Agrarian Revolution* (New York, 1975), pp. 370–6).
100 Skocpol, *States and Social Revolutions,* p. 155.
101 *Ibid.,* p. 120.
102 *Ibid.,* p. 156.
103 See A. Oberschall, 'Protracted conflict', in Zald and McCarthy, *The Dynamics of Social Movements,* pp. 56–8; and G. Marx, 'External efforts to damage or facilitate social movements: some patterns, explanations, outcomes and complications', in *ibid.,* p. 96.
104 See J. McCarthy and M. Zald (eds.), *The Trend of Social Movements in America: Professionalization and Resource Mobilization* (Morristown, 1973). Charles Perrow differentiates between two currents within the theoretical school which conceives of mobilisation in terms of resources: the first, represented by Oberschall and Tilly, accounts for mobilisation in a very Clausewitzian manner, regarding it as the continuation of politics by other, more violent means; McCarthy and Zald, reckoned to be the guiding spirits of the second current, reintroduce into the analysis of collective mobilisation a perspective involving costs and benefits and a calculus of an economic type, based upon notions such as flexibility, loyalty to a product, change and so on. As far as Perrow is concerned, McCarthy and Zald have 'suppressed Freud but replaced him, not by Marx or Lenin, but by Friedman' (C. Perrow, 'The sixties observed', in *ibid.,* pp. 199–200).
105 See Birnbaum, *La Logique de l'Etat.*
106 For a similar line of argument, see A. Touraine, F. Dubet, Z. Hegedus and M. Wieworka, *Les Pays contre l'Etat: luttes occitanes* (Paris, 1981).
107 C. Tilly, L. Tilly and R. Tilly, *The Rebellious Century,* pp. 84–5.

108 The relation posited between the state, democracy and mobilisation is not, however, wholly clear in this account.

109 See C. Tilly, L. Tilly and R. Tilly, *The Rebellious Century, 1830–1930*, pp. 48–55. Furthermore, these forms of mobilisation are by no means mutually exclusive.

110 E. Shorter and C. Tilly, *Strikes in France: 1830–1968* (New York, 1974). Thus, after the 1880s, 'The great mobilization meant that local groups of workers all over France joined hands in order to concentrate more efficiently their efforts upon the apparatus of the central state' (pp. 345–6).

111 See *ibid.*, chapter 12.

112 *Ibid.*, p. 327. For an application of Shorter's and Tilly's model, see James Cronin, *Industrial Conflict in Modern Britain* (London, 1979).

113 See, for example, G. Adam and J.-D. Reynaud, *Conflits du travail et changement social* (Paris, 1978); or C. Crouch and A. Pizzorno, *The Resurgence of Class Conflict in Western Europe since 1968* (London, 1978).

114 Tilly, *As Sociology Meets History*, chapter 6.

115 T. W. Margadent, *French Peasants in Revolt, the Insurrection of 1851* (Princeton, 1979), p. 104.

116 *Ibid.*, pp. 337, 155.

117 See M. Agulhon, *Le Cercle dans la France bourgeoise, 1810–1848* (Paris, 1977).

118 See the detailed analysis of the role played by the *chambrées* and the secret societies, in Provence, in the mobilisation against the *coup d'état*, in M. Agulhon, *The Republic in the Village* (Cambridge, 1982). On the role of local societies during this period, see also P. Vigier, *La Seconde République dans la région alpine* (Paris, 1963), vol. 2, pp. 183–6.

119 From this point of view, this perspective is again close to that of Anthony Oberschall.

120 J. Merriman, *The Agony of the Republic: Repression of the Left in Revolutionary France, 1848–1851* (New York, 1978), p. 59. See the whole of chapters 3 and 6 on the role of associations, groups and mutual aid societies in the countryside and in the towns.

121 Margadent, *French Peasants in Revolt*, p. 231.

122 *Ibid.*, p. 104.

123 *Ibid.*, p. 343. I also have in mind here H. Gerphagnon's thesis for the University of Paris, I, 'La Résistance au coup d'état à Clamecy (Nièvre)' (1981).

124 R. Aminzade, *Class, Politics and Early Industrial Capitalism: A Study of Mid-Nineteenth-Century Toulouse* (New York, 1981), chapter 6 and pp. 197–8.

125 See, for example, E. Bloch, *Thomas Münzer als Theologe der Revolution* (Frankfurt, 1962) and, by the same author, *The Principle of Hope* (Oxford, 1986). For a similar line of argument, see M. Abensour, 'L'Utopie socialiste: une nouvelle alliance', in *Le Temps de la réflexion* (Paris, 1981). I would acknowledge, however, that it is extremely difficult to assess the specific weight of ideologies in the development of collective action.

126 It is, furthermore, this single possibility which Mancur Olson has in mind when he describes 'the apparent tendency for revolutionary movements to draw their adherents from those with the *weakest* class ties ... some scholars contend that those who are déclassé, or "alienated" from the major groups of their society, are the most likely to turn to radical religious or political movements like communism, the John Birch Society, and the like' (*The Logic of Collective Action*, p. 109, n. 29).

127 See G. Mosse, *The Nationalization of the Masses* (New York, 1975).

128 See G. Mosse, *The Crisis of German Ideology* (New York, 1964), chapters 11 and 16.

129 H. Arendt, *The Origins of Totalitarianism*, p. 387.

130 *Ibid.* See B. Crick, 'On rereading *The origins of totalitarianism*', in M. Hill (ed.), *Hannah Arendt: The Recovery of the Public World* (New York, 1979).

131 See E. Lederer, *State of the Masses* (New York, 1940). For him, 'The totalitarian state is a mass state and no other state can ever destroy the social structure to such an extent ... That is why the masses are amorphous and stratification is abolished' (pp. 46, 31). See also S. Neumann, *Permanent Revolution* (New York, 1942). William Kornhauser also uses the example of Nazi Germany to illustrate his own conception that mass society functions as an atomised system in which intermediate groups have been eliminated (*The Politics of Mass Society*, chapter 3).

132 F. Neumann, *Behemoth* (New York, 1944), p. 401.

133 R. Heberle, *From Democracy to Nazism* (New York, 1970, first published in 1945), p. 122. For a similar line of argument, see T. A. Tilton, *Nazism, Neo-Nazism and the Peasantry* (London, 1975), p. 67.

134 B. Hagtvet, 'The theory of mass society and the collapse of the Weimar Republic', in S. Larsen, B. Hagtvet and J. Myklebust (eds.), *Who Were the Fascists?* (Bergen, 1980), pp. 90–1.

135 *Ibid.*, p. 104.

136 W. S. Allen, *The Nazi Seizure of Power* (New York, 1973), p. 20.

137 *Ibid.*, chapter 14.

138 See J. Noakes, *The Nazi Party in Lower Saxony, 1921–1923* (London, 1971), p. 143.

139 C. P. Loomis and J. A. Beegle, 'The spread of German Nazism in rural areas', *American Sociological Review*, 11 (1946). For a similar line of argument, see Heberle, *From Democracy to Nazism*. The Nazi vote therefore has a strong contextual basis, with it being mainly the rural and Protestant areas which gravitated towards the party (in the state of Prussia or in the north and centre of Germany) rather than the Ruhr and the Rhine. See Nico Passchier, 'The electoral geography of the nazi landscape', in Larsen *et al.* (eds.), *Who Were the Fascists?*, p. 297.

140 See R. Lepsius, 'The collapse of an intermediary power struggle: Germany 1933–1934', *International Journal of Contemporary Sociology* (September–December 1968).

141 See R. Hamilton, *Who Voted for Hitler?* (Princeton, 1982), chapter 3.

142 C. Brown, 'The nazi vote: a national ecological study', *American Political Science Review* (June 1982), p. 296.

143 See H. A. Winkler, 'From social protectionism to National-socialism: the German business movement in comparative perspective', *Journal of Modern History* (March 1976); and J. Kocka, 'Zur Problematik der deutschen Angestellten', in M. Mommsen *et al.*, *Industrielles System und politische Entwicklung in der Weimarer Republik* (Düsseldorf, 1974).

144 Hamilton, *Who Voted for Hitler?*, pp. 90, 121.

145 See T. Childe, 'The social bases of the National socialist vote', *Journal of Contemporary History*, 11 (1976), pp. 17–42.

146 See the debate on this point between K. O'Lessker ('Who voted for Hitler? A new look at the class basis of nazism', *American Journal of Sociology* (July 1969)) and P. Shiveley ('Party identification, party choice and voting stability: the Weimar case', *American Political Science Review* (December 1972), p. 1216).

147 P. Merkl, 'The nazis of the Abel Collection: why they joined the NSDAP', in Larsen *et al.* (eds.), *Who Were the Fascists?*, pp. 270–1. See also Barrington Moore, *Injustice: The Social Bases of Obedience and Revolt* (New York, 1978), p. 409.

148 See, for example, E. Shils and M. Janowitz, 'Cohesion and disintegration in the Wehrmacht in World War II', *Public Opinion Quarterly*, 12 (1948); P. Lazarsfeld, B. Berelson and H. Grandet, *The People's Choice* (New York, 1968); and T. Newcomb, 'The Bennington study', in S. Swanson and T. Newcomb (eds.), *Readings in Social Psychology* (New York, 1952). For a general presentation of this issue, see Birnbaum, *La Fin du politique*, pp. 93 ff.

149 See D. Abraham, *The Collapse of the Weimar Republic* (Princeton, 1981), chapter 5.

150 See chapter 7.

2 States, free riders and collective movements

1 E. Durkheim, *The Rules of Sociological Method* (London, 1982), p. 129. It is worth bearing in mind that Durkheim also maintains that 'It is . . . from the individual that emanate the ideas and needs which have determined the formation of societies. It is from him that everything comes, it is necessarily through him that everything must be explained. Moreover, in society there is nothing save individual consciousness' (p. 125).

2 Durkheim, *The Rules of Sociological Method*, p. 52.

3 M. Weber, *Economy and Society* (Berkeley and Los Angeles, 1968), vol. 1, p. 4.

4 Weber, *Economy and Society*, p. 18.

5 Quoted in M. Mommsen, 'Max Weber's political sociology and his philosophy of world history', *International Social Science Journal*, 17 (1965), p. 25.

6 This is, however, what Raymond Boudon tries to do in *The Logic of Social Action* (London, 1981), chapter 1.

204   Notes to pages 44–9

7   K. Popper, *The Open Society and its Enemies* (London, 1945), vol. 2, p. 98.
8   Weber, *Economy and Society*, p. 27.
9   G. Simmel, *Sociologie et épistémologie* (Paris, 1981), p. 174.
10 E. Durkheim, *Professional Ethics and Civic Morals*, trans. C. Brookfield (London, 1957), pp. 79–80.
11 K. Polanyi, *Trade and Market in the Early Empires* (Glencoe, 1957), chapter 10. It is nevertheless worth noting that Max Weber himself also ranks the different types of intentionality in a hierarchy and, by emphasising that it is essentially in modern societies that the most rational actions occur, reintroduces a kind of evolutionist approach. Georg Simmel, like Weber, in dating the emergence of an individual capable of adopting a genuinely intentional approach, appears to be distancing himself from his own purely analytic position.
12 See J. Lively and J. Rees, *Utilitarian Logic and Politics* (Oxford, 1978).
13 L. Dumont, *Essais sur l'individualisme* (Paris, 1983), p. 35.
14 Dumont, *Essais*, p. 23.
15 C. B. Macpherson, *The Political Theory of Possessive Individualism* (Oxford, 1962).
16 R. Nisbet, *The Sociological Tradition* (London, 1966), chapter 3.
17 A. Macfarlane, *The Origins of English Individualism* (New York, 1978), chapter 7.
18 One may also draw a sharp contrast between France and England if one concludes, as Claude Nicolet does, that 'France is perhaps the only country in Europe never to have acknowledged the "great transformation" . . . the birth certificate of modernity'. In remaining faithful to the revolutionary ideal, influenced by models from the ancient world, France thus refused the 'great transformation', the entrance into modernity which economic individualism represents (see C. Nicolet, *L'Idée républicaine en France* (Paris, 1983), pp. 479–80).
19 See A. Oberschall, *Social Conflict and Social Movements* (New Jersey, 1973); and C. Tilly, *From Mobilization to Revolution* (Reading, 1978).
20 See C. Tilly, *The Vendée* (New York, 1967).
21 See A. Cochin, *L'Esprit du Jacobinisme* (Paris, 1979).
22 See A. Aulard, *Histoire politique de la Révolution française* (Paris, 1901).
23 See P. Birnbaum, *La Logique de l'Etat* (Paris, 1982), pp. 193–213.
24 See M. Agulhon, *The Republic in the Village* (Cambridge, 1982); and T. W. Margadent, *French Peasants in Revolt, the Insurrection of 1851* (Princeton, 1979).
25 See E. Wolf, *Peasants Wars of the Twentieth Century* (London, 1973).
26 See T. Skocpol, *States and Social Revolutions* (Cambridge, 1979).
27 See J. Scott, *The Moral Economy of the Peasant* (New Haven, 1976), chapter 7; and J. Paige, *Agrarian Revolution* (New York, 1975), pp. 375–6.
28 Consider the example of German soldiers in the Second World War who, according to Shils and Janowitz, were motivated not by their commitment to Nazi ideology but by their fusion with their group conceived as a whole (see E. Shils and M. K. Janowitz, 'Cohésion et désagrégation de la Wehrmacht pendant le dernière guerre mondiale', in H. Mendras (ed.), *Eléments de sociologie: textes* (Paris, 1968)).
29 C. Calhoun, *The Question of Class Struggle* (Chicago, 1982), p. 228. Ira Katznelson has also shown that to the extent that the American working class is organised at the local level in homogeneous quarters, and to the extent that the place of residence is not separated from the workplace, one can expect 'holistic results' (see I. Katznelson, *City Trenches* (New York, 1981), pp. 52–3).
30 Calhoun, *The Question of Class Struggle*, p. 229.
31 Scott, *The Moral Economy of the Peasant*, pp. 166–7.
32 See A. Przeworski and M. Wallerstein, 'The structure of class conflict in democratic capitalist societies', *American Political Science Review*, 16 (1982); and B. Ollman, 'Toward class consciousness next time: Marx and the working class', in I. Katznelson *et al.* (eds.), *The Politics and Society Reader* (New York, 1975).
33 M. Hechter, 'A theory of group solidarity', in M. Hechter (ed.), *The Microfoundation of Macrosociology* (Philadelphia, 1983), p. 19.
34 S. Popkin, *The Rational Peasant* (Berkeley, 1979), p. 253. On the Popkin–Scott debate, see B. Cumings, 'Interest and ideology in the study of agrarian politics', *Politics and Society*, 4 (1981). Similarly, one could have shown, in the kibbutzim, which are, however, highly structured

groups, how free-rider strategies also emerge, which the authorities then attempt to control. See M. Spiro, *Kibbutz: Venture in Utopia* (New York, 1963), pp. 90–109. Some authors have even gone so far as to reinterpret the workings of primitive societies, such as that of the Nuer, on the basis of methodological individualism. See R. Bates, *Essays on the Political Economy of Rural Africa* (Cambridge, 1983), chapter 1.

35 See J. Rancière, *La Nuit des prolétaires* (Paris, 1981).
36 See M. Taylor, *Community, Anarchy and Liberty* (Cambridge, 1982), p. 53; and J. Elster, *Ulysses and the Sirens* (Cambridge, 1979), p. 146. There is a similar line of argument in M. Laver, *The Politics of Private Desires: A Guide to the Politics of Rational Choice* (London, 1981), pp. 50ff. On the whole debate, see R. Hardin, *Collective Action* (Baltimore, 1982); B. Barry and R. Hardin, *Rational Man and Irrational Society* (London, 1982); T. More, *The Organisation of Interests* (Chicago, 1982); and R. Boudon, 'Individual choice and social change: a no-theory of social change', *British Journal of Sociology* (March 1983). For a different perspective, see A. Touraine, *La Production de la Société* (Paris, 1973).
37 See P. Birnbaum, *Les Sommets de l'Etat* (Paris, 1977).
38 See, for example, E. Suleiman, *Les Hauts Fonctionnaires et la politique* (Paris, 1976).
39 On 'stalactite' and 'stalagmite' mobilisations, see P. Nettl, *Political Mobilisation* (London, 1967).
40 P. Grémion, *Le Pouvoir périphérique* (Paris, 1976); J.-P. Worms, 'Le préfet et ses notables', *Sociologie du travail*, 3 (1966); J.-C. Thoenig, 'La relation entre le centre et la périphérie en France', *Bulletin de l'Institut International d'Administration Publique* (October–December 1975).
41 See S. Krasner, *Defending National Interest* (Princeton, 1978).
42 T. Skocpol and K. Finegold, 'State capacity and economic intervention in the Early New Deal', *Political Science Quarterly* (Summer 1982), p. 271. See also T. Skocpol and J. Ikenberry, 'The political formation of the American welfare state in historical and comparative perspective', *Comparative Social Research*, 6 (1983); and S. Skowroneck, *Building a New American State* (New York, 1982).
43 See M. Levi, 'The predatory theory of rule', *Politics and Society*, 4 (1981).
44 D. North, *Structure and Change in Economic History* (New York, 1981), p. 53. Brian Barry has also emphasised how ideologies may serve to divert actors from an approach founded purely on personal interest. He makes particular mention of nationalism, which remains a lively force in modern societies (see B. Barry, *Sociologists, Economists and Democracy* (London, 1970), pp. 39–45). Hannah Arendt distinguishes the citizen from the bourgeois, who seeks only to maximise his own personal interest, and, placing special emphasis upon the case of Rosa Luxemburg, suggests that she 'was very much concerned with the world and not at all concerned with herself' (in Hill (ed.), *Hannah Arendt: The Recovery of the Public World*, pp. 310–30).

3 The state and mobilisation for war: the case of the French Revolution

1 R. Bendix, *Nation-Building and Citizenship* (Berkeley, 1977), p. 74.
2 See G. A. Kelly, 'Who needs a theory of citizenship?', *Daedalus*, 108, 4 (1979), pp. 27–8.
3 A. de Tocqueville, *The Ancien Regime and the Revolution*, translated by S. Gilbert (London, 1976).
4 A. Soboul, *Les Soldats de l'an II* (Paris, 1959), p. 273.
5 J. L. Talmon, *The Origins of Totalitarian Democracy* (London, 1952), pp. 167–72.
6 T. Skocpol, *States and Social Revolutions* (Cambridge, 1979), p. 186.
7 J. Michelet, *Histoire de la Révolution française*, vol. 2 (Paris, 1961–2), pp. 964–5.
8 W. Kornhauser, *The Politics of Mass Society* (London, 1960).
9 H. Arendt, *The Origins of Totalitarianism* (New York, 1951), pp. 316–17.
10 A. Oberschall, *Social Conflicts and Social Movements* (New Jersey, 1973). See F. Chazel, 'La mobilisation politique: problèmes et dimensions', *Revue française de science politique*, 25 (1975).
11 See C. Tilly, *From Mobilization to Revolution* (Reading, 1978), p. 238; and E. Shorter and C. Tilly, *Strikes in France, 1830–1968* (New York, 1974).
12 I have in mind here the mobilisation from above described as 'stalactite' mobilisation by J. P.

Nettl (*Political Mobilisation* (London, 1967), pp. 271–2). But Nettl applies it in the main to Third World countries.

13 *Archives parlementaires*, 20 April 1791, vol. 25, p. 227.
14 Jean-Paul Bertaud, *Valmy* (Paris, 1970), p. 191.
15 *Archives parlementaires*, vol. 17, p. 434.
16 *Archives parlementaires*, January 1792, vol. 37, p. 560.
17 E. Shils and M. K. Janowitz, 'Cohésion et désagrégation de la Wehrmacht pendant la dernière guerre mondiale', in H. Mendras (ed.), *Eléments de sociologie: textes* (Paris, 1968), p. 276.
18 See Max Weber's remarks in *Economy and Society*, vol. 2, pp. 1149, 1155.
19 Tilly, *From Mobilization to Revolution*, p. 77.
20 *Archives parlementaires*, vol. 37, p. 555.
21 *Archives parlementaires*, vol. 37, p. 516.
22 *Archives parlementaires*, 1 August 1792, vol. 47, p. 362.
23 *Archives parlementaires*, vol. 47, p. 363.
24 *Archives parlementaires*, 11 June 1793, vol. 59.
25 *Archives parlementaires*, 23 August 1793, vol. 72, p. 676.
26 M. Reinhard, *L'Armée et la Révolution pendant la Convention* (Paris, 1957), p. 116.
27 J.-P. Bertaud, *La Révolution armée* (Paris, 1979), pp. 133, 167.
28 A. de Tocqueville, *L'Ancien Régime et la Révolution* (Paris, 1953), vol. 2, p. 290.
29 S. Finer, 'State and nation-building in Europe: the role of the military', in C. Tilly (ed.), *The Formation of National States in Western Europe* (Princeton, 1975), pp. 144–5.
30 S. F. Scott, 'The French Revolution and the professionalization of the French Officer Corps, 1789–1793', in M. Janowitz and J. Van Doorn (eds.), *On Military Ideology* (Rotterdam, 1971), pp. 26–7.
31 Reinhard, *L'Armée et la Révolution*, pp. 190, 204.
32 M. Foucault, *Discipline and Punish* (Harmondsworth, 1977), p. 162.
33 D. D. Bien, 'La réaction aristocratique avant 1789', *Annales* (January–February 1974), pp. 41–3; *Annales* (March–April 1974), pp. 522–3.
34 W. Fisher and P. Lundgreen, 'The recruitment and training of administrative and technical personnel', in Tilly (ed.), *The Formation of National States in Western Europe*.
35 Guibert, 'Essai général de tactique', in 'Stratégiques', *L'Herne* (Paris, 1977), p. 145.
36 C. von Clausewitz, *On War* (London, 1976), p. 593.
37 See J.-Y. Guiomar, *L'Idéologie nationale* (Paris, 1974).
38 *Archives parlementaires*, 27 April 1791, p. 369.
39 S. F. Scott, 'Les officiers de l'armée de ligne à la veille de l'amalgame', *Annales historiques de la Révolution française* (March 1968), p. 457.
40 Dubois-Crancé's report, *Archives parlementaires*, 7 February 1793, pp. 359–61.
41 *Archives parlementaires*, 7 February 1793, p. 364. On the amalgamation, see J. Godechot, *Les Institutions de la France sous la Révolution et l'Empire* (Paris, 1968), pp. 363ff.
42 *Archives parlementaires*, 23 August 1793, vol. 72, p. 677.
43 Quoted in Reinhard, *L'Armée et la Révolution*, p. 123.
44 J. Jaurès, *L'Armée nouvelle* (Paris, 1977), pp. 153–5.
45 M. Reinhard, *Le Grand Carnot* (Paris, 1950), pp. 152, 344.
46 For the École de Mars, see A. Baczko, 'Utopies pédagogiques de la Révolution française', *Libre*, 8 (1980). For the Polytechnique, see T. Shin, 'La profession d'ingénieur, 1750–1920', *Revue française de sociologie* (January–March 1978).
47 On 28 January 1793, speaking of the organisation of the Ministry of War, Saint-Just declared: 'I support the establishment of a stewardship such as Sieyès has presented it to us; this is the best means for bringing economy, responsibility and discipline into administration' (*Archives parlementaires*, vol. 57, p. 739). On the same day, in the course of the same discussion, Jean Debry also emphasised the need for a 'division in the various functions such as will facilitate the exercise of them'. Likewise, on 31 January 1793, Sillery observed that the 'functions' to which the minister has been appointed 'are absolutely alien to him and that for colleagues he only has people without any knowledge . . . One of the worst scourges which we have to fear at the moment is the ignorance of the administrators. We are surrounded entirely by people who

believe themselves to have all the talents needed to administrate because they have the capacity to draw upon a few theoretical phrases.' I would note also that the decree of 23 August 1793, which organised the *levée en masse*, stipulated explicitly in its article 5 the creation by the state of manufactories, businesses, workshops and factories.

4 Ideology, collective action and the state: Germany, England, France

1 See K. Marx, *The German Ideology* (London, 1964).
2 See F. Engels, *The Origins of the Family, Private Property and the State*, in K. Marx and F. Engels, *Selected Works* (London, 1969), vol. 3.
3 See B. Badie and P. Birnbaum, *Sociology of the State* (Chicago, 1983), chapter 1.
4 A. Gramsci, *Selections from the Prison Notebooks* (London, 1971), p. 12.
5 P. Anderson, 'The antinomies of Antonio Gramsci', *New Left Review*, 100 (1976–7), p. 26. Adam Przeworski criticises Perry Anderson's interpretation of Gramsci's work by showing that, in Gramsci's view, states in the West use both force and consensus depending upon the relations between social classes. At the same time he ignores, as do Gramsci and Perry Anderson, the specificity of states in the West, and its consequences for the mode of government. See A. Przeworski, 'Material bases of consent: economics and politics in a hegemonic system', in M. Zeitlin (ed.), *Political Power and Social Theory*, vol. 1 (Greenwich, Connecticut, 1980), pp. 58–60.
6 Anderson, 'The antinomies of Antonio Gramsci', p. 29.
7 See P. Anderson, *Lineages of the Absolutist State* (London, 1974).
8 Stein Rokkan, for his part, draws his conceptual map of Europe according to the various procedures of national construction, and not according to the different types of state which have taken shape there. For example, he attributes the genesis of communism to the schism produced long ago by reaction to the Reformation. In Protestant countries, the resultant osmosis between political and religious élites favoured consensus, and rendered subsequent upsurges of communism impossible; in Catholic countries, the antagonism between those élites favoured dissension and later the appearance of communism. This explanation is primarily culturalist and ignores differences in state construction, for example between France and England, which appear in the same column in the conceptual map of Europe. See S. Lipset and S. Rokkan, 'Cleavage structure, party systems and voter alignments: an introduction', in *Party Systems and Voter Alignments* (New York, 1967); and S. Rokkan, 'Cities, states and nations', in S. Eisenstadt and S. Rokkan (eds.), *Building States and Nations* (London, 1973), vol. 1.
9 See, for example, S. Lipset, *L'Homme et la politique* (Paris, 1963), chapter 2.
10 See L. Althusser, 'Ideology and ideological state apparatuses', in *Lenin and Philosophy and Other Essays* (London, 1971).
11 See Barrington Moore Jr., *Social Origins of Dictatorship and Democracy: Lord and Peasant in the Making of the Modern World* (Boston, 1958).
12 See A. Gerschenkron, *Economic Backwardness in Historical Perspective* (New York, 1962).
13 See G. Roth, *The Social Democrats in Imperial Germany* (Ottawa, 1963), pp. 10–11. According to Lassalle, 'it is the state's function to perfect the development of freedom, the development of humankind in freedom' (F. Lassalle, *Discours et pamphlètes* (Paris, 1903), p. 188).
14 See A. Bergonioux and B. Manin, *La Social-démocratie ou le compromis* (Paris, 1979), p. 65. See also D. A. Chalmer, *The Social Democrat Party* (New Haven, 1964).
15 See G. Woodcock, *Anarchism* (London, 1963), pp. 404–9; and A. R. Carlson, *Anarchism in Germany* (Metuchen, New Jersey, 1972).
16 On the differences between the anarchists and Marx over the attitude to be adopted towards the state and the possibilities of transforming it, see P. Thomas, *Karl Marx and the Anarchists* (London, 1980), p. 334.
17 See P. J. Proudhon, *La Révolution sociale démontrée par le coup d'état du 2 décembre* (Paris, 1936).
18 P. J. Proudhon, *De la capacité politique des classes ouvrières*, in *Œuvres complètes*, vol. 3, p. 264.
19 K. Marx, *The Eighteenth Brumaire of Louis Bonaparte*, in *Surveys from Exile* (Harmondsworth, 1973), p. 237.
20 A. de Tocqueville, *L'Ancien Régime et la Révolution* (Paris, 1953), p. 122.

21 P. Ansart, *Naissance de l'anarchisme* (Paris, 1970), p. 131.
22 Y. Lequin, *Les Ouvriers de la région lyonnaise (1848–1914)*, vol. 2 (Paris, 1970), p. 131.
23 E. Droz, *P.J. Proudhon* (Paris, 1909), p. 34.
24 A. Kriegel, *Le Pain et les roses* (Paris, 1973), pp. 95–6. Jacques Julliard also likens Pelloutier to Proudhon, while pointing out the differences between their views on socialism and the idea of war (see J. Julliard, *Fernand Pelloutier et les origines du syndicalisme d'action direct* (Paris, 1971), pp. 209–10).
25 See F. Ridley, 'Revolutionary syndicalism in France: the general strike as theory and myth', *International Review of History and Political Science*, 3, 2 (1966).
26 Quoted in Julliard, *Fernand Pelloutier*, p. 341.
27 F. Pelloutier, *Histoire des bourses du travail* (Paris, 1971), p. 99.
28 J. Maîtron analyses all these currents in *Le Mouvement anarchiste en France* (Paris, 1975).
29 M. Perrot, *Les Ouvriers en grève, France 1871–1890* (Paris, 1974), vol. 2, p. 703.
30 See M. Perrot, 'Le congrès de la scission', *Le Monde*, 9 December 1979.
31 See H. Dubief, *Le Syndicalisme révolutionnaire* (Paris, 1969).
32 M. Perrot, 'Les socialistes français et les problèmes du pouvoir (1871–1914)', in M. Perrot and A. Kriegel, *Le Socialisme français et le pouvoir* (Paris, 1966), p. 19.
33 Quoted in Dubief, *Le Syndicalisme révolutionnaire*, p. 12. See also C. Willard, *Les Guesdistes* (Paris, 1965), part 2, chapter 11.
34 Madeleine Rébérioux shows how Jaurès later drew nearer to syndicalism, in *Jean Jaurès: La classe ouvrière. Textes présentés par M. Rébérioux* (Paris, 1976), pp. 14–15. See also, by the same author, 'Les tendances hostiles à l'Etat dans la SFIO (1905–1914)', *Le Mouvement social* (October–December 1968); and 'Jean Jaurès et le marxisme', in C. Bourgeois (ed.), *Histoire du marxisme européen*, vol. 1 (Paris, 1977), p. 233.
35 See M. Rébérioux, 'Le socialisme français de 1871 à 1914', in J. Droz (ed.), *Histoire générale du socialisme* (Paris, 1974), vol. 2, p. 196.
36 A. Kriegel, *Communismes ou miroir français* (Paris, 1974), p. 149.
37 C. Buci-Glucksmann, 'Pour un eurocommunisme de gauche', in O. Duhamel and H. Wever (eds.), *Changer le PC?* (Paris, 1972), p. 133.
38 G. D. H. Cole, *Socialist Thought, Marxism and Anarchism* (London, 1961), vol. 2, pp. 336–7.
39 F. Bédarida, 'Sur l'anarchisme en Angleterre', in *Mélanges d'histoire sociale offerts à Jean Maîtron* (Paris, 1976), p. 23.
40 See Badie and Birnbaum, *Sociology of the State*, part 3.
41 See Woodcock, *Anarchism*, p. 18.
42 See A. Carter, *The Political Theory of Anarchism* (London, 1971), pp. 10–11.
43 See D. Apter, 'The old anarchism and the new – some comments', in D. Apter and J. Joll (eds.), *Anarchism Today* (London, 1971), pp. 8–10.
44 See D. Stafford, 'Anarchists in Britain today', and E. de Jong, 'Provos and Kabouters', in Apter and Joll (eds.), *Anarchism Today*.
45 H. Pelling, *A History of British Trade Unionism* (London, 1963), p. 115.
46 See F. Bédarida, 'Le socialisme en Grande-Bretagne de 1875 à 1914', in Droz (ed.), *Histoire générale du socialisme*, p. 356.
47 On party–union relations in various leading cases, see J. Julliard, 'Les syndicats et la politique', in P. Birnbaum and J. M. Vincent (eds.), *Critique des pratiques* (Paris, 1978). See also A. Pizzorno, 'Les syndicats et l'action politique', *Sociologie du travail* (April–June 1971).
48 See H. Drucker, *Doctrine and Ethos in the Labour Party* (London, 1979), chapter 1. See also L. Panitch, Introduction to *Social Democracy and Industrial Militancy* (Cambridge, 1976). Tom Nairn is one of the few authors to establish a relationship between the nature of the Labour Party and the relative weakness of the British state, in 'The nature of the Labour Party', *New Left Review*, 27 and 28 (1964). In 'The decline of the British state', *New Left Review*, 101 (1977), p. 23, he rapidly extends his study of the relationship between the 'backward' state and the working class, placing emphasis also on the separation between the intellectuals and the working class.
49 J. Julliard, 'Théorie syndicaliste révolutionnare et pratique gréviste', *Le Mouvement social* (October–December 1968), p. 60.
50 See G. Adam and J.-D. Reynaud, *Conflits du travail et changement social* (Paris, 1978), pp. 59–61.

See also the comparative article by C. Crouch, 'The changing role of the state in industrial relations in Western Europe', in C. Crouch and A. Pizzorno (eds.), *The Resurgence of Class Conflict in Western Europe since 1968*, vol. 2 (London, 1978), chapter 8.

51 See A. Flanders and M. A. Clegg, *The System of Industrial Relations in Great Britain* (Oxford, 1954).

52 See G. Lyon-Caen, 'Critique de la négociation collective', *Droit social* (September–October 1979). We may perhaps adduce as further evidence the rediscovery of the role of the conciliation boards (*conseils de prud'hommes*), which obviate recourse to the state and testify to its withdrawal from employer–employee relations. See Pierre Can's thesis 'Sociologie des conseils de prud'hommes' (Paris, Ecole Pratique des Hautes Etudes, 1979).

53 See W. Korpi and M. Shalev, 'Strikes, industrial relations and class conflict in capitalist societies', *British Journal of Sociology* (June 1979), p. 181.

54 See C. Crouch, *Class Conflict and the Industrial Relations Crisis* (London, 1977).

55 Very briefly, for lack of space, let us observe in conclusion that in Italy the state has not succeeded in institutionalising itself and differentiating itself completely according to the French model. It continues to be infiltrated by civil society. In place of the relationship between state and civil society, therefore, we find a power structure composed of several élites and not, as in the United Kingdom, a dominant class. This situation, accompanied by a belated industrialisation accomplished in reality neither on the initiative of the state nor on that of a dominant class, long lent strength to community structures in resisting the development of social and political movements, whether Marxist or anarcho-syndicalist in inspiration. Although such movements took an increasingly organised shape towards the end of the nineteenth century, it should nevertheless be said that, in the setting of 'clientelism', the main feature was individual or small-group anarchism. See, for example, R. Hostetter, *The Italian Socialist Movement* (Princeton, 1958), chapter 13; Woodcock, *Anarchism*, chapter 11; and S. Tarrow, *Peasant Communism in Southern Italy* (New Haven, 1967), chapters 3 and 4.

5 Individual action, collective action and workers' strategy: the United States, Great Britain and France

1 As regards the myth of social mobility, see P. Birnbaum, *La Structure du pouvoir aux Etats-Unis* (Paris, 1971); and J. Heffer, 'Pourquoi n'y a-t-il pas de socialisme américain?' *Histoire* (March 1980).

2 See A. Hirschman, *Exit, voice and loyalty* (Princeton, 1970).

3 See J. Karabel, 'The failure of American socialism reconsidered', in R. Miliband and J. Saville (eds.), *The Socialist Register* (London, 1979); and I. Katznelson, *City Trenches* (New York, 1981).

4 See A. Przeworski and M. Wallerstein, 'The structure of class conflict in democratic capitalist societies', *American Political Science Review*, 16 (1982); and B. Ollman, 'Toward class consciousness next time: Marx and the working class', in I. Katznelson *et al.* (eds.), *The Politics and Society Reader* (New York, 1975).

5 See B. Fireman and W. Gamson, 'Utilitarian logic in the resource mobilization perspective', in M. Zald and J. McCarthy (eds.), *The Dynamics of Social Movements* (Cambridge, 1979).

6 See P. Foner, *History of the Labour Movement in the United States* (New York, 1955), vol. 2.

7 K. Marx, *Critique of the Gotha Programme*, in *The First International and After*, edited and introduced by D. Fernbach (London, 1974), p. 355.

8 K. Marx, *Grundrisse, Foundations of the Critique of Political Economy (Rough Draft)*, translated with a foreword by M. Nicolaus (London, 1973), p. 884.

9 K. Marx, in 'Unpublished letters of K. Marx and F. Engels to Americans', *Science and Society*, 2 (1938), pp. 218–31.

10 See S. M. Bialer and S. Sluzar (eds.), *Sources of Contemporary Radicalism* (Boulder, Colorado, 1977).

11 See J. Lasslett, *A Short Comparative History of American Socialism* (New York, 1977); and R. Dahl, *Polyarchy* (New Haven, 1971).

12 L. Hartz, *The Liberal Tradition in America* (New York, 1955), p. 6.

13 W. Sombart, *Why is there no Socialism in the United States?* (New York, 1976), p. 19. See also R. Boudon, *The Logic of Social Action* (London, 1981).

14 See T. Lowi, *American Government: Incomplete Conquest* (New York, 1976).

15 R. Merton, *Eléments de théorie et de méthode sociologique* (Paris, 1965), p. 128. See V. O. Key, *Politics, Parties and Pressure Groups* (Crowell, 1964); and F. Sorauf, *Party Politics in America* (Boston, 1973). See also, more recently, A. B. Callow, *The City Boss in America* (New York, 1976); and M. Johnson, 'Patrons and clients, jobs and machines: a case study of the uses of patronages', *American Political Science Review* (June 1979).

16 See S. Rothman, 'Intellectuals and the American political system', in S. M. Lipset (ed.), *Emerging Coalitions in American Politics* (New York, 1978).

17 S. M. Lipset, 'Radicalism or reformism: the sources of working class politics', *American Political Science Review*, 77 (1983).

18 See S. M. Lipset, 'Radicalism in North America: a comparative view of the party systems in Canada and the United States', *Transactions of the Royal Society of Canada*, 4, 14 (1976), p. 25.

19 Selig Perlman was even more deeply conscious of this factor than Sombart, in *A Theory of the Labor Movement* (New York, 1966). See J. Lasslett, 'The American tradition of labor theory and its relevance to the contemporary working class', in I. Horowitz, J. Legett and M. Oppenheimer (eds.), *The American Working Class, Prospects for the 1980s* (New Brunswick, 1979).

20 See T. Lowi, 'Why is there no socialism in the United States? A constitutional analysis', unpublished article.

21 See L. Warner, M. Meeker and K. Eells, *Social Class in America* (Chicago, 1949); S. M. Lipset and R. Bendix, *Social Class in America* (Chicago, 1949); S. M. Lipset and R. Bendix, *Social Mobility in Industrial Society* (London, 1959); P. Blau and J. Duncan, *The American Occupational Structure* (New York, 1967); J. Roach, L. Gross and O. Gurselin, *Social Stratification in the United States* (New Jersey, 1969); and R. Coleman and L. Rainwater, *Social Standing in America* (London, 1979).

22 Quoted in G. Gurvitch, *Le Concept des classes sociales* (Paris, 1954), pp. 79–80.

23 J. Schumpeter, *Imperialism and Social Classes* (Oxford, 1951), p. 140.

24 *Ibid.*, p. 165.

25 J. Schumpeter, *Capitalism, Socialism and Democracy* (London, 1943), pp. 375, 45.

26 See H. Gutman, *Work, Culture and Society in Industrializing America* (New York, 1976); D. Montgomery, 'To study the people: the American working class', *Labor History* (Autumn 1980); and D. Gordon, R. Edwards and M. Reich, *Segmented Work, Divided Workers: The Historical Transformation of Labour in the United States* (Cambridge, 1982).

27 See E. Shorter and C. Tilly, *Strikes in France* (Cambridge, 1974), pp. 306–30; J. T. Dunlop, 'Structure of collective bargaining', in G. G. Somers (ed.), *The Next 25 Years of Industrial Relations* (Madison, 1973); and H. A. Clegg, *Trade Unionism under Collective Bargaining: A Theory Based on Comparison of Six Countries* (Oxford, 1976).

28 See, for example, A. M. Ross and P. T. Hartman, *Changing Patterns of Industrial Conflict* (New York, 1960).

29 P. K. Edwards, *Strikes in the United States, 1881–1974* (Oxford, 1981), p. 226.

30 *Ibid.*, p. 229.

31 See Shorter and Tilly, *Strikes in France*, pp. 317–29; Edwards, *Strikes in the United States*, p. 234; G. Adam and J.-D. Reynaud, *Conflits du travail et changement social* (Paris, 1978); J. Cronin, *Industrial Conflict in Modern Britain* (London, 1979); and N. Kirk, *The Growth of Working-Class Reformism in Mid-Victorian England* (London, 1985).

32 R. T. McKenzie, *British Political Parties* (London, 1964), p. 13.

33 See I. Taylor, 'Ideology and policy', in C. Cook and I. Taylor, *The Labour Party* (London, 1980); H. Drucker, *Doctrine and Ethos in the Labour Party* (London, 1979); and P. Birnbaum, *La Logique de l'Etat* (Paris, 1981).

34 See C. Crouch and A. Pizzorno (eds.), *The Resurgence of Class Conflict in Western Europe since 1968*, vol. 1 (London, 1969); T. Nichols and H. Benyon, *Living with Capitalism* (London, 1977); and L. Panitch, *Social Democracy and Industrial Militancy* (Cambridge, 1976).

35 R. Price, 'Rethinking labour history', in J. Cronin and J. Schneer, *Social Conflict and the Political Order in Modern Britain* (London, 1982), p. 210.

36 See M. Mann, *Consciousness and Action among the Western Working Class* (London, 1973);

A. Marwick, *Class: Image and Reality in Britain and the USA since 1930* (New York, 1980); and D. Gallie, *Social Inequality and Class Radicalism in France and Britain* (London, 1983).

37 From this point of view it is crucial that we bring out the contrast between the present-day school, grouped around Raphael Samuel, which is concerned with narratives of working-class life (see R. Samuel (ed.), *People's History and Socialist Theory* (London, 1981)), and the more structuralist–Marxist perspective shared by those, such as Perry Anderson, Tom Nairn or Bob Jessop, who have been influenced by Althusser. The existence of such a contrast perhaps bears witness to the type of consciousness which British workers, belonging to a more pragmatic society (in which values and culture, as Edward Thompson's books have shown, play a crucial role), might be expected to have.

38 See D. Glass (ed.), *Social Mobility in Britain* (London, 1954).

39 See A. Giddens, *The Class Structure of Advanced Societies* (London, 1973).

40 See, for example, J. Goldthorpe (with C. Llewellyn and C. Payne), *Social Mobility and Class Structure in Modern Britain* (Oxford, 1980), pp. 42–62.

41 See Shorter and Tilly, *Strikes in France*; and Adam and Reynaud, *Conflits du travail et changement social*.

42 Consider, for instance, Brunet, the worker depicted in Sartre's *Roads to Freedom*.

43 A. Gorz, *Farewell to the Working Class* (London, 1982), pp. 35–6.

44 S. Mallet, *La Nouvelle Classe ouvrière* (Paris, 1969).

45 N. Poulantzas, 'Sur l'Etat dans la société capitaliste', *Politique aujourd'hui* (March 1970), p. 68.

46 N. Poulantzas, *Political Power and Social Classes* (Paris, 1968), p. 64.

47 L. Althusser, *Reading Capital* (London, 1970), p. 180.

48 M. Castells, *La Question urbaine* (Paris, 1972), pp. 314, 334. Similar arguments are presented in D. Bertaux, *Destins personnels et structures de classe* (Paris, 1977), pp. 47–9.

49 N. Poulantzas, *Classes in Contemporary Capitalism* (London, 1975), pp. 19, 17, 14.

50 *Ibid.*, pp. 33, 292.

51 A. Touraine, M. Wieviorka and F. Dubet, *Le Mouvement ouvrier* (Paris, 1984), p. 53.

52 A. Touraine, *La Conscience ouvrière* (Paris, 1966), p. 118.

53 *Ibid.*, p. 331.

54 A. Touraine, *La Société post-industrielle* (Paris, 1969), pp. 50, 99–101.

55 Touraine, *La Conscience ouvrière*, pp. 337–9.

56 *Ibid.*, pp. 13–14.

57 Touraine *et al.*, *Le Mouvement ouvrier*, p. 22.

58 *Ibid.*, p. 30.

59 It should be obvious enough that such general correlations are still extremely fragile. Thus, in a more limited, and in a way more extreme, manner, one can nowadays find more structural analyses of the American working class in the United States (for example, E. O. Wright, *Class, Crisis and the State* (London, 1978)) or of the British working class (for example, B. Hindess and P. Hirst, *Mode of Production and Social Formation* (London, 1977), J. Bloomfield *et al.*, *Class, Hegemony and the Party* (London, 1977) or, again, the journal *Capital and Class*). On the other hand, one can find studies in France which are more concerned with workers' values, such as Maurice Halbwachs, *La Classe ouvrière et les niveaux de vie* (Paris, 1913) and, in our own period, P. Henry, *Chombart de Lauw* (Paris, 1977), and J. Rancière, *La Nuit des prolétaires* (Paris, 1981). It is worth noting, however, that even in studies which are attentive to the question of values and ways of going about things, there is still a resistance to the idea of really studying the individual actors, and a basic solidarity is still taken for granted. Thus, for Luce Giard and Pierre Mayol, 'being a worker is not so much to do with being harnessed to a specific task as with participating – and this is the basic point – in an urban popular culture, in which crucial values of identification, turning mainly around *practices of solidarity*, predominate' (*L'Invention du quotidien* (Paris, 1980), p. 64).

60 M. Nadaud, *Léonard, maçon de la Creuse* (Paris, 1982), p. 122.

61 *Ibid.*, p. 194.

62 *Ibid.*, p. 154. George Duveau shows how in Lorraine or in Lyons workers have a taste for 'speculating', buying shares and so on. See G. Duveau, *La Vie ouvrière en France sous le Second Empire* (Paris, 1946), pp. 408–9.

63 Duveau, *La Vie ouvrière*, p. 119.

64 In A. Faure and J. Rancière (eds.), *La Parole ouvrière, 1830–1851* (Paris, 1976), pp. 160, 163, 166.
65 *Ibid.*, pp. 215–17.
66 *Ibid.*, pp. 298–301.
67 See A. Hirschman, *Shifting Involvements* (Princeton, 1982).
68 In Faure and Rancière (eds.), *La Parole ouvrière*, p. 95.
69 Rancière, *La Nuit des prolétaires*, p. 133.
70 D. Poulot, *Le Sublime* (Paris, 1980), pp. 139–41.
71 See D. Segrestin, *Le Phénomène corporatiste* (Paris, 1985).
72 Quoted by Rancière, *La Nuit des prolétaires*, p. 281.
73 See J. Lively and J. Rees, *Utilitarian Logics and Politics* (Oxford, 1978); and G. Ionescu, *Politics and the Pursuit of Happiness* (London, 1984).
74 See also A. Perdiguier, *Mémoires d'un compagnon* (Paris, 1978).
75 P. Dubois, *Les Ouvriers conservateurs* (Paris, 1981), pp. 117–18.
76 C. Thelot, *Tel père, tel fils?* (Paris, 1982), p. 78.
77 N. Mayer, 'Une filière de mobilité ouvrière: l'accès à la petite entreprise artisanale et commerciale', *Revue française de sociologie*, 18 (1977), pp. 28–30.
78 J.-P. Terrail, 'Familles ouvrières, école, destin social (1880–1980)', *Revue française de sociologie*, 25 (1984), p. 430.
79 Sondage SOFRES, *La France de 1983: une nation ou des classes?*, March 1983, p. 26.
80 Sondage SOFRES, *Le Classement idéologique des Français*, February 1985.
81 Sondage SOFRES, in *Le Nouvel Observateur*, 21 March 1984, p. 26.
82 M. Verret, *L'Espace ouvrier* (Paris, 1982).
83 Sondage SOFRES, *Dépolitisation des Français: mythe ou réalité?* (Paris, 1972), pp. 12, 14.
84 Sondage SOFRES, *La France de 1983: une nation ou des classes?*, p. 33.
85 R. Boudon, *Effets pervers et ordre social* (Paris, 1977), pp. 99–130.
86 See J. Capdevielle, E. Dupoirier, G. Grunberg, E. Schweisguth and C. Ysmal, *France de gauche, vote à droite: histoire d'un mythe* (Paris, 1981).
87 See P. Birnbaum, *Le Peuple et les gros: histoire d'un mythe* (Paris, 1984). In 1984 36% of workers voted for Reagan and only 22% for Mondale; 40% of them were in favour of a reduction in the role of the state. See SOFRES, *Opinion publique 1985* (Paris, 1985), pp. 257, 263.
88 A. Andrieux and J. Lignon, *L'Ouvrier d'aujourd'hui* (Paris, 1966), p. 163. See also J. Fremontier, *La Vie en bleu* (Paris, 1980), p. 313. 'There are fine places everywhere,' said one worker, 'it's just a question of finding them; with a small effort of will, one can manage to feather one's own nest' (in P. Molyneux and C. Merinari, *La Parole au capital* (Paris, 1978)).
89 See J. Kergoat, 'Combattivité, organisation et niveau de conscience dans la classe ouvrière', *Revue française des affaires sociales* (April–June 1982); and J. Kergoat, 'De la crise économique à la victoire électorale de la Gauche: réaction ouvrière et politiques syndicales', in M. Kesselman (ed.), *Le Mouvement ouvrier français, 1968–1982* (Paris, 1984), pp. 353–5.
90 S. Bonnet, *L'Homme de fer, 1960–1973* (Nancy, 1984), p. 375.
91 G. Noiriel, *Longwy: Immigrés et prolétaires, 1880–1980* (Paris, 1984), p. 348.
92 D. Kergoat, *Bulledor ou l'histoire d'une mobilisation ouvrière* (Paris, 1973), pp. 195–6.
93 The numerous strikes in, for example, the 1970s were in the main meant to defend standards of living. See 'Les grèves', *Sociologie du travail*, 4 (1973).
94 T. Baudoin and M. Collin, *Le Contournement des forteresses ouvrières* (Paris, 1983).
95 *Ibid.*, p. 42.
96 *Ibid.*, pp. 106, 128.
97 P. Dubois, *Les Ouvriers divisés* (Paris, 1981), pp. 79–81.
98 M. Verret, 'Mémoire ouvrière, mémoire communiste', *Revue française de science politique* (June 1984), pp. 415–16.
99 For Rolande Trempé, 'the miners became aware fairly early, from around 1869, of belonging to a specific group but it was only when they attained to a class consciousness in the 1890s that this group constituted a genuinely homogeneous whole' (*Les Mineurs de Carmaux, 1848–1914* (Paris, 1971), vol. 2, p. 928).
100 M. Perrot, *Les Ouvriers en grève* (Paris, 1974), vol. 1, p. 256.

101 *Ibid.*, vol. 2, p. 554.
102 *Ibid.*, vol. 2, p. 591.
103 See P. Birnbaum, *Dimension du pouvoir* (Paris, 1984).
104 S. Bonnet, *La Ligne rouge des hauts fourneaux* (Paris, 1981), pp. 122, 226, 253. See also Noiriel, *Longwy*, p. 84.
105 See R. Aminzade, *Class, Politics and Early Industrial Capitalism* (Albany, 1981), p. 197.
106 Y. Lequin, *Les Ouvriers de la région lyonnaise (1848–1914)* (Lyons, 1977), vol. 2, pp. 146, 147, 296.
107 G. Adam, 'Les structures syndicales', in G. Adam, F. Bon, J. Capdevielle and R. Moureaux, *L'Ouvrier français en 1970* (Paris, 1970), p. 31.
108 D. Segrestin, 'Pratiques syndicales et mobilisation: vers le changement?', in Kesselman (ed.), *Le Mouvement ouvrier français*, p. 263.
109 See S. Popkin, *The Rational Peasant* (Berkeley, 1979).
110 M. Hechter, 'A theory of group solidarity', in M. Hechter (ed.), *The Micro-Foundations of Macrosociology* (Philadelphia, 1983), p. 19.
111 See chapter 2.
112 See G. Michelat and M. Simon, *Classe, religion et comportement politique* (Paris, 1977). But, as Claude Thelot notes, 'leaving the working class to get employment does not change ways of voting much; leaving it in order to set oneself up in business overturns them altogether' (*Tel père, tel fils?*, p. 215).
113 C. Durand, *Conscience ouvrière et action syndicale* (Paris, 1971), p. 219.
114 See T. Lowi, 'Why is there no socialism in the United States? A constitutional analysis', unpublished article.

6 The state versus corporatism: France and England

1 See G. Therborn, 'The role of capital and the rise of democracy', *New Left Review* (May–June 1977).
2 L. Panitch, 'Recent theorizations of corporatism', *British Journal of Sociology* (June 1980).
3 P. Schmitter, 'Still the century of corporatism?', in P. Schmitter and G. Lehmbruch (eds.), *Trends toward Corporatist Intermediation* (Beverly Hills, 1979), p.13.
4 B. Nedelman and Kurt G. Meier remark that 'it remains unclear what its theorists understand by the concept of the State ... is it, for example, the government, or the administration, or the parliament, or is the State composed of all three of these units?' See B. Nedelman and K. Meier, 'Theories of contemporary corporatism: static or dynamic?', in Schmitter and Lehmbruch (eds.), *Trends toward Corporatist Intermediation*, p. 98.
5 Schmitter, 'Still the century of corporatism?', p. 22.
6 *Ibid.*, pp. 21–2.
7 See P. Birnbaum, 'State, Center and Bureaucracy', *Government and Opposition*, 4 (1980).
8 These remarks result from a long discussion with Philippe Schmitter.
9 J. T. Winkler, 'Corporatism', *Archives européennes de sociologie*, 17 (1976), p. 109. For Alan Cawson, who is attempting a synthesis between the arguments of Schmitter and of Winkler, corporatism can be explained by the needs of capitalism alone. See 'Pluralism, corporatism and the role of the state', *Government and Opposition*, 2 (1978), p. 193. The state there too remains the great absentee.
10 See Panitch, 'Recent theorizations of corporatism', p. 175.
11 L. Panitch, 'The development of corporatism in liberal democracies', in Schmitter and Lehmbruch (eds.), *Trends toward Corporatist Intermediation*, p. 130.
12 See chapter 4.
13 See L. Panitch, 'Trade unions and the capitalist state: corporatism and its contradictions', *New Left Review*, 125 (1981).
14 See C. Offe, 'Class rule and the political system', *German Political Studies*, 1 (1974).
15 See J. O'Connor, *The Fiscal Crisis of the State* (New York, 1973).
16 See N. Poulantzas, *Political Power and Social Classes* (London, 1973).
17 See J. Habermas, *Legitimation Crisis* (Boston, 1975).

18 C. Offe, 'The Attribution of public status to interest groups', in S. Berger (ed.), *Organizing Interests in Western Europe* (Cambridge, 1981), p. 147 (emphasis in original).

19 See B. Jessop, 'Corporatism, parliamentarism and social democracy', in Schmitter and Lehmbruch (eds.), *Trends toward Corporatist Intermediation*, p. 201. See also B. Jessop, 'The political indeterminacy of democracy', in A. Hunt (ed.), *Marxism and Democracy* (London, 1980), p. 77.

20 B. Jessop, 'Capitalism and democracy: the best political shell?', in G. Littlejohn *et al.* (eds.), *Power and the State* (London, 1978), p. 45.

21 *Ibid.*, p. 47.

22 B. Jessop, 'The transformation of the state in post-war Britain', in R. Scase (ed.), *The State in Western Europe* (London, 1980), p. 51.

23 *Ibid.*, p. 82.

24 C. Buci-Glucksman and G. Therborn, *Le Défi social démocrate* (Paris, 1981), p. 154.

25 See, e.g., *ibid.*, pp. 158, 169, 275, 278.

26 *Ibid.*, p. 127.

27 R. Salisbury, 'Why no corporatism in America?', in Schmitter and Lehmbruch (eds.), *Trends towards Corporatist Intermediation*, p. 218.

28 G. O'Donnell, 'Corporatism and the question of the state', in J. Malloy (ed.), *Authoritarianism and Corporatism in Latin America* (Pittsburgh, 1977), p. 48.

29 See C. Cook and I. Taylor, *The Labour Party* (London, 1980); and D. Howell, *British Social Democracy* (London, 1976).

30 R. T. McKenzie, *British Political Parties* (London, 1963); and H. Jenkins, *Rank and File* (London, 1980).

31 R. Miliband, *Parliamentary Socialism* (London, 1972).

32 S. Haseler, *The Tragedy of Labour* (Oxford, 1980).

33 H. Drucker, *Doctrine and Ethos in the Labour Party* (London, 1979).

34 P. Anderson, 'The origins of the present crisis', *New Left Review*, 23 (1964); T. Nairn, 'The nature of the Labour Party', *New Left Review*, 27 and 28 (1964). See also L. Panitch, 'Socialists and the Labour Party: a reappraisal', in R. Miliband and J. Saville (eds.), *The Socialist Register 1979* (London, 1980).

35 See D. Coates, *Labour in Power?* (London, 1980). The author refutes this thesis in a convincing manner.

36 See O. Freund, *Labour and the Law* (London, 1977).

37 See R. Hyman, 'La théorie des relations industrielles: une analyse matérialiste', *Sociologie du travail*, 4 (1979), p. 422; and A. Flanders and A. Fox, 'The reform of collective actions: from Donovan to Durkheim', *British Journal of Industrial Relations*, 7 (1969). See also H. A. Clegg, *The Changing System of Industrial Relations in Great Britain* (Oxford, 1979).

38 K. Middlemas, *Politics in Industrial Society* (London, 1975), pp. 373, 381.

39 See W. Grant and D. Marsh, 'Tripartism: reality or myth', *Government and Opposition*, 12, 2 (1977), pp. 194–211.

40 See J. Leruez, *Planification et politique en Grande Bretagne* (Paris, 1972).

41 See the excellent article by Andrew Cox, 'Corporatism as reductionism: the analytic limits of the corporatist thesis', *Government and Opposition*, 16, 1 (1981).

42 See S. Dunn, 'Vers la fin du "volontarisme" dans les relations industrielles en Grande-Bretagne', *Sociologie du travail*, 4 (1979); and F. Bédarida, E. Gibily and G. Rameix, *Syndicats et patrons en Grande Bretagne* (Paris, 1980).

43 See L. Panitch, *Social Democracy and Industrial Militancy* (Cambridge, 1976).

44 C. Crouch, *Class Conflict and the Industrial Relations Crisis* (London, 1977), pp. 48, 248.

45 *Ibid.*, p. 36.

46 D. Strinati, 'Capitalism, the state and industrial relations', in C. Crouch (ed.), *State and Economy in Contemporary Capitalism* (London, 1979), pp. 214–15.

47 See P. Stanworth and A. Giddens, *Elites and Power in British Society* (Cambridge, 1974); and I. Crewe, *Elites in Western Democracy* (London, 1974).

48 Perry Anderson thus overestimates the role of the state in Great Britain, the integration of the trade unions, and the development of corporatism. See Anderson, 'The limits and possibilities

of trade union action', in T. Clark and L. Clements (eds.), *Trade Unions under Capitalism* (Brighton, 1977).

49 G. Adams and J.-D. Reynaud, *Conflits du travail et changement social* (Paris, 1978), pp. 25–6, 97.

50 'Les Grèves', *Sociologie du travail*, 4 (1973).

51 W. Korpi and M. Shalev, 'Strikes, industrial relations and class conflict in capitalist societies', *British Journal of Sociology* (June 1979), p. 182.

52 M. Perrot, *Les Ouvriers en grève* (Paris, 1974), p. 689, table 2.

53 *Ibid.*, p. 703. Yves Lequin strongly underlines this constant recourse to the state by the working class, in *Les Ouvriers de la région lyonnaise (1848–1918)* (Lyons, 1977), p. 143, table 2.

54 *Ibid.*, p. 196, table 1.

55 E. Shorter and C. Tilly, *Strikes in France* (Cambridge, 1974), pp. 182, 327.

56 *Ibid.*, p. 40.

57 *Ibid.*, p. 41.

58 Quoted in A. Cottereau, *Etudes préalables à Denis Poulot, Le Sublime* (Paris, 1980), p. 52.

59 Adam and Reynaud, *Conflits du travail et changement social*, p. 59.

60 *Ibid.*, p. 243.

61 M. Durand, 'La grève: conflit structurel, système de relations industrielles ou facteur de changement social', *Sociologie du travail* (July–September 1979), p. 295.

62 S. Dassa, 'Le mouvement de mai et le système de relations professionnelles', *Sociologie du travail* (July–September 1970). See also J. Capdevielle, E. Dupoirier and G. Lorant, *La Grève du Joint Français* (Paris, 1975).

63 See J.-D. Reynaud, *Les Syndicats, les patrons et l'Etat* (Paris, 1978), p. 115. Sabine Erbes-Seguin shows, similarly, how in spite of the reforms that followed 1968 representatives of the workers have only a consultative role with their factory committees. See 'Les Deux champs de l'affrontement professionnel', *Sociologie du travail*, 4 (1977), p. 386.

64 See M. Schain, 'Corporatism and industrial relations in France', in P. Cerny and M. Schain (eds.), *French Politics and Public Policy* (New York, 1980).

65 J. Bunel and J. Saglio, 'La faiblesse de la négociation collective et le pouvoir patronal', *Sociologie du travail*, 4 (1977), p. 386. Studying the development of strikes in 1971, C. Durand and P. Dubois still stress that 'in more than two-thirds of the strikes, the employers do not show any excitement for conciliation' (C. Durand and P. Dubois, *La Grève* (Paris, 1975)).

66 The very important Commissions administratives taritaires, which works inside the state itself, is the one exception.

67 C. Gruson, *Origines et espoirs de la planification française* (Paris, 1968), p. 324.

68 See P. Bauchet, *La Planification française* (Paris, 1966), p. 8. Yves Ullmo shows also how the trade unions have been excluded from the discussion of programme contracts or from the Commissions Toutée discussions on salaries and public enterprises. Here again, this is an 'authoritarian' policy. See Y. Ullmo, *La Planification en France* (Paris, 1974), p. 285.

69 For a discussion of the PCF's views on the finalities of the plan, which explains why certain trade unions, such as the CGT, rejected the plan, see P. Herzog, *Politique économique et planification en régime capitaliste* (Paris, 1972).

70 See I. Boussard, *Vichy et la corporation paysanne* (Paris, 1980).

71 See Pierre Birnbaum, *The Heights of Power* (Chicago, 1982); and S. Cohen, *Modern Capitalist Planning: The French Model* (Berkeley, 1969), pp. 4–5, 51.

7 The Nazi collective movement against the Prussian state

1 J. Linz, 'Totalitarian and authoritarian régimes', in F. Greenstein and N. Polsby (eds.), *Handbook of Political Science*, vol. 3 (Reading, 1975), pp. 188–91.

2 J. Linz, 'An authoritarian régime: Spain', in E. Allardt and S. Rokkan (eds.), *Mass Politics* (New York, 1970), p. 255. See also Linz 'Totalitarian and authoritarian régimes', p. 264, for the distinction between totalitarianism and authoritarianism; and H. Arendt, *Between Past and Future* (New York, 1961), p. 96. As regards this debate and its application to contemporary political systems, see J.-F. Bayart, 'L'analyse des situations autoritaires', *Revue française de science politique* (June 1976).

3 Linz, 'An authoritarian régime: Spain', pp. 265–72.

4 It is worth noting that, in a situation where there is a complete lack of any institutionalised power, a 'praetorian' situation may develop (see S. Huntingdon, *Political Order in Changing Societies* (New Haven, 1968)), and that a totalitarian régime may be institutionalised and thereby come to resemble an authoritarian régime (this is how A. Mayer interprets the evolution of the Soviet régime, which he describes as 'administrative totalitarianism', in *The Soviet Political System* (New York, 1965)).

5 See H. Arendt, *The Origins of Totalitarianism* (London, 1961); M. Curtis, *Totalitarianism* (New Brunswick, 1980), pp. 2–9; and H. Spiro, 'Totalitarianism', in *International Encyclopedia of the Social Sciences*, vol. 16 (London, 1968), p. 109.

6 See D. Rustow, 'Transitions to democracy', *Comparative Politics* (April 1970).

7 C. Friedrich, 'The evolving theory and practice of totalitarian regimes', in C. Friedrich, M. Curtis and B. Barber, *Totalitarianism in Perspective* (London, 1969), p. 126.

8 Sigmund Neumann also places most emphasis upon the role of leader, in order to give a better account of power in a totalitarian régime, in *Permanent Revolution* (New York, 1942).

9 C. Friedrich and Z. Brzezinski, *Totalitarian Dictatorships and Autocracy* (Harvard, 1959), p. 17.

10 See A. Groth, 'The "isms" in totalitarianism', *American Political Science Review*, 58, 4 (1964), pp. 893–5.

11 Arendt, *The Origins of Totalitarianism*, p. 237.

12 *Ibid.*, p. 259.

13 *Ibid.*, p. 266.

14 See B. Badie and P. Birnbaum, *Sociology of the State* (Chicago, 1983).

15 H. Ekstein and D. Apter, *Comparative Politics* (New York, 1963), p. 434.

16 M. Curtis, 'Retreat from totalitarianism', in Friedrich, Curtis and Barber, *Totalitarianism in Perspective*, p. 59.

17 B. Barber, 'Conceptual foundations of totalitarianism', in Friedrich, Curtis and Barber, *Totalitarianism in Perspective*, p. 25.

18 L. Schapiro, *Totalitarianism* (London, 1972), p. 71.

19 Franz Neumann draws much the same distinction between totalitarianism and the absolutist state, in *The Democratic and Authoritarian State* (Glencoe, 1957), p. 245.

20 Schapiro, *Totalitarianism*, p. 74.

21 H. Buchheim, *Totalitarian Rule* (Middletown, 1968), p. 98.

22 H. Rauschning, *Germany's Revolution of Destruction* (London, 1939), p. 88.

23 According to Claude Lefort, totalitarianism 'implies a dedifferentiation of the instances which order the constitution of a political society. There are no longer final criteria in law, nor final criteria in knowledge such as might be out of the reach of power' (*L'Invention démocratique* (Paris, 1981), p. 100).

24 A. Hitler, *Mein Kampf* (London, 1969), p. 7.

25 *Ibid.*, pp. 357–8.

26 *Ibid.*, vol. 2, chapter 4. See E. Jackel, *Hitler idéologue* (Paris, 1973), chapter 4.

27 The 25 points in the programme of the NSDAP are presented in Walther Hofer, *Der Nationalsozialismus. Dokumente 1933–1945* (Frankfurt, 1957), pp. 28–31.

28 Speech given in 1935, reproduced in H. Buchheim, 'The SS – instrument of domination', in H. Krausnick, H. Buchheim, M. Broszat and H. Jacobven, *Anatomy of the SS State* (London, 1968), p. 201.

29 B. Mussolini, *Fascism, Doctrine and Institutions* (Rome, 1935), p. 11.

30 *Ibid.*, p. 25.

31 G. Mosse, *The Crisis of German Ideology* (London, 1966), p. 61.

32 *Ibid.*, p. 215.

33 See G. Mosse, *The Nationalization of the Masses* (New York, 1975).

34 O. Koellreutter, *Deutsches Verfassungsrecht*, quoted in J.-P. Faye, *Langages totalitaires* (Paris, 1973), pp. 85–6.

35 Quoted in Faye, *Langages totalitaires*, p. 86.

36 Quoted in *ibid.*, p. 47.

37 Quoted in *ibid.*

38 See L. Dupeux, *National-bolchévisme dans l'Allemagne de Weimar* (Paris, 1979), vol. 1, p. 52.

39 These texts have been analysed in *ibid.*, pp. 408–9.

40 See *ibid.*, p. 430. See also vol. 2, pp. 647–8.
41 See W. Wippermann, 'Nationalsozialismus und Preussentum', *Aus Politik und Zeitgeschichte*, 52–3 (1981), note 1.
42 W. Ebenstein, *The Nazi State* (New York, 1943), p. 52.
43 See R. Koehl, 'Feudal aspects of National Socialism', in H. Turner Jr., *Nazism and the Third Reich* (New York, 1972), p. 169. Conversely, as Louis Dupeux observes, the National Bolsheviks 'used to heap ridicule upon "the flight to the Middle Ages", with its Estates (*Stände*), its enfiefed property, its anti-industrial and anti-technological tendencies' (*National-bolchévisme*, vol. 1, p. 507).
44 Quoted in N. Poulantzas, *Fascism and Dictatorship* (London, 1979), p. 58.
45 Quoted in *ibid.*, p. 97.
46 Quoted in P. Ayçoberry, *La Question nazis* (Paris, 1979), p. 93.
47 A. Gisselbrecht, 'Le fascisme hitlérien. Présentation', *Recherches internationales*, 4 (1971), p. 29.
48 A. Thalheimer, 'Über den Faschismus', in R. Kühnl, *Texte zur Faschismusdiskussion*, vol. 1 (Hamburg, 1974). See also J. Dülffer, 'Bonapartism, Fascism and National-Socialism', *Journal of Contemporary History* (October 1976).
49 This is the case with, for example, Daniel Guérin, *Fascisme et grand capital* (Paris, 1965).
50 Poulantzas, *Fascism and Dictatorship*, p. 62 (translation modified).
51 *Ibid.*, p. 97.
52 *Ibid.*, part 7, chapters 3 and 4.
53 F. Pollack, 'Is national-socialism a new order?', in *Studies in Philosophy and Social Science*, 3 (1941), p. 443. Note, however, that Pollack quotes studies by Burnham (p. 441, note 3).
54 Pollack, 'Is national-socialism a new order?', p. 441, note 6.
55 F. Pollack, 'State capitalism. Its possibilities and limitations', in *Studies in Philosophy and Social Science*, 2 (1941), p. 201.
56 M. Horkheimer, 'L'Etat autoritaire', in *Théorie critique* (Paris, 1978), p. 332 (an article written in 1942).
57 Horkheimer, 'L'Etat autoritaire', p. 330.
58 In particular, A. R. L. Gurland, who maintains that, in the name of the monopolies, 'the state . . . gains power to advance the concentration of capital . . . at the expense of small business' ('Technological trends and economic structure', in *Studies in Philosophy and Social Science*, 2 (1941), p. 244). Martin Jay produces a remarkable analysis of the different approaches to Nazi power within the Frankfurt School in *The Dialectical Imagination* (Boston, Mass., 1973).
59 F. Neumann, *Behemoth* (London, 1942), pp. 183–4.
60 *Ibid.*, p. 214.
61 *Ibid.*, p. 181.
62 *Ibid.*, p. 56.
63 *Ibid.*, p. 375.
64 F. Neumann, *Behemoth* (New York, 1944), p. 630. Otto Kirscheimer, who also belonged to the Frankfurt School, likewise emphasised the distinction between state and bureaucracy and analysed the way in which the party 'captured the machinery of state' (*Politics, Law and Social Change* (New York, 1969), pp. 153, 155).
65 Neumann, *Behemoth* (1944), p. 632. Since this disappearance made it possible to forge an alliance between power in the economic sense and the head of the Nazi Party (p. 634), Neumann then reverted to a more classical Marxist perspective, which was more easily justified once it was explicitly acknowledged that the state as a specific locus of power had disappeared.
66 *Ibid.*, p. 470. See P. Ayçoberry, 'Franz Neumann. Behemoth', *Le Débat* (September 1982).
67 Arthur Schweitzer has emphasised the wide range of coalitions of interests which formed around the multiple power centres of the ruling class, with the business world (apart from IG Farben) being opposed to economic *dirigisme*, an opposition which was based upon the political voluntarism of the Nazi leaders. See *Big Business and the Third Reich* (London, 1964), pp. 43, 240, 241, 540. See also Henry A. Turner Jr., 'Le grand capital et la montée de Hitler au pouvoir', in D. Schoenbaum, *Hitler's Social Revolution* (New York, 1966), appendix. For a Marxist interpretation, see, on the other hand, D. Abraham, *The Collapse of the Weimar Republic* (Princeton, 1981), pp. 321–4.

68 See T. W. Mason, 'Primat de la politique et rapport de la politique à l'économie dans l'Allemagne national-socialiste', in Schoenbaum, *Hitler's Social Revolution*, appendix.

69 See H. Rosenberg, *Bureaucracy, Aristocracy and Autocracy: The Prussian Experience* (Cambridge, 1958); J. Gillis, *The Prussian Bureaucracy in Crisis, 1840–1860* (Stanford, 1971); G. Craig, *The Politics of the Prussian Army, 1640–1945* (London, 1979); F. Marstein Marx, 'Civil service in Germany', in L. White, *Civil Service Abroad* (New York, 1935); J. C. G. Röhl, 'Higher civil servants in Germany, 1890–1900', *Journal of Contemporary History*, 6 (1967); D. Lerner, *The Nazi Elite* (Stanford, 1951); W. Zapf, *Wandlungen der deutschen Elite, 1919–1961* (Munich, 1965); and W. Struve, *Elites against Democracy: Leadership Ideals in Bourgeois Political Thought in Germany, 1890–1933* (Princeton, 1973).

70 See also R. Dahrendorf, *Society and Democracy in Germany* (New York, 1969). On Italian fascism as a factor in the modernisation of society, see A. F. K. Organski, 'Fascism and modernisation', in S. Woolf (ed.), *The Nature of Fascism* (London, 1968). Organski disregards Nazism, on the grounds that it emerged in an already industrialised society. On the link between Nazism and modernisation, see also Wolfgang Sauer, 'National-socialism: totalitarianism or fascism', in H. Turner (ed.), *Reappraisal of Fascism* (New York, 1975); K. Bracher, 'Tradition und Revolution im Nationalsozialismus', in M. Funke (ed.), *Hitler, Deutschland und die Mächte* (Berlin, 1976); and A. Cassels, *Fascism* (New York, 1975).

71 On modernisation in Germany and the revolution 'from above', see Barrington Moore, *The Social Origins of Dictatorship and Democracy* (Boston, 1958); and E. Fraenkel, *The Dual State* (New York, 1969), p. 13.

72 Ebenstein, *The Nazi State*, p. 13.

73 Both Italy and Germany were unified relatively late, and, in this intermediate region of Europe, the definitive construction of a state was delayed. See J. Linz, 'Some notes toward a comparative study of Fascism in sociological historical perspective', in W. Laqueur (ed.), *Fascism* (London, 1976), p. 15. Linz here continues the line of argument sketched by S. Rokkan, in S. Lipset and S. Rokkan, *Party Systems and Voter Alignments* (New York, 1967). See also Juan Linz, 'Political space and fascism as late-comer', in S. Larsen *et al.* (eds.), *Who Were the Fascists?* (Bergen, 1980); and B. Hagtvet and S. Rokkan, 'The conditions of fascist victory', in Larsen *et al.* (eds.), *Who Were the Fascists?* On the relations between fascism and the administration in Italy, see E. Ragionieri, *Politica e amministrazione: Storia della Italia unita* (Bari, 1967); I. Rossiello (ed.), *Gli apparati statali dall' Unità al Fascismo* (Bologna, 1976); and, above all, A. Aquarone, *L'organizzazione dello stato totalitario* (Turin, 1965). See also A. J. Gregor, *Italian Fascism and Developmental Dictatorship* (Princeton, 1979). On the comparison between Nazi Germany and fascist Italy as regards institutions, see the often confused observations of Amos Perlmutter, *Modern Authoritarianism* (New Haven, 1981), pp. 111–14.

74 See Hofer, *Der Nationalsozialismus*, pp. 61–2.

75 See M. Broszat, *The Hitler State* (London, 1981), pp. 108–12.

76 Buchheim, *Totalitarian Rule*, p. 137. See also A. Grosser, *Dix essais sur le nazisme* (Paris, 1976), chapter 4.

77 H. Mommsen, 'National socialism: continuity and change', in Laqueur (ed.), *Fascism*, pp. 156, 171. See also J. Caplan, 'Bureaucracy, politics and the national socialist state', in P. Stachura (ed.), *The Shaping of the Nazi State* (London, 1978).

78 My presentation of this question depends upon the study by Hans Mommsen, *Beamtentum im Dritten Reich* (Stuttgart, 1966). Likewise, Frick wanted to maintain internal disciplinary structures, and so on.

79 Quoted in Broszat, *The Hitler State*, pp. 257–8. As regards this point, see the whole of chapter 7 of this same work.

80 See Schoenbaum, *Hitler's Social Revolution*, p. 225.

81 See Broszat, *The Hitler State*, chapters 8 and 9. In this sense, see also Frédéric Burin, 'Bureaucracy and national-socialism: a reconsideration of Weberian theory', in R. Merton (ed.), *Reader in Bureaucracy* (New York, 1952), pp. 42–3. John Steiner shows how civil servants became 'efficient "political soldiers"' and obeyed Hitler's totalitarian system' (*Power Politics and Social Change in National-Socialist Germany* (The Hague, 1976), p. 141).

82 See Koehl, 'Feudal aspects of National Socialism', pp. 161–2.

83 See Broszat, *The Hitler State*, chapter 9; H. Mommsen, 'Ausnahmezustand als Herrschaft-

stechnik des NS Regimes', in Funke, (ed.), *Hitler, Deutschland und die Mächte*; or H. Mommsen, 'Das nationalsozialistiche Herrschaftssystem', in *Jahrbuch der Universität Düsseldorf, 1970–1971*.

84 Karl Bracher, on the other hand, claims that the Hitlerian totalitarianism imposed by the Führer was 'intentional' in character (in *The German Dictatorship* (Harmondsworth, 1974), p. 423). See also the more recent essay by the same author, 'Zeitgeschichtliche Kontroversen', in *Um Faschismus, Totalitarismus, Demokratie* (Munich, 1976).

85 See K. Hildebrand, *Das Dritte Reich* (Munich, 1979) and T. Mason, 'Banalisation du nazisme? La controverse actuelle sur l'interprétation du national-socialisme', *Le Débat* (September 1982).

8 Territorial and ethnic mobilisation in Scotland, Brittany and Catalonia

1 See C. Enloe, *Ethnic Conflict and Political Development* (Boston, Mass., 1973).

2 See G. Haupt, M. Löwy and C. Weill, *Les Marxistes et la question nationale* (Paris, 1974).

3 See S. Berger, 'Bretons, Basques, Scots and other European nations', *Journal of Interdisciplinary History*, 3 (1972).

4 M. Hechter and W. Brustein, 'Regional modes of production and patterns of State formation in Western Europe', *American Journal of Sociology*, 5 (1980), p. 1075.

5 See M. Hechter, *Internal Colonialism* (London, 1975), chapter 3.

6 A. Touraine, F. Dubet, Z. Hegedus and M. Wieworka show that 'the Occitan movement, as is the case in other aspects with the Breton movement also, can only develop by defining itself as an anti-state movement', such that these movements are opposed to 'an omnipotent and centralising state' (*Les Pays contre L'Etat: luttes occitanes* (Paris, 1981), pp. 291, 299). Although these authors bring out the peculiar character of the type of state to which these nationality movements are opposed, it is nevertheless necessary to adopt a more comparative approach if one is to be in a position to assess the weight of the variable of the state in the formation of different kinds of nationality movement.

7 See G. S. Pryde, *The Treaty of Union* (Edinburgh, 1950). See also T. B. Smith, *Scotland* (Edinburgh, 1962), chapter 3.

8 J. Kellas, *The Scottish Political System* (Cambridge, 1973), p. 2.

9 A. Hirschman, *Exit, Voice and Loyalty* (Princeton, 1970).

10 Hechter, *Internal Colonialism*, pp. 67, 122.

11 See K. Webb, *The Growth of Nationalism in Scotland* (Harmondsworth, 1977), pp. 121–7.

12 T. Nairn, *The Break-Up of Britain* (London, 1977), chapters 2 and 3.

13 Hence the recent failure of the Scottish National Party. For a more systematic analysis, see J. Kellas and P. Fotheringham, 'The political behaviour of the working class', in A. MacLaren, *Social Class in Scotland* (Edinburgh, 1976).

14 See 'Minorités nationales en France', *Les Temps modernes* (August–September 1973); and M. de Certeau, D. Julia and J. Revel, *Une politique de la langue: la Révolution française et les patois* (Paris, 1975).

15 Quoted in P. Serant, *La Bretagne et la France* (Paris, 1971), p. 380.

16 See C. Bertho, 'L'invention de la Bretagne, genèse sociale d'un stéréotype', *Actes de la recherche en sciences sociales* (November 1980).

17 See J. Reece, *The bretons against France* (London, 1977).

18 R. Dulong, *La Question bretonne* (Paris, 1975), p. 202; see also R. Dulong, *Les Régions, l'Etat et la société locale* (Paris, 1978), p. 208. For a similar position, see Y. Guin, *Histoire de la Bretagne* (Paris, 1977). In *Jeux interdits à la frontière* (Paris, 1978), Louis Quere tends rather to emphasise the specificity of Breton nationalism and its attempts to construct a counter-state.

19 See D. Lomax, *The Reconquest of Spain* (London, 1978); and J. H. Elliott, *Imperial Spain, 1469–1716* (London, 1966).

20 See J. Linz, 'Early State-building and late peripheral nationalism against the State: the case of Spain', in S. Eisenstadt and S. Rokkan (eds.), *Building States and Nations* (London, 1973), vol. 2.

21 See S. Eisenstadt, 'Analyse comparée de la formation de l'Etat selon le contexte historique', *Revue internationale des sciences sociales*, 4 (1980).

22 P. Anderson, *Lineages of the Absolutist State* (London, 1974), p. 69. In much the same way, I. Wallerstein holds that 'Spain was an empire when what was needed was a medium-size state'

(*The Modern World-System*, vol. 1 (New York, 1974), p. 179).

23 P. Chaunu also emphasises the fact that the Empire was composed of 17 states, in 'L'empire de Charles Quint', in M. Duverger (ed.), *Le Concept d'Empire* (Paris, 1980), p. 253.

24 See P. Vilar, *Le Catalogne dans l'Espagne moderne* (Paris, 1962), vol. 3.

25 Quoted in F. Soldevila, *Historia de Catalunya* (Barcelona, 1963), p. 984. See also M. Devez, *L'Espagne de Philippe IV* (Paris, 1970).

26 This text, together with the quotation from Vives, are taken from the fundamental study by J. Rossinyol, *Le Problème national catalan* (Paris, 1974), pp. 4, 5.

27 For J. Fuster, 'the lag between centre and periphery has been a constant feature from the time of Charles V up until the present day; they are two zones which the state has not succeeded in fusing into one ... A genuine state would have avoided all that' (in Rossinyol, *Le Problème national catalan*, p. 245).

28 See M. Beltran, *La elite burocrática española* (Barcelona, 1977), p. 79; and A. L. Pina, *Poder y clases sociales* (Madrid, 1978).

29 See J. A. G. Casanova, *Federalismo y autonomia: Cataluña y el Estado español, 1868–1938* (Barcelona, 1979).

30 See M. Ranis, 'The State and the logic of centralization', unpublished article, American Political Association, New York, 1981.

31 See G. Camilleri and C. Galiay, 'Le statut d'autonomie de la Catalogne', *Revue française de science politique* (October 1980).

32 See J. Leruez, 'Régionalisme et politique au Royaume-Uni', *Revue française de science politique* (December 1979); B. Vernon, *Devolution* (Oxford, 1979); and H. Drucker and G. Brown, *The Politics of Nationalism and Devolution* (London, 1980).

9 Nation, state and culture: the example of Zionism

1 See I. Wallerstein, *The Capitalist World-Economy* (Cambridge, 1979); P. Anderson, *Lineages of the Absolutist State* (London, 1974); S. Rokkan, 'Cities, states and nations', in S. Eisenstadt and S. Rokkan (eds.), *Building States and Nations* (London, 1973).

2 See P. Birnbaum, *La Logique de l'Etat* (Paris, 1982).

3 See D. Feuerwerker, *L'Emancipation des juifs en France* (Paris, 1976); P. Hyman, *From Dreyfus to Vichy* (New York, 1983); and F. Molino and B. Wasserstein, *The Jews in Modern France* (Brandesi, 1985).

4 See E. Hamburger, 'One hundred years of emancipation', in *Leo Beck Year Book, 1969* (London, 1969); R. Rürup, 'Jewish emancipation and bourgeois society', in *Leo Beck Year Book, 1969*; and S. Lowenstein, 'The pace of modernization of German Jewry in the nineteenth century', in *Leo Beck Year Book, 1969*.

5 See Rokkan, 'Cities, states and nations'.

6 See E. Mendelsohn, *Class Struggle in the Pale* (Cambridge, 1970); P. Korzec, *Juifs en Pologne* (Paris, 1980); and J. Frankel, *Prophecy and Politics: Socialism, Nationalism and the Russian Jews, 1862–1917* (Cambridge, 1981).

7 See J. Reinharz, *Fatherland or Promised Land: The Dilemma of the German Jew* (Oxford, 1975).

8 K. Marx and F. Engels, *Manifesto of the Communist Party*, in *The Revolutions of 1848, Political Writings Volume I*, edited and introduced by D. Fernbach (London, 1973), p. 84.

9 V. I. Lenin, *The Position of the Bund in the Party* [1903], in *Collected Works*, vol. 7 (London, 1961), p. 101.

10 V. I. Lenin, *Critical Remarks on the National Question* [1913], in *Collected Works*, vol. 20 (London, 1964), p. 26.

11 See H. Tobias, *The Jewish Bund in Russia* (Stanford, 1972).

12 See Mendelsohn, *Class Struggle in the Pale*.

13 J. V. Stalin, 'Marxism and the national question', in B. Franklin (ed.), *The Essential Stalin* (London, 1973), p. 61.

14 *Ibid.*, pp. 63–4.

15 See H. Slovès, *L'Etat juif de l'Union Soviétique* (Paris, 1982).

16 B. Borochov, *Class Struggle and the Jewish Nation* (New Brunswick, 1984), p. 18.

17 *Ibid.*, p. 11.

18 *Ibid.*, p. 57.
19 O. Bauer, 'The concept of nation', in T. Bottomore and P. Goode (eds.), *Austro-Marxism* (Oxford, 1978), p. 103.
20 See Bottomore and Goode (eds.), *Austro-Marxism*.
21 O. Bauer, cited in R. Wistrich, *Socialism and the Jews* (London, 1982), p. 337.
22 O. Bauer, cited in Wistrich, *Socialism and the Jews*, p. 340.
23 See Wistrich, *Socialism and the Jews*, p. 316.
24 Quoted in *ibid.*, p. 331.
25 See G. Mosse, 'German socialists and the Jewish question in the Weimar Republic', in *Leo Beck Year Book, 1969*.
26 See Wistrich, *Socialism and the Jews*, pp. 144–57.
27 H. Cohn, 'Theodore Herzl's conversion to Zionism', *Jewish Social Studies* (April 1970), pp. 101–10.
28 T. Herzl, *L'Etat juif* (Jerusalem, 1954), pp. 29–30.
29 *Ibid.*, p. 115.
30 D. Vital, *The Origins of Zionism* (Oxford, 1975).
31 Herzl, *L'Etat juif*, p. 55.
32 T. Herzl, *The Complete Diaries of Theodore Herzl* (New York, 1960), vol. 1, pp. 162, 174.
33 See B. Badie and P. Birnbaum, *Sociology of the State* (Chicago, 1983).
34 See J. Kornberg, 'Ahad Ha-'Am and Herzl', in J. Kornberg (ed.), *At the Crossroads: Essays on Ahad Ha-'Am* (Albany, 1983).
35 See C. Klein, *Le Caractère juif de l'Etat d'Israël* (Paris, 1977); and C. Liebman, D.-Y. Eliezer, *Civil Religion in Israel* (Berkeley, 1984).
36 In Ahad Ha-'Am, *Ten Essays on Zionism and Judaism* (London, 1922).
37 Quoted in D. Vital, *Zionism, the Formative Years* (Oxford, 1982), p. 28.
38 *Ibid.*, p. 26.
39 See Badie and Birnbaum, *Sociology of the State*.
40 Quoted in Vital, *Zionism, the Formative Years*, p. 31.
41 See P. Birnbaum, 'Les pogromes russes et la naissance du sionisme', *Le Monde*, 9 May 1982.
42 Quoted in S. Avineri, *The Making of Modern Zionism* (London, 1981), p. 68 (italicised in the original).
43 A. Herzberg, *The Zionist Idea* (New York, 1959), p. 63.
44 Herzberg, *The Zionist Idea*, p. 65.
45 See B. Kimmerling, *Zionism and Territory* (Berkeley, 1983).
46 L. Pinsker, *Autoemancipation* (London, 1947), p. 25.
47 See Vital, *The Origins of Zionism*, p. 131.
48 Quoted in Vital, *Zionism, the Formative Years*, p. 345. See also Y. Manor, *Naissance du sionisme politique* (Paris, 1981).
49 Vital, *Zionism, the Formative Years*, pp. 355–6.
50 For another perspective on these tendencies, see D. D. Elazar and S. Cohen, *The Jewish Polity* (Bloomington, 1985), p. 213.
51 E. Gellner, *Nations and Nationalism* (Oxford, 1983), p. 36.
52 Quoted in J. Reinharz, *Chaim Weizmann: The Making of a Zionist Leader* (New York, 1985), p. 387. As regards relations between Ahad Ha-'Am and Martin Buber, however, see J. Reinharz, 'Ahad Ha-'Am, Martin Buber and German Zionism', in Kornberg (ed.), *At the Crossroads*; and on the ties between Ahad Ha-'Am and Weizmann, see B. Halpern's contribution to the same volume.
53 M. Buber, *A Land of Two Peoples*, ed. P. R. Mendes-Flohr (New York, 1983), p. 36.
54 Gellner, *Nations and Nationalism*, pp. 2, 55.
55 A. Schapira, *Berl: The Biography of a Socialist Zionist* (Cambridge, 1984), p. 258.
56 Quoted by Avineri, *The Making of Modern Zionism*, p. 167.
57 Quoted by Avineri, *The Making of Modern Zionism*, pp. 167–8.
58 S. Swirski, 'Community and the meaning of the modern state: the case of Israel', *Jewish Journal of Sociology* (December 1976).
59 G. Scholem, *Fidélité et utopie* (Paris, 1978), pp. 54–5.

10 The state, the police and the West Indians: collective movements in Great Britain

1 M. Foucault, *Discipline and Punish* (Harmondsworth, 1977), translated by A. Sheridan, p. 203.
2 See, for example, J. Aubert and R. Petit, *La Police en France* (Paris, 1981), pp. 77–85; P. Stead, *The Police of France* (London, 1983); and J.-J. Gleizal, *Le Désordre policier* (Paris, 1985).
3 Quoted in L. Radzinowicz, *A History of English Criminal Law* (London, 1956), vol. 3, p. 442.
4 See N. Rosenblum, *Bentham's Theory of the Modern State* (Cambridge, Mass., 1978), chapters 5 and 6. See also L. J. Hume, 'Jeremy Bentham and the nineteenth-century revolution in government', *Historical Journal*, 10 (1967).
5 See, for example, John Lea, 'Discipline and capitalist development', in B. Fine *et al.* (eds.), *Capitalism and the Rule of Law* (London, 1979), pp. 80, 81.
6 On the influence of Bentham's project on prison construction in France, see J. Léonard, 'L'historien et le philosophe, à propos de *Surveillir et punir*', in M. Perrot (ed.), *L'Impossible Prison* (Paris, 1980), p. 13; and M. Perrot, '1848. Révolution et prison', in Perrot (ed.), *L'Impossible Prison*. As regards the English prisons, see B. Fitzgerald and J. Sim, *British Prison* (Oxford, 1979).
7 C. Reith, *The Blind Eyes of History* (London, 1952), p. 130.
8 R. Fosdick, *European Police Systems* (Montclair, NJ, [1915], 1969), pp. 15–23. On the complex relations between types of state and types of police, see D. Bayley, 'The police and political development in Europe', in C. Tilly (ed.), *The Formation of National States in Western Europe* (Princeton, 1975); and D. Bayley, 'Police function, structure and control in Western Europe and North America: comparative and historical studies', in N. Morris and M. Tonry (eds.), *Crime and Justice* (Chicago, 1979).
9 D. Hay, 'Property, authority and the criminal law', in D. Hay, *Albion's Fatal Tree* (Harmondsworth, 1977).
10 Michel Foucault notes that, with the exception of England, the whole of the criminal process in Europe, including France, remained secret until the sentence was pronounced (*Discipline and Punish*, p. 35). If it was public in Great Britain, it was because criminal law had a quite different function there.
11 E. P. Thompson, *The Making of the English Working Class* (London, 1964), p. 808. See also E. J. Hobsbawm, *The Age of Revolutions* (London, 1973).
12 See R. A. Schweitzer, C. Tilly and J. Boyd, *The Texture of Contention in Britain 1828–1829*, Centre for Research on Social Organization, paper 13 (April 1980).
13 J. Stevenson, *Popular Disturbances in England, 1700–1870* (London, 1979), pp. 322–3. Charles Tilly also reckons that the term 'combat' is a little excessive for the 1820s, since the protest meetings and processions were generally peaceful and orderly (*Britain's Everyday Conflicts in an Age of Inequality*, Centre for Research on Social Organization, paper 11 (February 1981), p. 51).
14 See Frank Munger's thesis, 'Popular Protest and its Suppression in Early Nineteenth Century Lancashire, England', quoted in C. Tilly, *How (and to some extent why) to study British Contention*, Centre for Research on Social Organization, paper 21 (June 1981).
15 See T. A. Critchley, *A History of Police in England and Wales* (London, 1967).
16 The police did nevertheless increase the size of their units towards the end of the nineteenth century, and crime seemed to fall as a consequence. See C. Tilly *et al.*, *How Policing Affected the Visibility of Crime in Nineteenth-Century Europe and America*, Centre for Research on Social Organization, paper 115, pp. 80–2. For a treatment of the establishment of a 'new police force' during the nineteenth century, see C. Dijnaut, 'Les origines de l'appareil policier moderne en Europe de l'Ouest continentale', *Déviance et société*, 4 (1980).
17 See also S. Bowes, *The Police and Civil Liberties* (London, 1966); and T. Bowden, *Beyond the Limits of the Law* (Harmondsworth, 1978), chapter 9.
18 See J. Stevenson and C. Cook, *The Slump: Society and Politics during the Depression* (London, 1979), chapter 10.
19 On the other hand, Allan Silver reckons that, from the nineteenth century on, the reinforcement of policing was connected to the problem of maintaining order in the industrial towns (A. Silver, 'The demands for order in civil society', in D. Bordua (ed.), *The Police* (London, 1967)).

20 In 1985, the same causes gave rise to still more violent episodes, in which several people were killed.
21 See National Deviancy Conference (ed.), *Permissiveness and Control* (London, 1980).
22 See D. Butler and D. Stokes, *Political Change in Britain* (London, 1974), p. 306; and A. Phizacklea and R. Miles, 'Working-class racist beliefs in the inner city', in R. Miles and A. Phizacklea (eds.), *Racism and Political Action in Britain* (London, 1979).
23 See Miles and Phizacklea, *Racism*; and Martin Walker, *The National Front* (London, 1977).
24 See S. Hall *et al.*, *Policing the Crisis* (London, 1978).
25 John Lambert has likewise shown that in Birmingham a very small proportion of offenders come from the immigrant population, but this fact has done nothing to undermine police stereotypes in this respect. See J. Lambert, *Crime, Police and Race Relations* (Oxford, 1970), p. 125.
26 See B. Rose-Smith, 'Police powers and terrorism legislation', in P. Hain (ed.), *Policing the Police*, vol. 1 (London, 1979).
27 See T. Bunyan, *The Political Police in Britain* (London, 1978).
28 See J. Rollo, 'The Special Patrol Group', in P. Hain (ed.), *Policing the Police*, vol. 2 (London, 1980).
29 See D. Campbell, 'Society under surveillance', in P. Hain (ed.), *Policing the Police*, vol. 2.
30 See B. Cox, J. Shirley and M. Short, *The Fall of Scotland Yard* (London, 1977).
31 R. Mark, *Policing a Perplexed Society* (London, 1977), p. 7. See also D. Halloway, 'Maintaining public order in Britain', unpublished article, Edinburgh, October 1977.
32 Quoted in Halloway, 'Maintaining public order'.
33 By March 1981, the regular police forces of England and Wales numbered some 117,000. See *The Government's Expenditure Plans, 1981–1982* (London, March 1981), p. 97.
34 See D. Peirce, P. Grabosky and T. Gurr, 'London: the politics of crime and conflict, 1800 to the 1970s', in T. Gurr, P. Grabosky and R. Hula (eds.), *The Politics of Crime and Conflict* (London, 1977), pp. 80, 204.
35 Michael Hechter treats this nationalist, and at times communist, thrust in the Celtic peripheries as a response to authoritarian measures taken in the centre (*Internal Colonialism* (London, 1975), chapter 9). It is worth noting, however, that the integration of Scotland into Great Britain was achieved quite voluntarily, an indication of the basically limited nature of this resistance.

Conclusion: the end of the state? From differentiation to dedifferentiation

1 See P. Nettl, 'The state as a conceptual variable', *World Politics* (July 1968); S. Finer, 'State building, state boundaries and border control', *Social Sciences Information*, 13, 4–5; C. Tilly (ed.), *The Formation of National States in Western Europe* (Princeton, 1975); K. Dyson, *The State Tradition in Western Europe* (London, 1980); and B. Badie and P. Birnbaum, *Sociology of the State* (Chicago, 1983).
2 See S. Krasner, *Defending National Interests* (Princeton, 1978); and T. Skocpol and J. Ikenberry, 'The political formation of the American welfare state in historical and comparative perspective', *Comparative Social Research*, 6 (1983).
3 See P. Bachrach, *The Theory of Democratic Elitism* (Boston, 1967); and C. Pateman, *Participation and Democratic Theory* (Cambridge, 1970).
4 See B. Barber, *Strong Democracy* (Berkeley, 1984).
5 See H. Boyte, *The Backyard Revolution: Understanding the New Citizen Movement* (Philadelphia, 1981).
6 See N. Poulantzas, *State Power and Socialism* (London, 1980).
7 See S. Carrillo, *Eurocommunismo y Estado* (Barcelona, 1977).
8 A. de Tocqueville, *Democracy in America* (New York, 1969), p. 523.
9 *Ibid.*, p. 60.
10 See J. Lively, *The Social and Political Ideas of A. de Tocqueville* (Oxford, 1965); and P. Manent, *Tocqueville et la nature de la démocratie* (Paris, 1982).
11 A. de Tocqueville, *The Ancien Régime and the Revolution* (London, 1966), p. 70 (translation modified).

12 See Barrington Moore, *Social Origins of Dictatorship and Democracy* (New York, 1967); and G. Hermet, *Aux frontières de la démocratie* (Paris, 1983).
13 See C. Nicolet, *L'Idée républicaine en France* (Paris, 1982).
14 See P. Grémion, *Le Pouvoir périphérique* (Paris, 1976).
15 See J. Rondin, *Le Sacré des notables: la France en décentralisation* (Paris, 1985).
16 R. Nozick, *Anarchy, State and Utopia* (Oxford, 1974), p. ix.
17 See B. Manin, 'A Hayek et la question de libéralisme', *Revue française de science politique* (February 1983).
18 See J. Paul (ed.), *Reading Nozick* (Ottawa, 1981); and L. Rouban, 'La philosophie formelle de l'Etat selon R. Nozick', *Revue française de science politique* (February 1984).
19 See Skocpol and Ikenberry, 'The political formation of the American welfare state'.
20 See G. McLennan, D. Held and S. Hall (eds.), *State and Society in Contemporary Britain* (London, 1984); and J. Leruez, 'Privatisation et dénationalisations', in J. Leruez (ed.), *Le Thatcherisme* (Paris, 1984).
21 See H. Lepage, *Demain le libéralisme* (Paris, 1978); P. Rosanvallon, *La Crise de l'Etat-Providence* (Paris, 1981); and G. Sorman, *L'Etat minimum* (Paris, 1985).
22 See J.-F. Revel, *Le Rejet de l'Etat* (Paris, 1984).
23 See M. Taylor, *Community, Anarchy and Liberty* (Cambridge, 1982).
24 See P. Schmitter, 'Still the century of corporatism?', in P. Schmitter and G. Lehmbruch (eds.), *Trends Towards Corporatist Intermediation* (London, 1979).
25 See K. Middlemas, *Politics in Industrial Society* (London, 1975).
26 See A. Barker (ed.), *Quangos in Britain* (London, 1982).
27 See M. Heisler and R. Kvavik, 'Patterns of European politics: the "European polity model"', in M. Heisler (ed.), *Politics in Europe* (New York, 1974); and J. Olsen, 'Integrated organizational participation in government', in P. Nystrom and W. Starbuck (eds.), *Handbook of Organisational Design* (Paris, 1981).
28 See A. Cawson, 'Varieties of corporatism: the importance of the meso-level of interest intermediation', in A. Cawson (ed.), *Disappearing Democracy? Organised Interests and the State: Studies in Meso-Corporatism* (London, 1985).
29 See P. Birnbaum, *La Logique de l'Etat* (Paris, 1982); and P. Schmitter, *Neo-corporatism and the State* (Florence, 1984).
30 See E. Suleiman, *Politics, Power and Bureaucracy in France* (Princeton, 1974); and P. Birnbaum, *The Heights of Power* (Chicago, 1982).
31 See J. Keeler, 'Corporatism and official union hegemony: the case of French agricultural syndicalism', in S. Berger (ed.), *Organizing Interests in Western Europe* (Cambridge, 1981).
32 See S. Cohen, *Modern Capitalist Planning: The French Model* (Berkeley, 1977); and R. Kruisel, *Le Capitalisme et l'Etat en France* (Paris, 1984).
33 See M. Dagnaud and D. Mehl, *L'Elite rose* (Paris, 1982).
34 *Le Monde*, 22 September 1981.
35 See P. Clastres, *Society against the State* (Oxford, 1977); and C. Castoriadis, *The Imaginary Institution of Society* (Oxford, 1987).
36 See P. Birnbaum, *Dimensions du pouvoir* (Paris, 1984); and P. Cerny and M. Schain, *Socialism, the State and Public Policy in France* (London, 1985).
37 See F. Dupuy and J. C. Thoenig, *L'Administration en miettes* (Paris, 1985).
38 See P. Riddell, *The Thatcher Government* (Oxford, 1983).
39 See T. Skocpol, *States and Social Revolutions* (Cambridge, 1979).
40 See E. Shorter and C. Tilly, *Strikes in France* (Cambridge, 1974).
41 See C. Tilly, *The Vendée* (Cambridge, Mass., 1964).
42 H. Buchheim, *Totalitarian Rule* (Middletown, 1968), p. 91.
43 Rauschning, *Germany's Revolution of Destruction*.
44 See E. Frankel, *The Dual State* (New York, 1941).
45 See R. Koehl, 'Feudal aspects of National Socialism', in T. T. Henry (ed.), *Nazism and the Third Reich* (New York, 1972), pp. 161–2.
46 S. M. Broszat, *The Hitler State* (London, 1981); and H. Mommsen, 'Ausnahmezustand als Herrschaftstechnik des NZ Regimes', in M. Funke (ed.), *Hitler, Deutschland und die Mächte* (Düsseldorf, 1976).

47 See Birnbaum, *Dimensions du pouvoir*.
48 A. Kazancigil and E. Usbudun (eds.), *Atatürk, Founder of a Modern State* (London, 1981), p. 51.
49 See S. Mardin, 'Religion and secularism in Turkey', in Kazancigil and Usbudun (eds.), *Atatürk, Founder of a Modern State*.
50 See M. Heper, 'Atatürk and public bureaucracy', in J. Landau (ed.), *Atatürk and the Modernisation of Turkey* (London, 1984).
51 See Badie, *Culture et politique* (Paris, 1983).
52 See B. Toprak, 'Politicisation of Islam in a secular state: the National Salvation Party in Turkey', in S. Amir Arjomand (ed.), *From Nationalism to Revolutionary Islam* (London, 1984).
53 See C. Moore, *Politics in North Africa* (Boston, 1970); and M. Camau, 'L'Etat tunisien: de la tutelle au désengagement', *Maghreb-Machrek* (January–March 1984).
54 See B. Lewis, 'The returned of Islam', *Middle East Review*, 1 (1979); and M. Hermassi, 'La société tunisienne au miroir islamiste', *Maghreb-Machrek* (January–March 1984).
55 See J. Leca, 'Une capacité d'intégration défaillante', *Esprit* (June 1985).
56 See S. Neumann, *Die Parteien der Weimarer Republik* (Stuttgart, 1965).
57 See G. Smith, *Democracy in Western Germany* (London, 1979).
58 See N. Johnson, *Government in the Federal Republic of Germany* (Oxford, 1973).
59 See F. Scharpf, 'The joint-decision trap: lessons from German federalism and European integration', unpublished article, Florence, 1985.
60 See K. Dyson, *Party, State and Bureaucracy in Western Germany* (London, 1977); K. von Beyme, *Die politische Elite in der BRD* (Munich, 1971); and K. Schontheimer and H. Röhring (eds.), *Handbuch des politischen Systems der Bundesrepublik Deutschland* (Munich, 1977).
61 See. J. Linz, 'Totalitarian and authoritarian regimes', in F. Greenstein and N. Polsby (eds.), *Handbook of Political Science*, vol. 3 (Reading, 1975).
62 See R. Paxton, *Vichy France* (London, 1972).
63 See P. Novick, *The Resistance versus Vichy* (London, 1968); and J. Mourgeon, *La Répression administrative* (Paris, 1967).
64 See M. Shaw (ed.), *War, State and Society* (London, 1984).
65 See J. Nye and R. Keohane, 'Transnational relations and world politics', in R. Keohane and J. Nye (eds.), *Transnational Relations and World Politics* (Harvard, 1972).

Index